Alex Pettes
July 2011

TWENTY-FIRST-CENTURY
IRVINGS

Harvey Sawler

NIMBUS
PUBLISHING

For David Rodd
Businessman, Gentleman and Friend
(1940–2006)

Nimbus Publishing Limited
PO Box 9166
Halifax, NS B3K 5M8
(902) 455-4286

Printed and bound in Canada

Design: Reuben Hall
Author photo: Sharon French

Library and Archives Canada Cataloguing in Publication

Sawler, Harvey, 1954-
Twenty-first-century Irvings / Harvey Sawler.
ISBN 978-1-55109-608-7

1. Irving family. 2. J. D. Irving Limited. 3. Irving Oil Limited.
4. Industrialists—New Brunswick—Biography. 5. Capitalists and finan-ciers—New Brunswick—Biography. 6. Family-owned business enterprises—Succession—New Brunswick. I. Title.

HC112.5.I78S39 2007   338.092'27151   C2007-902902-7

We acknowledge the financial support of the Government of Canada through the Book Publishing Industry Development Program (BPIDP) and the Cana-da Council, and of the Province of Nova Scotia through the Department of Tourism, Culture and Heritage for our publishing activities.

Author's Note

This book began in 2005 as an investigation into the current and oncoming generations of Canada's Irving family. With unparalleled dominance in forestry, energy, transportation, and countless other enterprises, the Irvings are the undisputed monarchs of entrepreneurship in Atlantic Canada and one of the richest families in the world.

But this is more a story about who the Irvings are than it is one about numbers, statistics, and holdings. Those themes have largely been tackled in previous books, which have focused on the famed industrialist K.C. Irving (1899–1992) and, to some degree, his three sons, Jim (J.K.), Arthur, and Jack. Beyond those books and the daily press, the only substantive media exposure relating to the family was a 2001 CBC television documentary, *Unlocking the Mystery: The Irvings As You've Never Seen Them Before*. Given the Irvings' renowned zeal for secrecy, the CBC documentary was nothing short of a coup. In it, two generations of the Irving family speak directly on camera, but K.C.'s sons filled the lion's share of the air time. In light of the passage of time, the new generations of family members rising through the ranks, and the preoccupation of Canadian Maritimers with all things Irving, it seemed like a good time to update their remarkable story.

If they kept with tradition (the CBC documentary being one of the rare exceptions), the Irvings would be unlikely to cooperate in the telling of their own story. For more than a decade, I'd been casually acquainted with seventy-eight-year-old Jim Irving (known to the public as J.K.) and his nephew, forty-some-year-old Kenneth. J.K. and I were once board members of an organization called Bouctouche Bay Eco-Tourism Inc., although our roles were significantly different: mine was as an ex-officio provincial government bureaucrat while his was as the private citizen who laid a couple of million of his personal bucks on the table to build the award-winning attraction known as the Irving Bouctouche Dune. Kenneth and I had met through mutual friends on a few social occasions. Telephone and e-mail inquiries were made to both J.K. and Kenneth, and efforts were also made through intermediaries to communicate with some other family members. The silence was deafening.

Most of 2006, then, was spent putting several key questions to a diverse group of informed interview subjects. How has the family remained so dominant and powerful? Who is providing the required vision and leadership in the absence of K.C. and his sons, all three of whom are retired or near retirement? How is the family unit doing? And just where are they headed in the twenty-first century? When first contacted, interview subjects paused nervously to ask if the Irvings were cooperating with the project. Some, whether they had good or seemingly bad things to say, chose not to continue. This normally had to do with a relationship, job, or contract-related matter. It is very difficult to get people on the record if there is the slightest hint they don't see eye to eye with the Irvings.

By default, it seemed I would have to make do with these external points of view. While again and again interviewees began by claiming they had "nothing much to say," what they did say took us a long way toward unravelling the Irvings' reputations as relentlessly tough, efficient, and highly private business people. The interview sources help uncover who the Irvings are as humans and as individuals. The external viewpoints also provide reasonable and logical analysis of how much longer the Irving business legacy can possibly hope to continue, given that it has already surpassed the normal lifespan of a family business.

Just after I had finished my research, an e-mail arrived from out of the blue. The sender was Saint John–based Mary Keith, vice president of communications for J. D. Irving Ltd. Keith had been my target contact in attempting to reach J. K. Exactly a year to the day from my original request for an interview, Keith wrote that J. K. had suddenly decided to talk to me. Shortly thereafter, J. K. and I had a brief telephone conversation, during which he agreed to an interview. What resulted was an unencumbered, day-long interview conducted in his Saint John office, aboard an Irving plane travelling to and from his boyhood home of Bouctouche, NB, and during an emotional visit to a nondescript, off-road thicket and fishing pond once known as Irvingdale. And there was more: shortly thereafter, he arranged for a private viewing and note taking of newly acquired genealogical reference material that would radically alter the complexion and direction of this book.

Finally, there is an unavoidable, uncomfortable presumptuousness in writing about the Irvings. This is the matter of seeming to be on a first-name basis with the members of the family. Face to face with J. K., there's a certain formality at play; it's always a matter of "Mr. Irving." With Kenneth, who is laid-back and younger, "Kenneth" is cool, but only on a social level. But considerable liberty has been taken with the use of their first names and initials, as well as those of the rest of the family. This liberty provides greater clarity for the benefit of the reader. There are simply too many Irvings to keep track of without resorting to first names. So to the seven generations of Irvings referenced throughout the text—George, Jane, Herbert, J. D., K. C., J. K., Jean, Arthur, Sandra, Jack, Kenneth, Tasha, Arthur Jr., John Jr., Jim, Robert, Judith, Mary Jean, Stewart, Kate, and Jamie—I respectfully seek your indulgence.

Contents

Foreword

You can love them or you can hate them, but you have to respect them. Further, you cannot help but be fascinated by them. That pretty much sums up the range of feelings that people have about the Irvings.

But who are the Irvings? They are a family as simple and as complex as any other, composed of many individuals that are quite different from one another. The Irving parents look at their children and say, like other parents, "How can these children come from the same genes? How can these children have been brought up in the same house and yet be so different?" Yet, despite this diversity, there is definitely an Irving culture, an unmistakable family air. This book is about how that family air has been shaped, how the family culture has been maintained and passed down through six generations in spite of strong, distinct, and diverse personalities.

Thanks to the generosity of J. K. Irving, who provided the author with unprecedented access to the family history, *Twenty-First-Century Irvings* recounts the previously unknown story of the early Irving generations. The narrative also explores the unmistakable traits that have been passed down to all the Irvings, painting a portrait of the contemporary Irvings and of Irving culture.

But the mere description of the Irving family is not what makes this a must-read. What makes this book important is that it methodically shows how the Irvings have remained a constant, progressive economic force for more than 150 years, outstripping the tenure of every other Canadian business family by decades. This book discovers that Irving culture, values, and success have all been achieved through one method—good parenting. The Irvings face the same human struggles as all modern families; their lives have been no more perfect than yours or mine. However, generation after generation, Irving parents and Irving children have simply spent time together.

The book also uncovers the power of emotion. Read carefully and you will see that behind their reputation for hard-nosed business, all of the Irvings are more driven by emotion than they are by empiricism. To most, that will be a surprise. But emotional attachment to their parents, children, businesses, employees, and region plays a much bigger part in the decision-making process of the Irvings than in most other corporations.

As the family expands and becomes more dispersed, as they marry and move to different cities, their bond is naturally threatened. As the expanding family pyramid makes it difficult for each member of the family to spend significant amounts of time together, the author cautions that the secret ingredient in creating the family's success—spending time together—will no longer work its magic, and that the Irvings have perhaps their greatest challenges ahead of them.

—FRANCIS P. MCGUIRE,
former deputy minister of the Department of Economic Development and Tourism for the Province of New Brunswick and current president of Major Drilling International Ltd. (Moncton, NB).

Irving Family Business History

1
George Irving
(1779–1863)
(m. Jane)
Scottish immigrant and Kent County, New Brunswick farmer.

2
Herbert Irving
(1823–1907)
(m. Catharine)
*Farmer, lumberman, community volunteer, Justice of the Peace,
businessman and 'informal financial institution'*

3
James Durgavel (J.D.) Irving
(1860–1933)
(m. Minnie, m. Mary)
*Farmer, lumberman, gristmill, carding mill, sawmill operator,
coal storage shipper, general merchant, and entrepreneur.*

4
Kenneth Colin (K.C.) Irving
(1899–1992)
(m. Harriett, m. Winnifred)
*Industrialist, businessman and entrepreneur involved in energy,
retail, forestry and countless other businesses.*

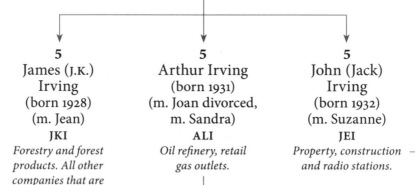

5	**5**	**5**
James (J.K.) Irving (born 1928) (m. Jean)	**Arthur Irving** (born 1931) (m. Joan divorced, m. Sandra)	**John (Jack) Irving** (born 1932) (m. Suzanne)
JKI	**ALI**	**JEI**
Forestry and forest products. All other companies that are not operated by **ALI** *and* JEI	*Oil refinery, retail gas outlets.*	*Property, construction and radio stations.*

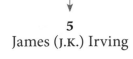

5
James (J.K.) Irving

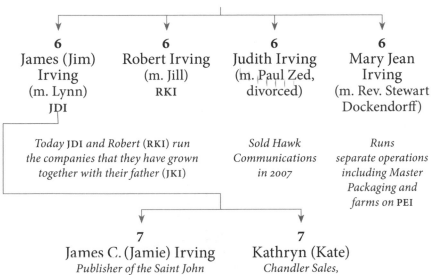

| **6**
James (Jim)
Irving
(m. Lynn)
JDI | **6**
Robert Irving
(m. Jill)
RKI | **6**
Judith Irving
(m. Paul Zed,
divorced) | **6**
Mary Jean
Irving
(m. Rev. Stewart
Dockendorff) |

Today JDI *and Robert* (RKI) *run
the companies that they have grown
together with their father* (JKI)

*Sold Hawk
Communications
in 2007*

*Runs
separate operations
including Master
Packaging and
farms on* PEI

7
James C. (Jamie) Irving
*Publisher of the Saint John
Telegraph-Journal*

7
Kathryn (Kate)
*Chandler Sales,
Moncton*

5
Arthur Irving

6
Kenneth Irving
(m. Tasha)

6
Arthur Leigh Irving
(m. Iris)

*Today Kenneth and Arthur Leigh run the companies that
they have grown together with their father* (ALI)
Arthur's daughters Jennifer, Emily and Sarah are not in the business.

5
John (Jack) Irving

6
John Irving Jr.
(m. Elizabeth)
Harvard MBA *grad focused on real estate holdings.*

(Jack's daughter Anne and son Colin are not in the business.)

More than two dozen younger cousins aren't in the business.

Sources: Mary Keith, VP of Communications, J. D. Irving, Ltd.
The Irving Family History, researched by Burton Glendenning

Introduction—Myths and Truths

The public have an insatiable curiosity to know everything,
except what is worth knowing.

—OSCAR WILDE

There have been six generations of Irvings since K. C.'s great-grandparents George and Jane immigrated to New Brunswick, Canada, from Dumfries-shire, Scotland, in 1833. That makes seven generations of Irvings in Canada. Most people are unaware that the Irving story is such a multi-generational one—with three generations preceding K. C. and three in his wake. And while there has been a passing interest in K. C.'s father, J. D. Irving, it is really K. C. and his uncanny ability to create and run outstanding and successful businesses that have been the focus of Irving-related attention. It's as though K. C. emerged from the ether in the early 1930s and everything he wrought was of his own volition and imagination.

Valued at a reported $5.9 billion US, today the Irvings sit at number 129 on the 2007 *Forbes* world billionaires list. (They have ranked higher, but the world order is changing so rapidly there are 178 new names on the 2007 *Forbes* list compared to just the year previous.) In Canada, only Toronto's Thomson and Weston families appear ahead of the Irvings. And the Irving empire has such sectoral and regional dominance that only America's Morgans, Vanderbilts, and Rockefellers merit a valid comparison among family businesses. This dominance is a much more important factor in the Irving story than their fluctuating position on the *Forbes* list. And the generations preceding and succeeding K. C. are actually key to understanding the Irving story. That the world thinks of the Irvings as having begun with K. C. is really the largest myth that surrounds them.

The bare-bones fact is that K. C. was not the original Irving entrepreneur. Nor was he the poor Bouctouche farm boy he's often been portrayed as. Rather, he was the pivot man in a relentless relay of effort now spanning more than fourteen decades. His great-grandfather George suffered in poverty, but soon thereafter a phenomenon took hold—what we today casually refer to as entrepreneurship. A lone son would single-handedly change the family's fortunes forever. That son would transfer his skills and knowledge to his son, and he to his son, a boy named K. C. As a result, from K. C. onward, being an Irving (principally a male Irving) meant that you were the bearer of that legacy, with all the attendant privileges and responsibilities.

There is no diminishing the fact that K. C. hoisted the bar high, achieving astonishing feats, sprinting harder and faster than anyone of his time, leaping beyond the highest imaginable point and fearlessly generating controversy and a mythical reputation for toughness as he thrust along. But like all who have come after him, K. C. was crafted and schooled into being an Irving. While K. C. the man has evolved into a mythical figure, the rest of the family exposed up to now through daily media, in books, and in the CBC documentary *Unlocking the Mystery*, are merely seen as supporting players to the Irving mythology. K. C. has been the marquee name, the others playing as the chorus or the ensemble.

This book deals with the sixteen key individuals who've served on the front lines of the many Irving enterprises over the 174 years since the family's arrival in Canada—thirteen men and three women who come from and who represent one of the most unique family and business cultures in all of North America. The Irving name is as synonymous with the city of Saint John and the province of New Brunswick as "Kennedy" is with the city of Boston and the state of Massachusetts. In New Brunswick, even the first names of many Irvings are highly recognizable, even though little is known about the individuals themselves. That they prefer to remain unknown is their business, but it might also be a handicap, as their mythical secrecy tends to overshadow so much of what they do. Most of the book's interview subjects claim much of what the Irvings do is intended for the public good.

Inside and outside of New Brunswick—in Nova Scotia, Prince Edward Island, Newfoundland and Labrador, eastern Quebec, and northern Maine—the Irving name is more dominant than any other on the landscape. The way it usually appears in Northeast cities, towns, villages, and hamlets is in big blue capital letters, the iconic signage signifying their hundreds of gas stations, convenience stores, and restaurants. To locals, these businesses are colloquially known as "the Irving," landmarks and guideposts as relevant to community life as the local post office or town square. *Turn left at the Irving. Turn right at the Irving. Across from the Irving. I'll meet you at the Irving. If you've gone by the Irving, you've gone too far.*

Beyond the highly visible Irving gas stations, there are other businesses too numerous to name or to count; there are holdings in Maritime Canada so abundant you just never know when you're walking on Irving land. And they have influence that subtly or directly permeates every aspect of daily and political life. You could fit all those Irvings that are currently business-active in a passenger van, but they are, in a sense, everywhere. Most of us awaken each day with mundane issues and concerns clouding our minds: the family's health and welfare, work, and money matters. When the Irvings awaken, their thoughts go to personal matters, as well as issues of public visibility and associated vulnerabilities. Their work thoughts impact thousands of individual breadwinners every single day. Indirectly, they put bread on the tables of countless people. And their money thoughts determine whether or not hundreds or thousands more people will get to go to work at new jobs in the days, months, and years to come.

Myths

The Irvings have always been surrounded by myth—stories handed down through time that attempt to explain what is unknown about them. Such myths have almost invariably painted negative images that the public, given its own imperfect nature, has been delighted to adopt. Humanity, after all, has proven to have an insatiable appetite for myths: Apollo dragging the sun across the sky by driving a golden chariot drawn by fiery horses; a cherry tree, an axe, and George Washington unable to tell a lie; Louis Riel as a larger-than-life hero. Myths begin as an attempt to explain something that cannot otherwise be explained; elaboration aggrandizes the small truths they're based on.

Since no one really knows about the Irvings' business but the Irvings themselves, people have tended to turn to rumour and speculation. In the oral tradition of the New Brunswick woods, coffee shops, and other gathering places, stories emerging from minor scraps and third-hand anecdotes are distorted into full-blown myths, myths that grow more bloated over time. This is the other way that myths emerge, through the retelling of stories or information. When people have only tidbits of information, they tend to exaggerate or alter facts to improve the story. The more storytellers there are in the chain, the more extreme the result.

In *Anne of Green Gables*, heroine Anne Shirley breaks a writing slate over the head of her classmate, charmer Gilbert Blythe, when he calls her red pigtails "carrots." Gilbert shrugs off the incident by apologizing for having irked her so, but by the time news of the incident reaches clear across Avonlea, Gilbert is said to be lying in a Halifax hospital bed within an inch of his life, with a team of doctors at hand. Such is the Maritime culture. For every parcel of land K. C. or his descendants have ever purchased, there's a story that casts them as bonanza ranchers who cut the fences and poison the well water of their hard-working, impoverished victims—anything to snatch away the deed and force their neighbours off their land. Such exaggerators never live in glass houses. During interviews for this book, concepts such as "Maritime envy" and "alibi for failure" were put forward to explain why the Irving mythology was an inevitability. Some disenfranchised people have told stories of their own experiences with the Irvings (or retold stories handed to them by others) and supplanted inaccuracies to compensate for details they didn't know or because they simply couldn't otherwise explain what had happened.

Over time, no matter how justified a criticism of the Irvings might have been, it was bound to become overstated, reaching mythological status.

Most Irving mythology revolves around the life and times of K. C. His most extreme public image is that of a powerful tycoon, a work-obsessed, hard-nosed dealmaker who took no prisoners, who crushed unions and competitors without pity, who would sue anyone who dared touch an errant Irving-branded log, and who used vertical integration as if it were an evil conspiracy. He is seen by some as a man with too much power, a man who couldn't give a square damn about the environment, who owned rather than employed people, and who took his fortune and hoarded it in a Caribbean tax haven.

The Irvings do simple things like everyone else, things that illustrate their basic humanity. They do things like shop for fish sticks at the supermarket; go for an impromptu Saturday afternoon haircut and chat with the person waiting in the chair next to them; cheer from the sidelines at their children's soccer games; go to Moncton Wildcats hockey games; and drive themselves around town in modest vehicles. K. C. operated on this level of simplicity too; he loved cream soda, Kit Kat chocolate bars, and ice cream. All Irvings, it's said, love ice cream. And K. C. and his descendants have done nice things for people and their community. But when you become mythological in status, the largest events and controversies remain uppermost in the public mindset.

In spite of their individual ordinariness, there is a definite mystique surrounding how the Irvings create and manage so many different types of businesses so well and how it is that they've maintained the family glue up to now. This book does much to explain what makes them tick, but their extreme business acumen is such a mystery that it seems they do not fully understand it themselves. Asked how it was that his father K. C. could afford to spend inordinate amounts of time labouring over how many words would be contained in a single telegram to save mere pennies—this while huge mills were chugging along in the background—J. K. Irving admitted that he simply could not explain it. It's just the way it was, the way things happened.

And as stated, the Irving mystique is all the more magnified by the secretive way the Irvings conduct their affairs, which is their right, but not necessarily their finest characteristic. It is the Irving sense of secrecy that makes much of the public immediately suspicious of their actions. Going back to the core of why mythology exists at all—people's tendency to explain in their own terms that which they cannot otherwise explain—the Irvings have no one to blame but themselves, because of their secrecy, for much of the mythology that has been created around them.

The Irvings are not really who the public thinks they are, in part because their public image has been downtrodden by their propensity for secrecy, and in part because, like everyone else, they are changing with the times. By keeping their doors closed most of the time, they lose the only means to say what's on their minds. Instead, when pressed, they use PR spokespeople to state their case. Too often, this approach is reactive and comes off sounding clinical or routine instead of sincere. They probably feel that they've been burned by the media and that responding is just not worth the time and effort when they've got businesses to run. They may be partly right, because there are other uncontrollable factors at play when it comes to the media and public attitudes about big business in the Maritimes. But one thing is clear: the longstanding and current approach is not working.

The Irvings have harboured disdain for the part of the public attitude that is suspicious of everything they do and is so ready to criticize, often with little or no knowledge of the information at hand. It is surely that disdain that has brought J. K., more than any other family member, out of the Irving secrecy closet. Twenty years ago, J. K. attempted to set the public record straight on some Irving controversies while giving a speech at a large Saint John business function—a rare event. His cooperation in providing information for this book makes it clear that setting the public straight about his family remains one of J. K.'s ambitions.

Truths

There is truth to the point that the Irvings are secretive and that secrecy has hurt them in many ways. Apprehension about them within governments and among local community stakeholders has slowed the rate of progress on many projects and it has hurt their pride on a personal level. But there are, of course, truths that run deeper than the Irving purview.

Donald Savoie is a professor at the University of Moncton, as well as a renowned author and expert on the subject of Canadian and international public administration, governance, expenditure management, and relations between politicians and public servants. Savoie provides advice on a range of measures to improve accountability, strengthen transparency, and improve management in the public sector. That's just the start of his impressive list of credentials, which also includes authorship of thirty-five books on these subjects.

He happens to come from just outside K. C. Irving's hometown of Bouctouche. If you want to get Savoie all riled up, just mention someone dumping on the Irvings for being all-consuming, all-dominating, omnipresent business monsters who stifle and snuff out entrepreneurs. "That's absolute crap," says Savoie. This attitude, which he calls an "alibi for failure," is used by naysayers against the Irvings and other people who are successful in Atlantic Canada. Thus people use the Irvings as an alibi for any number of their own failures, for any number of reasons: not working hard enough; being under-capitalized; not negotiating effectively; being short on ambition, aptitude, or vision; failing to take care of their customers. Savoie used to hear this kind of thing most frequently twenty years ago, in the mid-1980s, particularly around Saint John. It's something you will hear less in places like Moncton. The difference has to do with the extreme concentration of Irving interests in Saint John, particularly in older industries (pulp and paper mills), and with K.C.'s hard-boiled public image. In places like Moncton, Irving money and investment are much more welcome and the people are receptive to the Irvings because everything they're doing is new (the tissue and diaper plant), and because of the local can-do attitude.

Savoie has strong opinions about this alibi for failure: "It's not sensible. If you want to start a business, start a business. Go for it. If you want to compete, compete. Do you think the Irvings are going to go and stifle out a little entrepreneur? If you get big, they'll look at you. If you get bigger, they'll really look at you. But don't blame the Irvings for the shortcomings of your own energies, enterprise, and vision." Savoie says he is convinced that Atlantic Canada doesn't need any excuses. "We can make it. Forget the alibi. Just look at the Irving business model. Look how it grew against incredible odds, ab-solutely incredible odds. The old guy did it and these guys are continuing to do it, inspired by that same model. And don't assume that what the Irvings want to do is always take advantage of things."

The Irvings have fixations unlike any other business family in Canada. There is no doubt that they have obsessive-compulsive tendencies toward work, details, cleanliness, and family. This book leads us to the dozen or more individuals left in K.C.'s wake, exploring their traits, characteristics, compulsions, and practices. These are a combination of the "Irving DNA"—hard work, patience, perseverance, undying loyalty, respect, moderation, at-tention to detail, deal making—and individual traits. In addition, we'll meet some of the "honorary Irvings," people who have been taken in by the Irv-ings and have learnt the family's formula for success.

After the gap of thirteen years since the last book on the Irvings was pub-lished, it's not only time to catch up with Canada's prolific captains of in-dustry and their personal and business adventures, it's also time to come to terms with the inevitability of their next-generational transition, from hands-on industrialists to a new breed of hands-on philanthropists at a level previ-ously unheard of in Atlantic Canada. As time goes on, there is no escaping these important questions: What will happen when the emerging generation takes the mantle, those great, great, great, great-grandchildren of the first Irving immigrants to New Brunswick, of whom so much will continue to be expected? Will they evade the dreaded business family bug known as "affluenza"? Will they remain the family they've been for a century and a half, or will they disperse themselves into separate family units? And finally, will they outlive the mythologies that surround them by taking full control of their public image?

The book's answers are based on interviews, on emerging evidence concerning the state of the Irving family, and on the instructive histories of other business families that have given rise to the logical expectation that the Irving party just can't go on forever. The current generation of Irvings is the seventh since the family's arrival in Canada, the sixth to be leaders in business. This means they have already defied all the odds, shattering the records of the Morgans, Vanderbilts, Rockefellers, and other business families that have also been prolific and multi-generational. The Irvings we've come to know as industrial power brokers are a generation or less away from a dramatic shift in the roles they will play in Atlantic Canada. Will they do it the old-fashioned Irving way—quietly, discreetly and effectively? Or will modern times and diverging, even competing, personalities overtake any hope for order?

PART I

Generations

1. Clan Eryvine—The First Generation

Genealogy is all about detective work, about piecing together parts of a puzzle. With the Irvings, as with most Scottish immigrants to North America, the investigation begins with distant clan heritage. This process is well known to Fredericton archivist Burton Glendenning, an individual with a penchant for detail and a probing mind who was well-suited for the job when J.K. Irving came looking in 2002 for someone to research and document the family history. J.K. wanted to retrieve the Presbyterian history of Bouctouche before it was lost or forgotten forever. Gradually and by the late 1940s, the generations-old Presbyterian connections to the community had all but disappeared with the influx of francophone Catholics, who are still the prevalent denomination today.

Glendenning's initial fact-finding was pretty standard fare. The Irving Scottish clan origin was in the Old English forms of Erewine and Erwinne, derived from Erwini from between 1124 and 1165. Derivations were associated with early Celtic monarchs of Scotland—Duncan Eryvine, who settled at Bonshaw, Scotland, brother of Crinan, who claimed descent from the High Kings of Ireland. The lands of Dumfriesshire are associated with the name Irvine, specifically Annan town, the Annan River and Annan Parish, all in Annandale. Together with their coat of arms, this is standard clan genealogy. But what Glendenning went on to discover astonished and delighted both he and J.K. If not for the curiosity of J.K. in commissioning Glendenning's investigation, the original Irving story would have remained unknown.

Glendenning uncovered pieces of the Irving puzzle that had never before been public knowledge, things that the Irvings themselves are probably still coming to terms with. These include references to new names such as George and Herbert Irving, old places like Dumfriesshire, Kirkcudbrightshire, Lot number 3734, the Renauld Road, and Irvingdale, and legal things including wills, promissory notes, and letters of patent. Central to what Glendenning uncovered is that the Irvings were once as impoverished as any other family in New Brunswick, which, given how far they've come, has got to make an already proud clan feel all the prouder. Times were tough for most early nineteenth-century immigrants to Canada. The Scottish-born Irvings were no exception.

Like many of their contemporaries, they arrived empty-handed, subsided off the rigour of the Canadian landscape, and feared God. That the Irvings experienced such tough slogging in the early days makes it all the more remarkable that the matriarch of the family defied the odds of her time and lived to be a centenarian and then some. The following headline appeared in the February 12, 1889, edition of the *Moncton Times*:

"103 Years of Age: A Case of Remarkable Longevity in Kent County." The headline was in reference to George Irving's late wife Jane (Stitt), who was born at Kirkcudbrightshire, Scotland, in 1787 and died at Mill Branch, Kent County, New Brunswick, on February 6, 1889. Dumfriesshire native George had died twenty-six years earlier than his wife, but he didn't do so bad either, outlasting most of his contemporaries by making it to the ripe age of eighty-four. For a couple who arrived in the New World in 1833 with nothing but eight children in tow (two more arrived after they settled in New Brunswick), they must have had incredible determination and robust constitutions. Many of George and Jane's descendants have also enjoyed longevity—for example, all three of their great-great-grandsons, all in their late seventies, remain in good health. However, this is not a story about life expectancy. It's a story about life's expectations.

When K. C.'s grandson and namesake Kenneth Irving's fourth child was born—a fourth girl—he let it slip to an acquaintance that he was relieved, saying he always wanted to have four girls. It wasn't so much that he absolutely needed to have four girls. It was more that he wasn't so sure he wanted a boy. "Much is expected of the men in this family," he said. In Kenneth's words, you can detect the weight of a lifetime spent being a male Irving. It's the load he has carried, like the others in his extended family, since the days when he was first coached to stand and stare into K. C.'s eyes, being taught how to present himself, how to shake a person's hand firmly and to ask the typical Irving question, "How are we doing?"

Much has been expected of the men in the Irving family ever since George Irving cobbled together three pounds sterling in 1837 as the first instalment for the survey and registration of the first piece of land the family would own in New Brunswick: Lot number 3734, ground zero of the empire to be. It cost the family fifteen pounds and no doubt much anxiety. It would take until May 1846—another nine years—before they could afford to complete the payment, an additional 11 pounds, cumulatively representing their second, third, fourth, and final instalments, earning them true title of one hundred acres on the northwest side of a tract known as Mill Branch, Kent County, New Brunswick. It was the commonly sized land grant of the day. It was land that was barely arable, not a spread of profit-producing forest. Of all the numbers associated with the long Irving legacy, this first one hundred acres is the most important one. If only George and his wife Jane could have stood on that first lot and seen the landscape and their family's future holdings unfurl before them. Together with their ten children (Elizabeth, Mary, Herbert, Thomas, Janet, Nancy, George, Jessie, John, and Margaret), George and Jane had already been living on the British land grant as poor squatters for more than three years before being able to make that first payment. That fact and their devout Protestantism defined them. Lot number 3734 is a symbol of the humble origins the Irvings shared with the other immigrants of their time. Who would have expected that any family in poverty-riddled nineteenth-century New Brunswick would go from that single lot, barely paid for, to become number 129 on the list of the world's richest people? When put in those terms, it is a breathtaking accomplishment.

2. From Rags to Riches—The Second Generation
GEORGE > HERBERT

It's a cliché, but it's true: the Irvings are an old-fashioned rags-to-riches story. Perhaps, therefore, it has become purely instinctive for Irvings to so aggressively pursue the things they do. None of them, from J. D. on down, has wanted to see their ancestors' hard work squandered on their watch. None of them wants to be responsible for turning theirs into a rags-to-riches-to-rags story, like the stories of so many other business families both large and small.

George and Jane Irving must have worked feverishly in their pursuit of the relative prosperity of their time. They were no doubt a stable and reliable influence. But it was one of their ten children who would dramatically turn the family tide. Emerging from the brood of ten, Herbert Irving was twenty-five years old in 1848, when he received his first land grant of sixty acres at Coal Branch, Weldford Parish, Kent County, New Brunswick. He was born on March 22, 1823, in Dumfriesshire, Scotland, and died in Bouctouche, New Brunswick, on September 19, 1907. In those intervening years, he was responsible for inventing the Irving entrepreneurial spirit. It was on his first sixty acres that he began his work as a farmer. Unlike his father, who never budged from his Bouctouche farm, Herbert grew by acquiring a second lot of 110 acres and quickly began making his presence felt in the community as a farmer, as a businessman, and as a volunteer in various assigned capacities over the years: he was a constable from 1853 to 1858; a constable and boom master of Weldford in 1858; a constable and fence viewer when he moved his family to nearby Chockpish, in Richibucto Parish, in 1858. In Chockpish he acquired an additional 375 acres, 100 of which were recorded as "improved." This is where he remained until 1884. When he returned to Bouctouche in 1884, Herbert Irving was appointed surveyor of roads. On June 13, 1885, he and his wife Catharine Dergavil were accepted as members of the Presbyterian church meaning they had been fully immersed into the community.

"The farm Herbert started was fascinating," says Burton Glendenning, "because it was built on the latest in scientific agriculture." He is referring to Herbert's inspired decision to import prized bulls from Nova Scotia and Ontario, a good brood mare from Scotland, and new varieties of apples. He was involved in the agricultural societies of his day, a sign of his advancing sophistication as a farmer. He was even forward-thinking in his use of fertilizers and other farming techniques. To put Herbert's growth as a farmer and businessman in context, consider that as early as 1860 (a mere sixteen years after his father had barely scraped together a few pounds to finish paying for the family's original land grant) his net worth was recorded at $3,440, including land, buildings, and machinery. He employed three hired hands on the Richibucto farm, including a woman who worked in the household. Meanwhile, a single hired hand harvested twenty-five tons of hay on the original holding of land back at Coal Branch, in Bouctouche. The following year, the Richibucto farm produced a goodly harvest, including two hundred pounds of cheese, nine hundred pounds of butter, eight hundred pounds of pork, five hundred bushels of potatoes, six hundred bushels of oats, seventy-five pounds of wool, and cloth valued at one hundred dollars. By 1863, Herbert emerged as an active member of the Kingston Agricultural Society, winning recognition and cash prizes for both his produce and his cattle, including second-best bull ($1.00), second-best cow ($1.50), third-best wheat ($1.50), second-best butter ($1.25), and third-best cheese ($1.00).

But beyond his efforts in livestock, cheese, butter, and pork, Herbert was busily emerging as something far more dynamic than a successful and prize-winning farmer—he had made himself into what Glendenning describes as a land developer and the area's "informal financial institution." If lot number 3734 is the symbolic foundation of the future Irving holdings, then Herbert's growth marks the symbolic turning point in the rags-to-riches yarn. He was the unofficial local bank at a time when there was no requirement for letters of patent or for an act of the legislative assembly for a person to lend money. In fact, it was not until 1926 that Herbert's grandson K. C. received the family's first official letters of patent from the government permitting him to loan money, or as Glendenning's research says, "to guarantee the performance of contracts."

What were Herbert's loans being used for? Mortgages—lots and lots of mortgages, including, ironically, the one on the Presbyterian church, where not too long before he and Catharine had been accepted as parishioners. There was a local need for cash, and Herbert's enterprising ways and hard work had produced enough to bankroll his neighbours and many others throughout the area. "He was everywhere and banks weren't everywhere," says Glendenning. Banks were in far-flung places like Moncton, Fredericton, and Saint John while Herbert was virtually next door. He was considered a respectable individual who, in a short span of time, bought, sold, and financed a hoard of properties. Consider that between 1858 and 1884 (the year he supposedly entered semi-retirement), Herbert undertook an average of eleven mortgage transactions per year. Even after slowing down, between 1884 and 1891, he conducted an average of seven such transactions annually. The list of surnames appearing on those early mortgages is too vast to list, but a random selection includes Guguen, MacLeod, Sawyer, Hudson, McEwen, Collet, Melanson, Belliveau, Mills, McKie, and dozens more.

At the same time that he was busily lending money hand over fist, Herbert's own land holdings were growing dramatically, as illustrated by his acquisition of Crown land grants, which were additional to property acquired through purchase, such as the 375 acres he bought in 1858. By the time Herbert was barely middle-aged, lot number 3734 was a comparatively small matter and probably didn't yet have the sentimental value it has today. Table 1 shows his land acquired through purchase, over the years. These are in addition to Herbert's Crown land grants.

TABLE 1
Herbert Irving's land acquisitions

YEAR	GRANT NUMBER	ACREAGE	LOCATION
1848	4367	60	Dundas
1853	5825	110	Weldford
1873	15347	98	Weldford Parish
1877	16890	32	Richibucto Parish
1878	17127	100	St. Mary's Parish
1879	17582	100	Richibucto Parish
1882	18912	90	Acadieville Parish
1884	19907	50	Harcourt Parish

This spirit of acquisition and capitalism are likely traceable, at least in part, to the Presbyterian culture of which Herbert was such a part. According to Max Weber (1864–1920), one of the founding fathers of sociology, the seeds of capitalism are found in the traditional Protestant work ethic. In *The Protestant Ethic and the Spirit of Capitalism,* written in 1904–05, Weber depicts capitalism as the most fateful force in modern Western life. He writes:

> The impulse to acquisition has existed always and everywhere and has in itself nothing to do with capitalism. Capitalism is the pursuit of profit, and forever renewed profit, by means of continuous, rational, capitalistic enterprise. This enterprise must be continuous, because in a capitalist society, anyone who did not take advantage of opportunities for profit-making would be doomed to extinction.

Weber's oft-cited text claims that there is a direct correlation between religious affiliation and social stratification. Catholics, he argued, show a stronger propensity to remain in their crafts, to become master craftspeople, while Protestants are attracted to "the upper ranks of skilled labour and administrative positions in factories. Protestants own a disproportionate share of capital." He argued that the increase of one's capital, in Calvinistic terms, was not just an ideal of subsistence, but an end in itself—"the ultimate purpose of a man's life. This is combined with the strict avoidance of all spontaneous enjoyment of life...the unalterable order of things in which they must live." Somewhere between Weber and sixteenth-century French theologian John Calvin, the Protestant connection with capitalism exists. Followers of Calvin believed that one could not get to heaven simply by performing good works or acts of faith. You were either among the chosen or you weren't. Wealth, however, was taken as a sign, by individuals and their neighbours, that you were one of the chosen; therein lies the encouragement to acquire wealth. The Protestant ethic allowed or commanded activities and disciplines that encouraged people to apply themselves rationally to the acquisition of wealth. People certainly regard the Irvings as being Calvinist in their lifestyle. It is widely known, for example, that they avoid alcohol and other such frivolities. If their success as capitalists is anything to go by, this approach has clearly worked for the Irvings so far, through seven generations.

Eventually, Herbert added "industrialist" to his job description, alongside farmer and informal banker. On October 17, 1883, he completed the acquisition of a steam sawmill from two gentlemen named George and John Robertson. It was the largest steam-powered mill in Kent County and was situated on the Bouctouche waterfront—the future location of a string of businesses under the purview of J. D. Irving. The mill was one of the few structures to survive "Le Grand Feu," the grand fire of September 22, 1892, which took eighteen houses, ten businesses, two barns, three warehouses, five hotels, four other businesses, and part of the span of the Bouctouche Bridge.

In 1891 Herbert divested himself of the sawmill, choosing son J.D. as his successor. At Herbert's death in 1907, resources were distributed amongst some of the children, with J.D. acquiring the family homestead in Bouctouche, as well as Herbert's "book debts, promissory notes and securities." The mortgage on the church was not bequeathed to J.D.; rather, it was held in trust by him, a modest, discreet way of demonstrating that the debt was forgiven. Herbert also left an amount of money for distribution to the poor of the parish and another amount to assist with the operation of a Sunday school, the first documented instances of Irving philanthropy, though certainly not the last.

3. Vertical Integration—The Third Generation
GEORGE > HERBERT > J.D.

The Irving men have a tendency to be central figures in their families and in their communities. In this regard, as well as in business, Herbert's son J.D. was no slouch. He was born in Galloway, Kent County (just north of Bouctouche, on the Northumberland Strait) on October 15, 1860. He was twice married, to Minnie Hutchison in 1884, and after her death, to Mary Gifford, in 1893. J.D. would live until 1933 and Mary until 1944.

In Douglas How and Ralph Costello's *Biography of K. C. Irving* (1993), the authors argue that J.D. was not only entrepreneurial—having run a general store, a power plant, a cold storage and freezer plant, a gristmill, a carting mill, a lumber business, an export business, three farms, and the sawmill— he was also the acknowledged central figure of the wider Irving family of his era, said to be the one whom siblings and the extended family would turn to for advice or aid. He was also into the fish and produce marketing business, a leading Liberal of his day, a pillar of the local Presbyterian church, and a philanthropist. How and Costello recount how J.D. responded to the tragedy of the 1917 Halifax explosion by gathering up as many windows and window-panes as he could find, and loading them and a handful of men onto a train to the Nova Scotia capital—all with no apparent gain. It seems J.D. had taken to philanthropy in the fashion of his father Herbert's devotion to the Presbyterian church. J.D. also shared his father's knack for setting the bar high in business and in farming, raising award-winning livestock, and following modern agricultural practices. J.D.'s agricultural efforts earned awards in 1912 for Champion Holstein Bull at the New Brunswick Provincial Exhibition in Saint John and for Reserve Champion Holstein Bull at the Maritime Exhibition in Halifax. Also like his father, he imported a mare from Scotland, this one acquired, coincidentally, from a man by the name of Robert C. Irving of Kirkcudbrightshire (home of J. D.'s grandmother Jane Stitt, though this Irving was apparently of no direct relation).

The Irvings' first foray into the media spotlight occurred when J. D. was written about in the December 1912 edition of the Maritime Farmer, where he was described as "a model to be emulated" for his work at the aptly named Bouctouche homestead, Sea View Farm. Unlike much of today's media relations, it was no doubt a gratifying experience. The Maritime Farmer congratulated J. D. for his ingenuity in vertical integration, the practice, much admired at the time, of producing things in one enterprise that would feed the needs of other enterprises. In those days, J. D. used the natural fertilizer harvested from the local bay for the growing of crops to feed his family, grew hay to feed his well-bred livestock, and processed the farm's outputs at the grist and carting mills he built on the Bouctouche waterfront. This is also near where he milled the wood he harvested. The Irvings have been practically crucified by some for their modern vertical integration practices, constantly accused of squeezing out small entrepreneurs by supplying themselves with whatever it is they need. (Dr. Savoie would classify this attitude under "alibi for failure.") A classic example of Irving vertical integration practices would be their end-to-end formula of harvesting wood, milling the wood, adding value to the wood, transporting the wood, and then selling it at one of their modern, sprawling Kent Building Supplies stores. Similarly, by owning Thorne's Hardware in Saint John, the Irvings could supply themselves with everything from hammers to generators to plumbing and electrical materials. On the grander scale, Irving ships work in synch with the Saint John Irving Oil refinery, eliminating any need to have third-party transporters.

It was the Irving milling operations, backed by the sawmill Herbert had passed on to J. D., that set the family's entrepreneurial and industrial future squarely on track. The momentum was evident in J. D.'s company letterhead, which at one time or another between 1881 and 1900 listed his business activities as general store, lumber mill, and gristmill operator, and fish dealer.

When he died on June 6, 1933 (an exact century after the arrival of his grandfather George from Scotland), J. D. had an estate valued at $88,307.80, on which succession duties were paid, a sizeable chunk in those days. Apart from ensuring his wife was cared for, he left his children combinations of land, goods, and cash from his estate, as well as shares in J. D. Irving Ltd. J. D.'s oldest son John Herbert seemed to take himself out of the business equation by moving to Halifax, according to J. D.'s *Moncton Times* obituary.

K. C. was to inherit the bulk of J. D.'s business holdings because the two were legally intertwined in the first two companies the Irvings ever owned.

The first was K.C. Irving Ltd., the letters of patent for which were dated November 22, 1926, and directors of which were listed as K.C., his father and his mother. But even more importantly, K.C. was listed as a director in J.D. Irving Ltd., the letters of patent for which were dated May 22, 1928. Although not verifiable, it appears clear by the nature and order of these incorporations that K.C. recognized the importance of the family getting its business affairs into legal order.

The letters of patent are revealing in terms of the breadth and scope of enterprise that both J.D. and K.C. were involved in. K.C. Irving Ltd. intended to carry out the business of everything from garage men to machinists and automobile outfitters, acting as financiers, real estate agents, and brokers. A single clause found within the letters of patent almost prophetically alludes to the company's future diversity and modern-day ventures; the clause reads: "To own and operate tanks, wagons, automobile trucks, boats, steamers or any other means or conveyances for the transportation, storing and sale of gasoline, oils or similar commodities." The letters of patent for J.D. Irving Ltd. are similarly vast in their diversity and complexity.

The expansiveness of J.D.'s and K.C.'s business vision very much replicated that of their predecessor Herbert, the first to leap from farming to land acquisition, then to financing, and finally into a form of industrial development. Reading the successive letters of patent, one gets the sense that J.D. and his son saw opportunity around every corner; they expected their business to expand exponentially in a very short period of time. Somewhere along this path, with K.C. having ventured into the city of Saint John, the formalization of their affairs into corporations became an essential precondition for further growth.

4. The Fulcrum—The Fourth Generation
GEORGE > HERBERT > J.D. > K.C.

It is without exaggeration to say that K.C. is, not was, the fulcrum, the pivotal man in the Irving story. Looking back from the twenty-first century, he still stands squarely at the centre of the family's multi-generational progression: the three generations before him and the three generations that have followed. In physics, the fulcrum does not create the force. The force was created by the combined business activities (as early as 1858) of Herbert and his son J.D., the latter remaining active until around 1930. During that span of more than seventy years, the two men unleashed enough entrepreneurial momentum between them that the Irving business machine became unstoppable. The fulcrum transfers the force from one place to another, changes the direction of the force, increases its magnitude, distance, or speed. This is an almost perfect description of the role that K.C. not only played, but continues to play. He may be deceased, but he is not gone. Although he died in 1992, he still acts as the centrepoint between the applied force of his grandfather and father and the resistant force of his descendants.

The resistant force is the ever-lingering threat that the descendants will eventually lose control of things, that they will not be able to continue keeping the family business on track in defiance of the odds. Just as surely as J.K., Arthur, Jack, their children and grandchildren think about K.C. every day of their waking lives, they count on his presence to guide them. It is because of K.C.'s overwhelming influence that the family has held together up to now. They feel his presence, they hear his voice, they mimic his actions in everything they do. They would feel ashamed before him if they didn't keep it all together. And he would be ashamed of them in turn.

The idea of K.C. as the Irving family fulcrum is more than just a metaphor. In day-to-day Irving life, it is very real. Before K.C.'s time was the first Irving era, during which the Irving corporate foundation was set in place and secured. It was an era that twenty-first-century Irvings would have difficulty relating to or being connected to without the linkage of their grandfather. After K.C. is the third era, that of those same twenty-first-century Irvings, in which things are constantly threatening to go off balance because of the widening diversity of players and personalities at play in the modern Irving corporate and family hierarchy. The only thing connecting the first and third eras is K.C. himself, still very much alive and inspirational to his sons, grandchildren, and great-grandchildren.

It's impossible for people to pass off their personal contact with K.C. as anything other than an extraordinary event. He may not have had charisma on the magnitude of a JFK or a Mother Theresa, but he definitely had a quality that could bring the room to him. Being tall and distinctive looking was definitely a physical advantage, but charisma is more than physical. It is also charm and the ability to influence people. It wasn't just that he possessed authority and power. His money paved the way for many things, but it was his charisma—his influence and ability to persuade—which cut the road first. When it came to K.C., influence and persuasion were never lacking. When he spoke, people listened. When he asked, people answered. When he said jump, people had a habit of asking, "How high?"

◆

It doesn't come up in interviews or in idle talk and it's not how he's remembered or imagined, but K.C. Irving, it turns out, was in fact once a little boy. Because his image is that of the imposingly tall, steely-eyed magnate in a dark suit, it's hard to picture K. C. frolicking about. But no doubt he did. He played in the woods, ran barefoot, swam in Bouctouche Bay, skipped stones, and did his share of chores around Sea View Farm. Although it seems unimaginable, at an early age he may even have spent idle time daydreaming. But even with what his grandfather Herbert and father, J. D., had built, could he ever have imagined the Irving empire that would come to be?

K. C. was born in Bouctouche on March 14, 1899, on the cusp of a new century that would unleash new forms of economic expansion, industrialization, and technology. In a Maritime Canadian context, he would play an important part in this unleashing. He attended Dalhousie and Acadia universities for short periods before heading to England in 1916 against his father's wishes for service in the Royal Flying Corps. In 1924, he opened his first garage in the community of Bouctouche. Living in an apartment atop the garage, he became known for his willingness to get out of bed for customers who would honk their horns looking for gas in the middle of the night—the precursor to the type of twenty-four hour service now offered at many Irving stations and stores. K. C. also wrote down his personal business mantra in 1924, the précis of which is: "Look after the customer and they'll look after you."

Three years later, on February 4, 1927, he married Harriett L. MacNairn of East Galloway, a community just north of Bouctouche. In 1931, K. C. was offered the first Ford Motor Company sales franchise in Saint John and relocated his family there from Bouctouche. So proud was he of his association with Ford that he drove their vehicles for the rest of his life. During the 1930s, he also embarked on a plant venture that would be the precursor to his oil refinery days— the blending and packaging of lubricants, including the first factory-sealed one-quart lubricant to hit the market in glass bottles. To K. C., the glass bottle was a way to provide customers with the assurance of quality and purity.

Over the decades that followed, his expansion into gas retail and service outlets occurred at a rate paralleled only by his own expansion into forestry, transportation, manufacturing, and related industries, all of which holds to the principle of vertical integration. The construction of an oil refinery, heralding a new chapter in the scale of Irving operation, was marked with an official opening ceremony held on July 20, 1960.

The magnitude of enterprise that grew out of K. C.'s time as the family fulcrum is only fairly explained by listing the interests that today are publicly detectable, though they may not be well-known by the public at large. These include:

· Irving Oil Ltd.
· J. D. Irving Ltd. and its various operations, from forest certification to

fisheries management to tree growing to a mass of saw, paper, and pulp mills found throughout Atlantic Canada, as well as in Maine and Quebec
· shipbuilding companies and subsidiaries
· Irving E-commerce
· transportation companies, including Midland Transport and Midland Courier, Sunbury, Kent Line, Atlantic Towing, and the NB Southern Railway
· construction companies, including Gulf Operators civil works, Barrington Industrial Services, Irving Equipment, York Steel, Strescon construction contractors, Marque Construction, FCC Engineering, and Ocean Steel
· retail interests such as Chandler Hardware, Plasticraft Signs and Graphics, Kent Building Supplies, Kent Homes, Universal industrial parts and repair, Irving Tissue, Source Atlantic industrial parts and equipment distributors, and Lexi-Tech International
· Cavendish Farms food processing company

Tracking, let alone operating, what K. C. and later his sons have wrought, is exhausting work.

There is a side to this industriousness that few people know about. According to *The Biography of K. C. Irving* by Douglas How and Ralph Costello, the three Irving siblings—Kenneth, Marion, and Lou—were each provided with their own violin by their father, J. D. He'd reportedly ordered them from the Williamson Company in Toronto for $25 apiece. In How and Costello's account of things, K. C. could play a tune, but was no virtuoso. Perhaps he was already too focused on becoming a maestro in his other chosen fields.

They say that a skilled violin-maker can walk into the woods and determine the quality and suitability of a tree by tapping on the trunk with the backside of a hatchet. K. C. too had the ability to walk into the woods and see things about trees that others would never appreciate or understand, things that he taught to his sons and to his grandchildren. He may have been mediocre at playing the violin, but he probably could have found the right maple, spruce, and ebony needed to build one.

In business, K. C. was never meant to be one string in the orchestral ensemble; he was destined to be the composer and conductor, indeed the maestro. In this pivotal role, he would be at the centre of everything. He would set aside his Williamson Company violin because he had something far more powerful to focus on: his opus, his symphony of enterprise. He did, however, cling to a favourite metaphor from his short-lived days as a violinist. He was known to say of people who couldn't get the job done in business that "they couldn't play the violin."

With wife Harriett, K. C. had three sons, J. K., Arthur, and Jack. Harriett died in May of 1976; K. C. later married Winnifred, who still divides her time between New Brunswick and the home they shared in Bermuda before his death on December 13, 1992.

◆

Saint John native Joel Levesque has had an unavoidable connection with the Irving family and Irving businesses all his life. His father worked for them. He's worked for them, both directly and indirectly. It's almost as though he's one of them. Many Saint Johners, because they're surrounded by Irving-ness and have been connected to the family and their companies one way or another, have similar Irving perspectives, but few have a story so acutely descriptive of K. C. as this one told by Levesque. As vice president of public affairs for Saint John–based Moosehead Breweries and a leader in the pub-lic relations field in Canada, Levesque knows that no matter what company, product, or service he is representing, the focus must always be on the cus-tomer. This lesson was taught to him personally by K. C. in an occurrence that has dramatically shaped his view, not only of the Irvings, but of how important the customer really is in the grand scheme of their businesses.

Christmas Eve, 1971, was an inhospitable night, with sleet and freezing rain pounding down on Saint John. There were two people scheduled to work until midnight at the Irving gas station near the Reversing Falls Bridge (the one that catastrophically exploded three years later, accidentally killing four people and putting the Irving name on the national news wires in the worst imaginable circumstance). Levesque (of the same generation as J. K.'s son Jim and Jim's cousin Kenneth) and another student named Dale Smith were winding down what was, because of the conditions, a pretty slow shift, when they suddenly had a visitor. As Levesque tells it, "At 11:00 PM on Christmas Eve, in pulls K. C. Irving and his wife in a shiny navy blue Meteor and he jumps out—and he's well into his seventies. He shakes our hands, 'Merry Christmas fellows. How's business? What's going on?'"

Levesque and Smith, taken aback, returned the salutation, including a "Thank you, Merry Christmas Mr. Irving." In those days, tiny gas islands were where pump jockeys spent their time between servicing cars, especially when the weather was cold and crappy. At K. C.'s urging, the three spent the next few minutes standing inside the glassed-in cubicle—little more than an over-sized telephone booth—that seemed crowded when there were only two occupants. No sooner had K. C. stepped inside than the phone rang. Lev-esque took the call from a man at St. Rose Church in the Saint John district known as Milford, behind the nearby Irving-owned pulpmill. The caller had just come out of the ten o'clock Christmas Eve mass with his family, had gotten stuck in a snow bank, and was enlisting the aid of a tow truck.

"So K.C. is in this little gas island with us and I'm talking on the phone with this customer and I'm apologizing to him that we don't have a tow truck," continues Levesque. "And K.C. overhears even though he's talking to my colleague, turns to me, and says, 'What's this all about?' just as I'm hanging up the phone. So I explain to him this chap was stuck in the parking lot and looking for a tow truck. 'And as you know, Mr. Irving,' I said, 'we don't have a tow truck.' K.C. looked around and spied a pile of twenty-pound bags of rock salt that were being sold at the station for use on winter driveways and icy stairways. He says, 'Put a couple of those in my trunk.' So I put a couple in his trunk. He reaches into his pocket and pays me for them, which struck me as so funny. I understand now, of course—because it was inventory—but as a seventeen-year-old I'm thinking, *Hey, Mr. Irving, this is your stuff. Why are you paying me for it?*"

K.C. asked Levesque if he knew where the fellow was calling from. Levesque named the church and K.C. responded with a self-assured, "Yes, yes I know." Off he went into the night in his blue Meteor with Mrs. Irving along for the ride, determined to find and help this individual. "So to me," says Levesque, still shaking his head after thirty-five years, "that was the single most important lesson I've ever had about customer service and building consumer loyalty. I'm thinking, *Geez, that guy's just phoned an Irving station. Five minutes later, K.C. Irving shows up to help him push his car out of the snow bank.* So tell me that guy is not going to buy Irving gas and Irving home heating oil for the rest of his life. I remember thinking: *That's brilliant.*" Even then, the teenaged Levesque recognized the lesson for what it was—the Irving mantra: *Look after the customer and they'll look after you.*

"That, to me," says Levesque, "is exactly how all of the Irving family behave. That's been my experience with them. They all behave that way. Customers come first, employees come first. They are tremendously loyal to their hardworking employees. They demonstrate great respect to those people." Levesque admits that it's not all roses. "They ask a lot of their employees. They really do, but it can also be very rewarding. 'If you can't stand the heat,' as my father used to say, 'get out of the kitchen.'"

K.C. left an indelible customer service imprint on teenaged pump jockey Joel Levesque, just as he did on his sons and grandchildren. In a roundabout way, he left this imprint for everyone who's a closet or self-confessed Irving watcher. He even went so far as to write down his customer service philosophy, authored as early as 1924. K.C.'s philosophy remains alive as it is still posted in many Irving operations and is frequently used in Irving training programs:

What is a Customer?

A customer is the most important person in your business.

A customer is not an interruption to your work—he is the purpose of it.

We are not doing him a favor by serving him.

He is doing us a favor by giving us the opportunity to do so.

A customer is not dependent on us—we are dependent on him.

A customer is not an outsider to our business. He is part of it.

A customer is not a cold statistic. He is a flesh & blood human being with feelings and emotions, biases & prejudices.

A customer is not someone to argue and match wits with. Nobody ever won an argument with a customer.

A customer is someone who brings us his wants.

It is our job to handle them profitably to him and ourselves.

If K.C. had such profound impact on Joel Levesque's life and future outlook through a single incidental act, it's easy to imagine the massive influence he had through the daily lessons given his sons and the frequent lessons given his grandchildren. It's also easy to imagine that the knowledge and wisdom behind K.C.'s teachings had to be the result of those taught by those who came before him. As always, K.C. is at the centre, the fulcrum, of the Irving story.

◆

K.C.'s habit of showing up from out of nowhere has become a family trait. Whether late on Christmas Eve or in the middle of a July afternoon, he liked to arrive unannounced. What better way is there to tell what's really going on in your plants and in your businesses. Following on his lead, it's just as likely for J.K., Arthur Sr., Jack, and their children to appear out of the blue at a gas island, in the aisle of a Kent Building Supplies electrical department, or in the employee locker room of a pulpmill.

Fredericton-based media consultant Arthur Doyle was a teenager the first time he recalls meeting K.C., but long before, when he was just knee-high to an Irving, he can recall his father, G. Arthur Doyle, talking about him. The senior Doyle was a plumbing contractor in Saint John who later branched out into apartment building construction and ownership. Doyle says his father admired K.C. because, although his entrepreneurship operated on a much larger scale, he'd come from the same "value set." Doyle's earliest memories about the Irvings involved driving with his father by the Golden Ball building at night and seeing the lights on in K.C.'s office. He recalls his father saying, "He's working tonight." But then, says Doyle, "Of course he was. He was always working."

One of Doyle's first summer jobs—he was eighteen at the time—was as the timekeeper at a site near the Saint John pulpmill, jointly owned in those days by Irving and Kimberley-Clark. The job paid sixty cents an hour, the minimum wage in those days for summer students. It wasn't exactly back-breaking work, Doyle confesses; it consisted mainly of sitting in a tiny hut filling out workers' timesheets while monitoring their comings and goings and recording what jobs they were on. He would write down what part of the project the carpenters, plumbers, electricians, and labourers were working on. He also toured the site a couple of times in the morning and in the afternoon, reporting to a site superintendent by the name of Art Monaghan, a "tough, hard-nosed" guy who knew exactly how to build things for the Irvings.

One hot, mid-July afternoon, Doyle was stationed in his hut, about to make his rounds, when a shiny black Ford pulled up nearby. The car's lone occupant emerged wearing a double-breasted, dark blue suit, a crisp white shirt, and black polished shoes, and sporting a bald pate. The man began walking over to the same mobile port-o-potty as a site worker who'd emerged from a nearby building. When the tradesman saw K.C. heading for the can, he quickened his pace, arrived first and closed and locked the door. Although Doyle had never met K.C., something about his look and demeanour said that this just had to be "the man." Doyle scurried from his hut, caught up to K.C. and apologized for the worker's actions. "Sir," he said, "I apologize for that. That's rude and he'll just be a minute. And if not, don't worry, I'll bang on the door." K.C. turned around and said, "No, no. He works here. I don't. The sooner he gets through and gets back to work, the better." Still not identifying himself, K.C. inquired of Doyle if he was the timekeeper and asked, "Do you mind if I look around the site?" Doyle never quite got over the impression K.C. made. "He was very serious, soft spoken, very polite," says Doyle, who made the offer of touring him around the site. "No, no, that's fine," was the response. "I think I can find my way around it."

K.C.'s sense of operational urgency, the fuel he used to propel his companies so far at such an alarming speed, is illustrated in another story told by Doyle. It was passed on to him by the late entrepreneur Joe Palmer, a principal partner in the Day and Ross company. It was ten o'clock on a Saturday night in the middle of winter, a bit of a wild night, with freezing rain, the whole bit. Palmer was at home in rural Hartland, New Brunswick, when his phone rang. Mrs. Palmer answered and told Joe there was a gentleman on the telephone. Joe picked up and heard, "Hello, Mr. Palmer, this is Kenneth Irving [meaning K.C.]." Even though Joe had never met or spoken with K.C., there was something about his voice that made Palmer believe immediately that it had to be him. K.C. was in his sixties at the time, "at the top of his game," as Doyle put it, when he could read a financial statement in five minutes and tell his men, 'Okay, lease that to this company. And take those forty-five trucks and say that they're not in this company. They're going to be owned by another company. And this construction project, keep the contractor owning this. We don't own this yet.' Or, 'The inventory of that oil is $2.9 million. Okay, I want that transferred over to this holding company.' And he'd look at all that in five minutes," professes Doyle.

This is not to portray K. C. as engaging in unconventional accounting of any sort. It's just to say that he had an uncanny acumen for knowing where everything in his businesses was and where everything in his businesses belonged in order to generate the most productivity, a skill he's said to have passed on to his three sons.

K. C. reportedly told Palmer he was interested in a piece of property Palmer owned on the other side of the river from Hartland, home of the world's longest covered bridge. "Well, look," K. C. reportedly said. "I'm interested in talking to you about buying that."

"Okay, that's possible," said Palmer. "I want a good price for it."

"Yes, of course you would. That's a good property."

"Okay, when do you want to send somebody to see me, Mr. Irving? How do you want to proceed?"

"Could you come over?"

So in the middle of that late Saturday night, in the freezing rain of rural New Brunswick, K. C. was either on a pay phone or at a neighbour's nearby house. Almost incredulous, Palmer ventured out into the dark in those terrible conditions, calculating as he went what he would want for the property. Palmer arrived to see K. C. waiting in a broad-brimmed hat, a full-length raincoat, and a pair of rubber boots. One of K. C.'s two Mr. Reids was with him (there were apparently two unrelated Mr. Reids under K. C.'s employ, one in finance, the other in operations). After their salutations, K. C. began pacing up and down the length of the property in question, ignoring the onslaught of rain. Then began the bargaining.

"So what do you want for it?"

"Well, no, how much are you offering?"

"No, no. How much do you want?"

This was a classic K. C. Irving rule: never state a price; try to get one out of the seller. Palmer apparently decided to go fat and overstated the price he actually thought it was worth.

"That's fine," said K. C. "That's great. That's fine." And the two shook hands. K. C. then reportedly went on to say it was too bad it was Saturday night and that Palmer's lawyer probably wouldn't want to work on Sunday, so they'd have to wait for Monday morning for their respective legal beagles to talk. K. C. wanted it settled Monday morning. Period.

Doyle says K. C. did not like to wait. "You could die. I could die. You could change your mind." *Now* was K. C.'s operative word. An Irving gas station still sits on that Hartland site to this day.

◆

Dr. Louis LaPierre tells a story told to him by J. K. about a visit with his father to the Saint John Irving pulpmill, on a foggy, rainy Bay of Fundy night. J. K. would have been, says LaPierre, in his late forties, perhaps his early fifties. He and K. C. walked in a back door of the mill and J. K. set about to wipe his glasses clean. Inside a nearby washroom, J. K. gave a roll of toilet paper a whirl and five or six squares unfurled. His father said, "Oh Jimmy, hold on." K. C. reached over and tore off a single square of the tissue, handed it to his son and reportedly said, "All you need is one." In telling the story, J. K. would admit to LaPierre that his father was a frugal man. LaPierre says that J. K. has a somewhat different makeup, hinting that when his father was not around, he may have used more than one square.

J. K. himself tells a story that more than confirms his father's frugality, as well as his extreme penchant for detail. "My father was a stickler for detail. Before we had fax machines and all these things, it used to be telegrams. I'd sit in my father's office by the hour and he'd send telegrams. He'd go over the telegram and he would count the words. If you had ten words or less, you got a certain rate." If a draft telegram had thirteen or fourteen words, K. C. would work at it until it contained ten words or less. "How can you say this in ten words?" he would say to his son. And he would really work at it. He would change the message this way and that way until he got it in ten words or less. But with so many other things to do in running the business, how could counting words in a telegram possibly have been productive? "That's the way it was. I can't explain it," admits J. K. "Whatever job he was doing, he paid attention to it and he worked at it. There was a pleasure for him in getting all of those details right. That was kind of the score card."

As J. K. told me about his father's fastidious act, he performed one himself. We were driving around Bouctouche, and J. K. called a local Irving employee on a cell phone, a man in his fifties who seemed like a jack of all trades. J. K. unexpectedly pulled up within a stone's throw of the Kent Homes manufacturing plant near the Bouctouche waterfront and parked the Ford he was driving. The employee pulled up behind us in an Irving truck. The employee and J. K. ambled across the lawn near the Kent Homes headquarters. They were discussing the placement of a power pole or some such mundane detail. In the midst of all the big deals and big decisions that go on in the background of every business day, J. K. was doing the K. C. thing almost unwittingly. Exactly where to place the pole suddenly seemed as important as his father's pursuit of telegrams containing ten words or less.

◆

The fact that K. C. eventually retired to Bermuda, causing widespread controversy by shielding himself from the Canadian tax regime (everyone knew it wasn't just about the weather), does not mean that he lost his influence over affairs at home. Although the sons were running day-to-day matters, they very much followed the direction their father had set out, and they continued to do what he wanted them to do. As J. K. said during his interview, "When my father gave me instructions, I carried them out. I respected him and what he wanted done, it was done." In the quiet retirement atmosphere of Bermuda, or even after his passing, K. C. was omnipresent.

It was in Bermuda that New Brunswick business person David Hawkins accidentally had one of the most enlightening experiences of his life: he met K. C. The experience came late in his career, but it was enlightening nonetheless. Hawkins was once a back-to-the-land quasi-hippie who went on to work in advertising with Nikon and Minolta, then with the RT Kelley agency in Toronto, and later in his hometown of Montreal. In 1978, he packed up his agency experience and moved to Sackville, New Brunswick. There, he attended Mount Allison University as a mature student and lay the groundwork for Hawk Communications, which over time became one of the busiest and most profitable advertising and communications agencies in Atlantic Canada.

It's a minor irony that Hawkins would end up selling the business in October 2001 to J. K.'s youngest daughter, Judith. The irony was that Hawkins had already established an inadvertent relationship with her grandfather, K. C., several years prior. In the late 1980s, Hawkins and wife Lorrie were vacationing in Bermuda, staying near what is now the Fairmont Southampton Hotel. "We just bumped into [K. C.]," says Hawkins. "I think a lot of people did during that era in Bermuda. Just by chance I happened to see him walking along and I recognized him and I just went up to him and I said, 'Hi. I'm from New Brunswick.' And he asked my name and so we talked back and forth, and then he said, 'Well, why don't you come over this afternoon for tea?' So we did. And I think other people have had a similar experience." Hawkins and wife Lorrie couldn't resist the invitation. He describes K. C.'s Bermuda home as "a little bungalow" nestled in the shadows of the Fairmont Resort. "It's a very simple, innocuous place that you wouldn't really notice normally. There's a huge, big mansion beside it, and at first we thought that was his place. There was no security or anything." K. C.'s second wife, Winnifred, still lives there part of the year, dividing her time between Bermuda and New Brunswick.

K. C. was in his late eighties at the time, but he was very welcoming and talkative. "You know, you didn't exactly have a conversation with him," Hawkins explains. "You listened." For Hawkins, whose very enterprise relied on his ability to talk and develop relationships, sitting there for hours and hours would have been a near-impossible challenge were it not for whose company he was keeping. This was one of two or three visits the Hawkins' would have with the Irvings in Bermuda, and there were at least as many more back in Saint John. "It was a wonderful experience for me, for both of us [i.e. Lorrie]. He was very, very good to me," says Hawkins. "He was exceedingly kind to me and generous, open, hospitable. I mean, I just couldn't say enough. I really couldn't." Hawkins believes their relationship was rooted in "a very simple thing," the fact that they were both entrepreneurs and both from New Brunswick. "Obviously, he could accomplish more in a day than I did in an entire business career, but just the same, we were on the same theme. It's almost like we were both interested in playing bridge. It didn't matter whether he was a much better bridge player than me, or I was better. You're just interested in the same topic."

After the initial niceties were out of the way between the two couples, K. C. and Hawkins would typically go off to the elder's office. "He was very, very open with me, sharing stories going back to his early childhood and at the end of the First World War when, as a teenager, he enlisted without his father's awareness. Sometimes, he'd repeat the stories, but I always kind of thought—he was quite elderly you know—I always thought that he repeated the stories that excited him and that interested him." The stories were primarily about business conquests, but sometimes they got more personal. Hawkins recalls him speaking about his father, J. D., always in a very respectful manner and usually with reference to what it was like growing up in Bouctouche.

One story that stands out for Hawkins is the tale of K. C.'s enlistment in the air force during the final months of the First World War. He was at Acadia but left there to enlist in the Royal Flying Corps to become a flyer. He showed Hawkins a picture, taken somewhere in Nova Scotia, of himself beside one of those old biplanes. In the photograph, K. C. is seen wearing all the typical flying regalia of that era, including the leather helmet. K. C. was a year shy of the required eighteen years of age, and told Hawkins he joined without his father's knowledge. "So here you have the great K. C., you know, the great Canadian entrepreneur, who at the time was just a student," says Hawkins. "In that context, he was an everyday Canadian kid doing what a lot of Canadian kids did at that time, which was enlist in the war to defend their country. He was a child, and then an adolescent and then a teenager—all of those things—just like all the rest of us, and people forget that, you know."

K. C. would also tell Hawkins stories about how J. D. Irving Ltd. came to lumber more efficiently, exemplified by the shift from the use of horses to the era of internal combustion engines and the advent of trucks. The trucks, he would say, were exciting because they could go straight up and over a hill. "If you fly over New Brunswick, you can see this," says Hawkins, referring to the patterns of logging roads found in rural Atlantic Canada. With horse-drawn logging, Irving's foresters were forced to go round and round and round a hill, from the base to the top, revolving "like a corkscrew." But in a truck, you could go right up the side of it and down the other side, or come back down the same side. (The straight logging road, we'll soon see, was a recurring theme in stories about K. C.)

K. C.'s storytelling illustrates how enthusiastic he remained in the autumn of his life. Hawkins believes the enthusiasm stemmed from the fact that K. C. could recall how he and his company were able to advance through technology and industrialization, even within the relatively unsophisticated economic culture that existed in New Brunswick fifty or sixty years ago. Hawkins says he was aware both then and today about how others saw and judged K. C., but he consciously chose not to be judgmental. "I don't think it's fair for someone with a 1990s consciousness, a thirty-year-old in 1990, to judge a man who at the time was ninety, based on what he had done sixty years before. New Brunswick was a very different place then. The world was a very different place then. And so, in my view, K. C. took the raw material of New Brunswick and moulded it as best he knew how, relative to the times. You know, you can't judge a person outside of their time. And so, you have to look at what he accomplished and how he did things during his time."

Although he knew K. C. only in passing, Hawkins still feels the effects of his mentorship. "He was more than just an acquaintance," says Hawkins. "He was a mentor for me and I listened carefully and he shared information and I was very grateful for that. And I continue to be grateful for that." Hawkins treasures a photo taken of himself and K. C. shaking hands at the Bermuda house, a reminder and a symbol of doing business on a handshake and the value of that. Neither had any idea at the time that K. C.'s granddaughter would eventually assume ownership and control of Hawkins's life's project.

K. C. spent much of his life showing people the way to business success—first and foremost, his sons and grandchildren. But there were countless others: students like Joel Levesque, Arthur Doyle, and David Hawkins, all fortunate enough to wander by chance encounter into K. C.'s virtual classroom. Throughout his career and long into retirement, he played a role that few people, if any, recognize: he taught and mentored people in preparation for their roles in the twenty-first-century business world using the fundamentals taught to him by nineteenth-century men. K. C. stands firmly in the middle, as the Irving fulcrum, the family's pivotal twentieth-century man.

5. Band of Brothers—The Fifth Generation
GEORGE > HERBERT > J. D. > K. C. > J. K., ARTHUR SR., & JACK

From the public's perspective, K. C.'s sons, J. K., Arthur, and Jack, are the three amigos. They have dramatically different styles, but the intimacy of the Jim, Art and Jack Farm company they created as boys remains alive in spirit through their lives and business actions over the decades. The three have always been close to one another thanks to the strong sense of equity that K. C. surely instilled in each of them. They've run separate parts of the empire, but did so in such close fashion that the public still talks today as though all things Irving are still one (see the Irving family tree). The three would teach their children, as Herbert, J. D., and K. C. had, the fundamental lessons and principles of Irving business success. Each would mentor their own offspring, passing along those same core lessons and principles, but naturally applied with their own individual spin. When there ceased to be one teacher, there ceased to be ideal uniformity in the lessons and principles being taught. When there ceased to be one teacher, the subtle magic of unanimity began to slip away.

With the arrival of the twenty-first century, the three brothers were in the midst of passing from their twentieth-century roles as hard-driving businessmen in the mirror image of their father, into more relaxed philanthropic activity. Each also remains preoccupied with being the head of their respective families, but none can truly lead the entire clan or spearhead the overall Irving business thrust. This is because there is no longer an overall Irving business thrust as there was in the days of K. C. and when his three sons were in charge and connected emotionally. Today there are myriad Irving business plans at play at any given time.

Here is where the first natural division in the Irving hierarchy emerged. No matter how much they wanted to, none of the fifth-generation Irvings could reach their entire extended family, with all of its nephews and nieces and great-nephews and great-nieces. They could impose the traditional Irving lessons and principles on their own, as K. C. had done with each of them, but they could not ensure continuity across the entire sixth generation. J. K. could not impose himself on Kenneth and Arthur Jr. Arthur Sr. could not impose himself on Jim, Robert, Mary Jean, or Judith. Jack could not impose himself on any of his brothers' broods. The classic true-to-life image of K. C. sitting on a park bench making corporate decisions with his three sons, the picture of harmony and unanimity, could not be replicated in the sixth generation. They would have to find an awfully long bench, with those at one end unable to hear the message of those at the other.

The best the three brothers could do was to continue to keep the teachings and philosophies of K. C. as front and centre as possible. Wallace and Harrison McCain co-founders of McCain Foods, had no such ideal to turn to, no K. C., no J. D., no Herbert, and this contributed to their corporate demise in the 1990s, brought about by destructive and highly public infighting over family business succession. If J. K., Arthur Sr., and Jack could condition their family members to keep K. C. on a pedestal, however artificially, then there would always be at least some hope for the survival of the classic Irving values and ideals.

◆

K. C. Irving died on December 13, 1992, at the age of ninety-three, but his presence continues to impose itself across the Maritimes and parts of New England, and into the lives of millions of people. No one in the Maritimes comes remotely close to casting a shadow as large as that of K. C., the driven, hard-working man who created an empire simply by following the simple philosophy of taking care of one customer at a time.

This shadow is both figurative and literal. Figuratively speaking, it touches every aspect of Maritime life: whenever you drive your car, heat your home, build your deck, eat your French fries, ship a package, read your morning paper, get your paycheque, buy a hammer, or watch a hockey game; and, of course, whenever you fill your conversation with stories, opinions, and idle talk about the Irvings. K. C.'s creations are so omnipresent that you can't even wipe your bum these days—or wrap your baby's bum—without an Irving product in hand.

In literal terms, if you're in the right spot at the right time, overlooking beautiful Bouctouche Bay during the evening golden hour, you can actually stand in K. C.'s shadow. Here, in what is now a model sustainable tourism community fringed by the Acadian Coastal Drive and the Northumberland Strait, K. C. is represented in bronze as the focal point of a memorial park by the water's edge, not far from the bustling Irving-owned Kent Homes factory. *The Standing Man*, as the sculpture is named, also happens to overlook the original site of Sea View Farm, the place where K. C. grew up and where the house in which he was born once stood (the huge house burned in 1944). Also nearby was the original Presbyterian church so important to the lives of Herbert and Catharine Irving in the latter half of the nineteenth century.

The park is just one in a string of projects in Bouctouche commemorating the Irving presence throughout the community. There is also a warm and faithful rendition of the Presbyterian church called the Irving Memorial Chapel and Plantation. Surrounded by trees and gardens, the chapel's design was inspired in part by Scottish kirks that J. K. and his wife Jean saw during a visit to Scotland, and it is an important symbolic place for the family. Stained glass windows overlook the final resting place of K. C. and Harriett Irving, one window for each of their grandchildren. Jean's vision and ideas are all over this and adjacent sites, including the Plantation, where Celtic stone walls built without mortar combine with more trees, shrubs, and flowers to create a peaceful walkabout. Irving commemorative imprints are found all around Bouctouche, an integrated effort to instill the value of heritage and history in the community and three-dimensional evidence of the hunger J. K. has for understanding and properly honouring his family's past.

The Standing Man and the park surrounding him are on the site of the Irving family's first industrial efforts—the gristmill, the carting mill, the power plant, the cold storage and freezer plant, and—within view at Sawmill Point—the first of what would become many sawmills. Because of K. C.'s long association with the forests, the park is populated with birch, oak, and maple trees. There are benches and granite curbs bordering curving walkways of finely crushed gravel. At the centre is the sculpture of K. C., one of hundreds of works commissioned during the life of the late Michael Rizzello, a British artist and member of the Order of the British Empire. Cast by Rizzello in 1995, the eight-foot figure stands atop a four-foot-high rock. It was Rizzello who called it *The Standing Man.*

The story of how the statue was erected in Bouctouche is really a story about the pride and passion the Irving family feels for their pivotal man. In the hearts and minds of K. C.'s sons, *The Standing Man* was originally intended for another symbolic place, Saint John's Loyalist Burial Ground, the historic cemetery that was transformed into a beautiful park in the heart of the city in 1848. For more than a hundred years, it was a lovely and gracious focal point of the city, but somewhere along the way it fell into serious neglect. Adjacent to the iconic Irving Golden Ball building on Union Street, the overgrown, dilapidated site could be seen by K. C. and his sons from their offices, every single day. Following K. C.'s death in 1992, the Irvings made a proposal to the city to renovate the dilapidated cemetery. But plans changed when Saint John city council rejected the proposal because it included the idea of honouring K. C. in the same blush.

It was a painful episode for J. K., Arthur, and Jack (and no doubt K. C.'s grandchildren), so much so that some time after the council voted against the Irving proposition, then deputy mayor Shirley McAlary, intent on finding some way to have the burial ground renovation go forward, contacted K. C.'s sons. In a very brief meeting in the Irving offices, with K. C.'s three sons present, the deputy mayor was subjected to an abrupt, pounding-on-the-table dressing down from J. K. He said that the family was through discussing the issue and that they were sick and tired of it all. The incident showed just how upset they were over the way their father's name and reputation had been treated. It was a boiling over of the Irvings' simmering resentment at the ongoing degradation of their family name. From the family's point of view, they were doing something valid and worthwhile for the city and its residents. Some on council, though, had viewed the offer as self-aggrandizement on the part of the family. McAlary wasn't responsible for the way things had gone at council, but she was the one who decided to revisit the issue, albeit with good intentions. Minutes later, on the walk back to her office, in front of the Paramount Theatre, McAlary was said to be on the verge of tears. The Irving brothers had been forceful.

But time heals all things. The horribly neglected burial grounds remained a civic blight; the mess was in the Irvings' faces every time they came and went from their offices. Out of the blue one day City Hall received a call from an official at Irving-owned Ocean Steel. The Irvings had changed their minds and decided to proceed with renovating the burial grounds after all, and they had given up on the idea of commemorating their father at the site. There was one condition: the only official the Irvings would deal with on the project was long-serving city manager Terry Totten. An agreement was soon struck. In typical Irving fashion, things proceeded quickly, the result being a meticulously planned and renovated park that the entire city would come to embrace.

The restoration was designed by Alex Novell, a landscape architect with the UK-based firm Novell Tullett. Novell's work was intended to reflect the old, the new, the past, and the future. The Canadian beaver is a recurring theme within the design, symbolizing the hard work, enterprise, and tenacious resolve of the city's founders—the Loyalists who first arrived in 1783— and those who followed. A fountain featuring another sculpture by the late Michael Rizzello is the centrepiece of the site. The project was undertaken to treat the property with utmost respect. Reparation involved resetting grave markers and crypts, fixing damaged stones, and replacing rusted and broken iron brackets with brass fittings. Arbourists and other workers used wooden implements while carrying out their work to ensure the roots of trees were not damaged. Some of them allegedly got up to some gold mining: it's said that a hoard of gold teeth, a tangible trace of the Loyalists buried there, was pocketed by workers. It was a clear-cut case of finders, keepers.

Using lighting, benches, and pathways, and using the natural trees and garden areas to their advantage, the Irvings brought the park back to life. So comprehensive was the plan that people were flying back and forth from

England to Saint John to Boston just to see how bricks should be inlaid to avoid frost-heaving. Materials such as granite were also brought in from the UK to suit the designer's tastes and demands. The overall undertaking was at such a level of quality that the city public works office still possesses, and uses as reference, a bound, hardcover maintenance manual that was provided some time after the speech-making and ribbon-cutting took place at the official re-opening of the park during the summer of 1995. No one knows what the Irvings really spent on the effort. And of course, being Irvings, they wouldn't just build something then walk away. It is not unusual even today for someone from the Irving organization to contact City Hall requesting that a public works crew visit the site to deal with one maintenance matter or another.

An inscription on the grounds' main commemorative plaque includes a passage from Revelation that speaks poetically of the Loyalists and their pluck, concluding with the lines:

> Under the Guidance of your hand, O'Lord
> They sought refuge and found solace on these shores
> May they rest in peace
> Knowing that their descendants now flourish.

What's missing, of course, are the words that, under the family's original plan, would also have commemorated K. C. Irving. The average Saint Johner no doubt takes for granted, or never really ever understood, exactly what J. K., Arthur, Jack, and the extended family went through—what they gave and what they gave up—on the way to achieving their vision for both the park and the commemoration of their father.

With K. C. seemingly unwelcome in the controversial city square, the family looked to Bouctouche as the perfectly logical—some would say, more suitable—alternative. In hindsight, even though Saint John was and remains the true stronghold of Irving businesses, the Bouctouche setting is the more endearing and appropriate place for the statue; in Saint John, K. C.'s presence would have been passive, almost lost, amid the burial grounds' many trees and man-made fixtures, while in smaller, uncluttered Bouctouche, the statue dominates. There is a bronze plaque embedded into a large rock situated opposite the sculpture. The inscription reads:

> Here, within sight of the farm where he was born, and the river where he swam as a boy, stands a monument in honor of the memory and accomplishments of Bouctouche's most famous son, Kenneth Colin Irving. Born March 14, 1899, he was one of Canada's leading 20th century industrialists, entrepreneurs and businessmen.

After serving with the Royal Flying Corps in the First World War, he returned to Bouctouche to sell Ford cars and build his first garage and service station.

In 1925, he moved to Saint John to take over the Ford dealership in that city. After establishing Irving Oil, his business and industrial base expanded rapidly into all Atlantic Provinces, Quebec, Ontario, the United States and beyond. A man of vision, an organizer and a builder, he provided jobs for thousands of people. A pioneer of reforestation, he planted hundreds of millions of trees in New Brunswick in a program that won him national and international recognition.

He returned to Bouctouche often and regularly. He never forgot his old friends and contributed in countless ways to the community. He spoke often of the practical, small town lessons and work ethics he learned here as boy. In his own words, Bouctouche was forever, "the home of my heart."

Dedicated by the people of Bouctouche in August, 1994.

"Home of my heart" indeed. The Bouctouche area had been home to the resilient Irving heart since 1833 and the arrival of K. C.'s great-grandparents George and Jane from Scotland. The statue depicts only K. C., but it could just as readily have been a rendering memorializing his predecessors too.

◆

Francis McGuire is the former New Brunswick deputy minister of economic development and tourism, longtime cohort and political aide to former premier Frank McKenna, and now the president of Moncton-based Major Drilling International. McGuire has seen just how far K. C.'s shadow extends and how his influence continues to affect his descendants personally and emotionally. During the mid-1990s, McGuire was involved in meetings with Kenneth and his father, Arthur Sr., during preparations to upgrade the Saint John Irving Oil refinery, an upgrade that's now recognized as a key factor in the company's overwhelming success today. (As detailed later, there are now plans for yet more expansion.) Discussions and planning for the 1990s upgrade took place over a four-year span, McGuire recalls. "I think most other companies would have just said, 'Screw it!' And I remember saying to Kenneth, 'Well, geez, Kenneth, why are you doing this? It would be cheaper to buy a refinery in Louisiana.'" Acknowledging McGuire's logic, Kenneth asserted his own: "Absolutely, but that's not what my grandfather wanted."

This devotion to what K. C. wants is a constant for the Irvings. When he was aged and for all intents and purposes out of the daily running of the business, K. C. would come home from Bermuda during the summer, spending much of his time at the family's Restigouche River salmon fishing lodge. "I'd be at the office [in Saint John]," says J. K. "My father would come on the radio because we didn't have a telephone at the camp at the time. 'Jimmy, what are you doing this afternoon?' K. C. would say. 'I've got something I should show you. Can you come up?' I said, 'Maybe I'll be up tomorrow.' 'No, this is quite important. Can you come up this afternoon?' But really, he wanted company. So I'd get in my plane and we'd fly off to get up there." There was no question in J. K.'s mind about what he would do. "When my father gave me instructions, I carried them out. I respected him, and what he wanted done, it was done."

McGuire calls J. K., Arthur Sr., and Jack "a band of brothers." They are the Three Musketeers—one for all, all for one. Although J. K. is a large man, he comes across as thoughtful, warm, and gentle. Beneath that placidity, however, is a man of strength and certainty, a man who is always tough enough to get the job done, the leader of the platoon, the John Wayne of the boys. Arthur Sr. is like a Spitfire pilot, a young James Cagney, the one you'd want providing cover from the air with a machine gun when the chips were down. "Damn the torpedoes," he'd be the first to say. Jack is the Fred MacMurray character, the quiet, understated one; not the leader of the platoon, but always there, always reliable.

These different yet complementary personalities have no doubt been vital in transitioning Irving enterprise into the modern business world. K. C.'s forceful ways, which Arthur seems to have inherited, don't really work anymore when applied in isolation. Arthur's thrust-forward personality is useful so long as J. K. and Jack are there to counterbalance and temper their brother. This is evident in the CBC documentary *Unlocking the Mystery*. Throughout the three brothers' interview, one can feel the forcefulness of Arthur's discourse as though sitting across the coffee table from him. With his chin forward, his eyes flashing determination, his hands whipping the air for emphasis, and his more placid brothers looking on quietly from off-camera, Arthur goes positively evangelical: "We want to be successful and we want to have a sense of accomplishment and of doing a good job. That's it! We're not in it for anything else! We want to employ a lot of good people. We want our people to be proud of us. We want to be proud of them and we want to keep going down the road to make this part of the country a better place to live. That's our drive. Every day! Every day! Every day! And not quit!" His hallmark is not ambiguity. It was almost exhausting watching him go at the CBC camera. Almost strategically on Arthur's heels, J. K. eases in quietly, speaking in soft, measured tones, taking the time to explain whatever his brother had just asserted. Jack, speaking when spoken to, is the most ordinary of the three, never the one to make headlines.

This tendency to play off one another is like a practised routine. It is no doubt the natural by-product of seven decades very much spent in one another's company. It all began when they were mere boys.

Many timeless lessons were taught by K. C. to his three sons through symbolic events they would never forget. There's no doubt that one of the specific lessons K. C. taught his sons was the art of taking care of the customer, that the customer is always king. It's the lesson K. C. demonstrated to Joel Levesque and his friend Dale Smith that blizzardy Christmas Eve in 1971. And it's the same lesson he taught his sons one distant New Year's Eve in Bouctouche. For their first business, K. C.'s sons, calling themselves the Jim, Art, and Jack Farm, had gotten 145 hens for the business of selling eggs. J.K. still has an original egg carton from that venture within easy reach in his Saint John office. He owned 60 per cent of the business, Arthur 30, and Jack 10. The brothers were in bed when K. C. and Harriett arrived home around 11:30 PM to find two cartons of eggs on a downstairs table. K. C. went straight to the bedroom and asked what the eggs were doing left downstairs. J.K. explained they were for Mrs. Carter. "I was going to deliver them, but I forgot and I'm going to take them up first thing in the morning." K. C. replied: "No. You were supposed to deliver those today. You go and deliver them." So near midnight on New Year's Eve, J.K. put his clothes on and marched them up to Mrs. Carter, weaving around the cars parked in the yard, knocking on the door, and crashing the Carters' New Year's Eve party. Whoever came to the door announced, "Oh, Mrs. Carter. Your egg man is here!" After an experience like that, J.K. never forgot about the importance of serving the customer's needs, no matter what. You just know that J.K. and his brothers have told this story dozens of times to their own children and grandchildren. No doubt, he and his brothers have imparted similar lessons, both large and small, which will be remembered long after they're gone.

It's said in modern marketing parlance that if you can't own the brand, you don't want it. K. C.'s sons are to be admired even today for the sheer simplicity of their little company's unmistakable name. No one was about to take away the brand "Jim, Art, and Jack Farm," so in that sense, the brothers were applying good old common sense to be what in today's terms is called "strategic." As they explained in *Unlocking the Mystery*, it was through the Jim, Art, and Jack Farm that the three first learned to work together and rely upon one another's strengths. The difference between the brief egg farm era and today is that the current corporation carries their shared surname, making what they own sometimes indistinguishable.

◆

"Irvingdale" has the ring to it of a quaint American village, bringing to mind images of white picket fences, front porches, a treed square with a monument and park benches, and friendly folks who wave to say "Hello." It's actually the site of the old Irving family summer cottage, a place basic enough that during the summers, it artificially put K. C.'s young post-Depression family as close as possible to the plain rural New Brunswick environs of their great-great-grandfather George, the impoverished Scottish immigrant of 1833.

Irvingdale was just one stop on the daylong tour of the Bouctouche area that forms the backdrop of J. K.'s interview for this book. After flying from the Saint John airport, the Irving plane landed on the family's "back-forty" private landing strip, a perfectly paved strip of highway that goes nowhere. J. K. grabbed a stack of box lunches of lobster and chicken sandwiches, fruit, and cookies prepared that morning in the kitchens of the J. D. Irving head office back in Saint John. He then led the way from the plane to a 90s model navy blue Ford Meteor. Easing his frame in behind the wheel, he proceeded to conduct a personal tour of the places and things that are most important to him and his family.

Today, Irvingdale is nothing more than a vacant, overgrown thicket near a small dam and a pond, a short stretch off the Acadian Coastal Drive north of the town of Bouctouche. The Irving family compound, the waterfront venue where the family has cottaged since the 1960s, is just a few short kilometres away. The road leading to Irvingdale is the old Renauld Road, so named for late local farmer Eric Renauld. Renauld was at times a surrogate father of sorts to young J. K., Arthur, and Jack when K. C. was away drumming up business in Saint John and elsewhere in the Maritimes. Harriett Irving would take her boys away from the year-round family home in Saint John to this, a place where they could run barefoot, bicycle, play, swim, and fish for trout. K. C. would spend time there only on periodic weekends, so it was left to Mr. Renauld to help keep an eye on things in between times. Renauld's sons Aubrey and Cleo were older than J. K., Arthur, and Jack, but the boys were chums to some degree.

The Irvingdale cottage was a humble place, a basic building with an outdoor two-holer, four bunk beds, no electricity, and access only by the old mud road that skirted the shores of the Northumberland Strait until the government of Allison Dysart began paving the New Brunswick back roads after being elected in 1935. Mother Nature was the cottage refrigerator; the Irvings kept their butter and milk in the pond to keep it cold. The milk came from a cow the family kept on the property. There was periodic running water thanks to an air pressure system K. C. had installed. Every weekend, he would prime it up and the flow would last until about Wednesday or so, when the system would lose its pressure. Unless Mr. Renauld helped out, this would leave the family waterless until K. C. returned once again from what in those days was a four-and-a-half-hour trek from his offices in Saint John. Parked in the Meteor facing the pond, J. K. is sentimental about this simple yet idyllic place where he grew up. The cottage is gone, but it is vivid in his mind. He's sentimental too about Mr. Renauld, the kind neighbour who was always there to help out in K. C.'s absence. Mr. Renauld got J. K. started on fishing when he was seven or eight years old, and once J. K. had gotten the hang of it, he'd frequently spend a couple of hours on his own fishing the pond in the evening from a small punt. J. K. points to a sweet spot in the pond, recalling where a spring ran cold and the trout would congregate. Mr. Renauld also took the Irving boys duck hunting some mornings. Arthur Sr. carried this experience forward by becoming one of the most widely recognized national figures within Ducks Unlimited.

This line of discussion reveals that the Irving boys were as ordinary as they could possibly be. The public thinks of them as grown up businessmen, ambitious men in suits, an image that tends to dehumanize them. But the Irvings have cherished childhood memories just like the rest of us. J. K.'s favourite Christmas present ever was a Flexible Flyer wooden sled he received at age seven or eight. His most memorable book as a boy was *Captains Courageous*, Rudyard Kipling's classic tale of tenacity, courage, loyalty, and humility. The 1897 novel follows the adventures of the arrogant and spoiled son of a railroad tycoon who is washed overboard from a trans-Atlantic steamship and rescued by fishermen on the Grand Banks. The valiant fisherman who serves as the story's protagonist transforms the boy—after many trials and tribulations—into an industrious, serious, considerate, and loving young man. The stakes in the Irving saga were never quite as dramatic, never quite as life and death as they are in *Captains Courageous*, but by many accounts the story of the Irvings is also riddled with tenacity, courage, loyalty, and humility. Kipling's novel is a story of life's lessons learned. So too is the story of how the Irvings have been captains of their ships over so many generations.

This talk of boyhood events prompts a hearty laugh and a story of near-perilous mischief that it seems J. K. hasn't talked of in years. Part of him is back suddenly in Irvingdale. There was a shotgun kept inside the cottage—a loaded shotgun. One afternoon, with Harriett out of the house and K. C. away on business, a visiting boyhood friend, George Dolan from the Miramichi, was toying with the shotgun when it accidentally discharged, leaving a gaping hole in the cottage's wooden floorboards. The boys were lucky none of them was blown away by the blast. Panicked, they conspired to cover the hole by moving the cottage ping-pong table and the mat it stood on. When their father returned home a day or two later, with George Dolan still a guest at Irvingdale, a perceptive K.C. recognized that something was out of place and discovered the hole. Before K.C. could even begin his investigation into what had happened, George Dolan had taken off up the Renauld Road, intent on hitchhiking home to the Miramichi by the main coastal road. From this story emerges the additional tidbit that K.C. was an adept ping-pong player, and that he had a knack for horseshoes too.

There's something about these candid reminiscences that makes it clear J.K. wants the world to believe the Irvings are genuine New Brunswick or Maritime people. It's always bothered and frustrated him that the public's view of the Irvings is so jaundiced in spite of what he sees as their good works. As the oldest of K.C.'s sons, he is by chronology, if not his quiet wisdom, the current patriarch of the family. As patriarch, he is taking on the campaign to put to rest the negative aspects of their collective persona. J.K. alludes during the Bouctouche visit to many things the family is doing to make that community (amongst many others) a better place to live. His demeanour is that of a man too modest to boast, but there are definitely things he wants to get out, like the fact that K.C. was giving to causes long, long ago. For example, when the family relocated to their more modern compound up the coast, K.C. donated the cottage at Irvingdale to a local Boy Scout troop, the last users of the facility before it eventually burned to the ground. The Irvings also used to welcome Bouctouche Red Cross youth swimming classes to their private swimming pool at the compound not far from Irvingdale on the Northumberland Strait. More than a thousand local kids have benefited from the program over the years. But when it comes to Irving philanthropy, Boy Scouts and the Red Cross are merely the tip of the iceberg.

◆

One doesn't get to be the patriarch of a family as complex as the Irvings without having paid one's dues, earned your stripes, and listened to what the last patriarch had to say about things. J.K.'s dues-paying began in earnest in the 1940s when he was no more than twenty and was working in the Madawaska-area woods in northwestern New Brunswick. They were starting to build roads with which to access the harvestable wood on lands that K.C. had bought. In those days, everyone was involved in what would now be considered primitive logging practices, pushing trees to this side and the other to create the road.

J.K. remembers the first road construction he oversaw. "We put a turn at the bottom of the hill and went up the hill. It was a terrible road. My father had come up to visit us, about December or January." J.K. was driving his father in a truck up this muddy, slippery hill "where you had to go like hell" by taking a run at it and then attempt to negotiate the turn up the hill. "I remember the first time I didn't make it," says J.K. So with his father seated beside him in the truck, he backed up and went at it again. K.C. remarked that they had carved out a terrible road. One can envision an impatient, no-nonsense K.C. in the passenger's seat rolling his eyes at this futile, repetitious effort. "So the next spring," J.K. explains, "we started to build a road out at Black Brook, across the tracks. And we were going to build this road, and it was all laid out, when father came up and he spent about three days there. No tractor could push any tree. Cut the road first, so we cut it. And then the thing was the stumps in the road. We'd dig a hole, put the stumps in and bury them. And we'd try and make it as straight as possible." K.C. was there to drill into his son and the other workers the idea that the efficient way to build the logging road was to build it as straight as you possibly could. The lesson of building the roads straight became for J.K. a metaphor for everything in life, the idea that you should always do the job right. "He drilled that into me and I think I got it."

It's not as though everything was already known about forestry techniques and technology in those times. In fact, those stumps they'd buried came popping out of the ground the next year because of frost upheaval. But when they did adopt practices that worked—like straightening out the road—each technique worked with the other, like compound interest, to arrive at the Irvings' current techniques in the forestry sector. The lasting lesson from that long-ago experience: it's a virtual crime to build a bend in a road on Irving forested land unless it's absolute necessary. J.K. recalls later having built a logging road near Chipman, New Brunswick, that went on as straight as a die for a six-mile stretch—so perfect "you could put a level on it." He had learned his straight roads lesson well. A few years after it had been built (in 1956), he was flying with K.C. over the site when his father pointed out a slight curve at the tail end of the road. J.K. rationalized that the variance was there because of the approach to an Irving camp. "You know, that wasn't good enough," recalls J.K. "I had to go back and re-survey it. We had to redo it." His father did more than just point it out. As far as K. C. was concerned, it wasn't the way it should be, and it simply had to be fixed.

Much of any Irving man's life, patriarch or otherwise, is about learning in the field the hard way. J.K. attended Acadia University in Wolfville, Nova Scotia, dutifully following in the family footsteps. But his choice of chemistry proved boring, and he left after just two years on campus. One summer was spent picking up a bit of French and scaling wood (scaling is done with a stick used for measuring wood by the cubic foot, the way wood is bought and paid for). He went to work on a logging drive near Rivière-du-Loup with a partner of his father, a native Quebecer by the name of Mr. Gaudreau. Calling himself a lousy student bored with chemistry, the idea of heading to Quebec seemed like a good notion at the time, but he had "no idea" what he was in for. He went to work for a man named Dufour, who reported to Mr. Gaudreau. "I showed up and I went to work. For three weeks, I thought I would die. It was tough work. We used to eat four times a day because you started at six o'clock in the morning, you lunched at ten-thirty, you lunched again at two o'clock and then you had supper at six o'clock. And it was a twelve-hour day, seven days a week." There were three hundred men involved in the drive effort.

One morning, during the half-hour break for the ten-thirty lunch, J. K. made the mistake of napping. Everyone returned to their duties except him. When he finally awoke, he rushed to join the rest of the crew hauling wood on their shoulders like a chain gang across a gravel bar. His temporary absence resulted in an encounter with a supervisor by the name of Levesque, a man who spoke almost no English whatsoever. Levesque was smoking a pipe, flipping it back and forth in his mouth. J. K. would later learn that the flipping of the pipe in Levesque's mouth was not a good sign; it meant he was being summoned. "I started to walk over to this guy and he was over sixty. As I got closer to him, he'd walk faster and I'd try to catch up. Finally, he stopped and turned around. He looked at me and he says, 'Dufour say Irving no more work. Send him home.' I'd gotten fired from the job of three weeks, which seemed like an eternity. Then he said, 'Dufour one son of a bitch, eh?' And then a big smile came across his face. I lived to fight another day." In the end, J. K. and Mr. Levesque became friends, but the lesson was not lost on him.

So committed was J. K. to staying on the drive, that when K. C. contacted him that August, intent on taking the entire family to the Canadian National Exhibition in Toronto, J. K. actually passed up the opportunity. "I like what I'm doing here and I'm not finished. I'm gonna finish this out," he told his father. What had made the difference between the three initial weeks of hell and wanting to stay was simple: J. K. liked being in the woods and he'd been whipped into shape by the experience. "We had a great crowd of men. I felt right at home there and we worked like the devil but we had a pretty good time, an interesting time. There were just a lot of very, very good people, and I learned an awful lot from them." Part of the log drive routine involved small competitions where two men would load a pulp log on one man's shoulders, logs so heavy you'd see red and blue stars in your eyes until after you dumped it off. Guys would be standing on the side hollering and cheering. J. K. explains, "You'd walk back and feel about two feet off the ground. You'd feel like you're walking on air" after discarding the load. The rest for J. K. is career history. He missed the CNE in Toronto; he never returned to Acadia; and he's been in the family enterprise every waking second since.

He spent the next few seasons (from April until September) working the logging drives on the tributaries feeding the St. John River. In the off season he worked in the woods cutting boom logs as long as thirty-two feet. "Actually, of all the things of my life, that's the area that I enjoyed the most," J. K. maintains. It was so clear that J. K. loved what he was doing, his mother Harriett told K. C., "You've got to get him back to town because we'll never get a tie on him again." The dichotomy of being prepped for the executive suite at J. D. Irving Ltd. and yet having a love of the woods was something J. K. had to personally resolve by blending the two together. The most important thing about those experiences in the woods and hanging around sawmills was that J. K. learned how to make things work. He adapted ways to bore holes in logs to make their handling easier; he learned how pulleys work; he learned about the importance of measuring things properly; and, most of all, he learned first-hand what it's truly like for the men who would spend their entire lives labouring under his management and control. He would be forever linked, as woodsman or corporate executive, to the logs branded with the distinctive green dots bearing the Irving brand.

No matter how much J. K. learned from the woods, from being around the tough men in the camps, it was K. C. who provided the greatest mentorship in his sons' refinement as individuals and as businessmen. J. K. has never forgotten spending the summer of 1938 flying with his father in a float plane to do business all over the Maritimes, in Prince Edward Island, Cape Breton, Shelburne, Bridgewater, and places in between. J. K. was ten years old when he experienced what became the standard practice for latter-day Irving generations: he watched his father at work, tuning into his every activity, every nuance, every business technique. Wherever they went, K. C. met with people and checked to ensure things were done correctly, right down to the nitty-gritty of making sure a tank was put up properly or that some valves were installed the right way.

J. K. says that if you work for the Irvings, you're allowed one honest mistake. You're even allowed a second honest mistake. Even Irvings of course, make mistakes. But if you make the same mistake a third time—that's strike three and you're out. He admits he has certainly made a few over the years. One of them was a doozy by any standard. It was a lesson he will never forget. The problem occurred in what's known locally as Indiantown, near Saint John. J. D. Irving Ltd. had bought a tugboat from an interest in the United Kingdom (one of several purchased after the Second World War) and had shipped it to Canada aboard a landing craft named the *Puffin*. No one, says J. K., could figure out quite how to get the tug off the *Puffin*'s deck until someone came up with the idea of transferring it to a laker named the *Richards*. The technique would involve cutting holes in the *Richards* to allow a controlled entry of water into the vessel at low tide. This would lower the *Richards* to the bottom and they would slide the tug from one surface to the other. A man in high rubber boots and a bullhorn in hand stood directing the pull and torque of a tractor. It was an unusual enough event that a crowd had gathered.

Thinking all was well and stabilized, everyone went home at the end of the job. But at three o'clock on Sunday morning, J. K. received a call. "Jimmy! Jimmy! It's terrible, the *Richards* broke!" Sure enough, the 7000-ton *Richards* had split in two because of a sizeable miscalculation in drilling. For the next six days, the bulk steel of the *Richards* was cut into pieces, right under the nose of ever-vigilant K. C., who watched from his office window. J. K. did not need to have the magnitude of the mistake explained to him; he had learned a huge lesson through the debacle about the handling of large-scale projects that require a certain type of expertise. What's more, it was clear to J. K. that his father recognized his son had learned his lesson.

Everything in Irving business life is about retaining lessons learned, whether it is how to pull your weight on a logging crew, K. C.'s insistence on building straight logging roads, scrimping on the cost of a telegram, or figuring out how many squares of tissue are required to clean one's glasses. Their father drilled J. K. and his brothers Arthur Sr. and Jack from the day they were born. As a result, throughout their lives, they have been highly disciplined, highly predictable, and able to support one another no matter what the situation. One could argue that the only lesson the brothers have not learned well has to do with the matter of secrecy and their communication style with the media. This may be the one lesson K. C. was not well-suited to impart.

6. Twenty-First-Century Irvings—The Sixth Generation

GEORGE > HERBERT > J. D. > K. C. > J. K., ARTHUR SR., AND JACK > JIM, ROBERT, MARY JEAN, JUDITH, KENNETH, ARTHUR JR., AND JOHN

The family business leaders of the sixth generation of Irvings are the first to be cousins instead of fathers, sons, and brothers. (See the Irving family tree.) The two with the highest profiles are Jim, eldest son of J. K. and eldest grandchild of K. C., and Kenneth, eldest son of Arthur Sr.

Jim and his younger brother Robert head up most of the dozens of companies that are not on the oil side, everything from forestry, mill and paper value-added operations to transportation to food processing. Jim principally controls J. D. Irving Ltd. Robert, the first of the family to be based in Moncton, is an emerging business figure in New Brunswick. Jim and Robert's sister Mary Jean lives in Charlottetown, PEI, where she runs separate operations, including Master Packaging and a number of potato farms that feed the family's Cavendish Farms processing facilities. Their younger sister Judith was involved in business for a period through the acquisition of a Moncton-based advertising agency, but left in February of 2007.

Kenneth is the key player at Irving Oil Ltd., with his brother Arthur Jr. in the marketing position. The other sixth generation cousin is John, son of Jack, who is principally involved in real estate holdings. Five other cousins— Jennifer, Emily, Sarah, Anne, and Colin—have chosen career paths outside of the family's corporate dynasty.

Every one of the sixth generation cousins had some degree of exposure to K. C. before he died in 1992, meaning that, for a time, they were under his shadow as well as under the influence of their own respective fathers. It's said that each of K. C.'s dozen grandchildren reacts differently to the shadow cast by him, and that although they have the image and legacy of their grandfather in common, they are emerging as individuals in their own right. There are seven players in the sixth generation of Irvings who are involved in one or more of the family businesses.

Jim and his siblings and cousins are mature enough now that they're carving their own ways in life, independent but still acting in accordance with the traditional influences of their three respective business-obsessed fathers. Of course, they are not clones of one another and it's not expected they could be—the farther they are from the trunk of the family tree, the more independent and individual they're bound to become. This is even more true of the seventh generation, only two of whom are currently in the family enterprise. J. K.'s grandchildren Jamie and Kate are working in family businesses, but their true capabilities and leadership qualities are yet to be exhibited.

The most visible of all of the twenty-first-century Irvings is forty-something Kenneth. He presents himself like a Southern gentleman, more mild-mannered than Clark Kent, like a reserved clergyman. In one-to-one situations, he is soft spoken in the extreme. This is in contrast to his cousin Jim (J. K.'s son), who is more direct, all business, and very different from his father, Arthur Sr. In terms of demeanour and approachability, Kenneth is more akin to his uncle J. K. Kenneth knows how to be an Irving businessman, but he does it in a style that has earned him (rightly or wrongly) a reputation for being more concerned about people than some of the other family members. He's also fun to talk to at a dinner party and diverts attention away from himself to the lives, careers, and interests of others in a room. But he's also got the Irving gene for being tough when need be.

In spite of that traditional Irving toughness, several sources have said that during a mid-1990s refinery strike, Kenneth is known to have truly agonized over the fact that a couple of hundred people were on strike for two years. They say he was tormented over what it was doing to the lives of the workers and their families. Said one source: "He knew in his heart of hearts that they had to see the strike through to the end for the sake of the future of the business. He absolutely knew that and was committed to seeing it through," and not, they say, just because of pressure from his father, Arthur. He knew full well on his own that if the company didn't get the concessions it was seeking from the union, the operation could find itself in trouble because of international competition. The Irving Oil refinery may look huge from South End Saint John, but it looks almost puny from Houston or Calgary. The sources say that what the Irvings were pursuing in terms of labour cost control was absolutely legit. But at the same time, Kenneth and his father knew and hoped that the folks on strike would see the light so that they could get back to work. Said one source: "You could see that it was keeping him (Kenneth) up at night worrying about it."

If the rest of the Irvings are typically under the radar, Kenneth's younger brother Arthur Jr. is a submariner. He does not have a public persona and sticks to running marketing at Irving Oil. Like his brother, he is said to have a good sense of humour and loves to have a good laugh. You're not going to see a gaggle of Irvings out drinking shooters in public or cracking a twelve-pack of Moosehead beer, but in private, when you get to know them, they do know how to have a good laugh. A couple will even enjoy a glass or two of wine. Unlike in their working lives, their social lives are all about moderation. The ways in which they let go are not over the edge, but even the moderate releases they do partake in are kept very discreet. Because of assured confidentiality, details cannot be revealed, but there are known instances involving Kenneth, family, and friends that illustrate their capacity to be playful and to enjoy a good laugh. They're not into skinny-dipping and other such reckless abandon, but they do enjoy gags so long as they're kept amongst family and their most trusted friends.

◆

Serious Kenneth was a keynote luncheon speaker at the first Reaching Atlantica conference held in Saint John in June of 2006. Francis McGuire, the former deputy minister of New Brunswick's Department of Economic Development and Tourism who went on to become president of Major Drilling International, has frequently remarked that Kenneth has developed into a smooth public speaker and that the Irvings should put him in the forefront to help improve the family's and their companies' images. Smooth and keynote he certainly was at Reaching Atlantica, seeming very comfortable with the freedom (and slight abandon) of speaking without notes and forsaking the crutch of a podium in favour of a lapel microphone and the unrestricted flow of the entire front of the ballroom of the Saint John Convention Centre. His coolness and composure are all the more remarkable given that a throng of raucous protesters tried and almost succeeded in breaking the security perimeter of the conference centre ballroom. The protestors were voicing their opposition to what they saw as the social and political threats to Canada embodied in the Atlantica concept. Pushed and promoted most vigorously by *Progress Magazine* publisher Neville Gilfoy of Halifax, the Atlantica idea promotes more north-south economic ties throughout Atlantic Canada, Maine, Vermont, New Hampshire, parts of Quebec, and upstate New York.

As the protesters made their presence known (several were arrested and charged), Kenneth did not miss a beat. He seemed rehearsed—almost overscripted—although he's been quoted as saying he just gets up and talks. Irving Oil public affairs guy Daniel Goodwin must have heart attacks over Kenneth's freehand style, preferring no doubt, as all public affairs professionals do, that such speeches be delivered from a prepared text. What is said in a public forum with the visibility of an event like Reaching Atlantica has "got to be part of the corporate plan" according to a media source, and reflect the corporate objectives—especially when your father is sitting less than twenty feet away and is "paranoid about the media," as Arthur Sr. has been described. But freestyle Kenneth did sound convincing. What made it so was that he truly seemed to believe in what he was saying.

Throughout his remarks to the Atlantica conference, Kenneth repeatedly acknowledged the presence of his father, who was seated at one of the front tables with his second wife, Sandra. It was as though there were two parallel themes during the address: one having to do with the oil industry, the other providing constant recognition to Arthur Sr. The speech was sprinkled with self-deprecating comments with a definite "Father Knows Best" undertone.

The purpose of Kenneth's participation was to help legitimize the Atlantic conference. The conference organizers had asked him to speak about the advantages of running a major corporation within the Atlantica zone. He did this, and also spoke to some of the disadvantages and threats. No one outside the Irving loop knew it at the time, but what he was actually doing was planting the seed—a big juicy teaser—for a forthcoming announcement that would make the Saint John, New Brunswick, and Maritime media swoon. That announcement came months later, during the first week of October 2006: Irving Oil Ltd. was actively seeking partners for the creation of a second oil refinery, a state-of-the-art project estimated at between $5 and $7 billion. For once in a blue moon, even the national media carried a Maritime story with gusto, even though it had nothing to do with horses and buggies, unemployment insurance, or one-toothed fishermen.

At the conference, Kenneth had begun the setup for the formal October announcement by saying that in the oil and other businesses, "scale really matters" in this day and age, so much so that in his family's corporate experience, 80 per cent of what investors are focused on when they come to the table is scale. Scale means that "there is a natural pull" for companies to join larger companies. He emphasized that this is true in every sector, from dairy to oil. It's evident in all aspects of the Atlantic Canadian economy now, from fishery companies to grocery stores. The overwhelming presence of Sobey's and the Atlantic Superstores (Loblaws in Atlantic Canada garb) have pretty well put the boots to the Coop and Clover Farm stores that were a vital part of the Maritime fabric and way of life for decades. While the two larger chains modernized and grew, Coop and Clover Farm got swept away almost overnight. Kent Building Suppliers and Home Depot also represent scale in their market. This degree of scale, Kenneth said, means that investments occur in increments of billions, which take a considerable amount of time to plan and assemble, something the Irvings aren't necessarily accustomed to. They've learned to be patient when it comes to watching trees grow, but not when it comes to deal making. They like to move things along rapidly, a definite trait handed down from K. C. and, one can assume, from even earlier in the Irving legacy, from J. D. and Herbert.

Saying nothing about the forthcoming oil refinery surprise, Kenneth told the conference that talks leading toward the Saint John liquefied natural gas (LNG) terminal project (another major Irving undertaking) began in 1999–2000 and the facility won't be operable until 2008. When you consider that oil sector investors have an interest and attention span of about two years and that the average oil industry CEO has a corporate presence of about five years, it's hard to understand how large-scale projects that aren't family-owned ever get off the ground at all. Alluding to those points, Kenneth jokingly thanked his "dad" for keeping him around as long as he has.

Against this interesting backdrop of scale, Kenneth said there are "three big dynamics" in the oil sector today: large competition, volatility, and the environment. On volatility, he said that the true driver behind gas and energy cost instability is the uncertainty about world conditions in the oil patch. On the environmental side, Irving Oil was previously primarily preoccupied with air and water quality within the confines of their main centre of operations, Saint John; making sure tanks didn't leak wherever they ran Irving gas stations and keeping their fleet of oil tankers afloat and out of harm's way.

But today, the focus is global, with issues such as greenhouse gases making the headlines. It was this global environmental shift in the oil sector that led the Irvings to stake out an edge in the marketplace by processing and marketing more environmentally friendly fuels. The decisions taken several years ago to pursue this line of products have turned out to be a strategic advantage for the company.

Getting back to the advantages of running a major corporation in New Brunswick, the Maritimes, or Atlantica (depending on your perspective), Kenneth said that hurricanes in 2005, epitomized by Katrina, illustrated how unreliable and vulnerable the Southern US oil conduit is for the thirsty Northeast US. When you hold Houston up against Atlantica as a preferred supplier of energy, Atlantica, he said, wins out. He got the audience's rapt attention by claiming that Atlantica is closer to Venezuela than Houston. "That's a great party trick if you happen to be in Houston," he said. Seems it was a great party trick at the Atlantica conference too: you could see people's faces go blank as they drew little maps in their heads and tried to calculate the distances between Saint John, Houston, and Venezuela, attempting to figure out whether Kenneth's sense of geography was accurate or wacko. Turns out it's a slight exaggeration, but only by a couple of hundred scant kilometres.

Kenneth argued that another key advantage unique to Atlantica is "relationships." The comment sounded a trifle trite at first, until he described how CEOs he has toured through the control room of the Irving Oil refinery have been surprised at the mood and conviviality of things. They can sense, he said, how people are connected to one another and to the job they're doing, implying that this is not the case elsewhere. Relationships or no relationships, transitions in the world of oil movement and supply are way beyond the control of the Irvings. Kenneth once told Moosehead Breweries' Andrew Oland that Alberta used to supply energy products to the United States and central Canada, but is now being drawn to markets in China. This means that refineries in Ontario, Quebec, and the Maritimes are destined to fill the void, with New England being the most prominent target market in the Irvings' sites.

The speech wound its way to the excitement of building an energy hub in Saint John and southern New Brunswick. Everyone in the room thought he was talking about the existing refinery, the forthcoming LNG terminal and pipelines, all which he said "play off one another." The second refinery cards were held close to his chest, everyone in the room seeing the LNG terminal alone as exciting enough investment news for Saint John. He said his family was trying to attract capital, people with know-how, and world-scale companies as partners, an example being Trans Canada Pipeline and the building of a one-hundred-megawatt power plant right inside the Saint John refinery. Still again, the second refinery capital initiative went without mentioning. Kenneth said it's important to "keep adding to the gene pool" within the Irving enterprises. The region needs new thinkers, people with new thoughts, to enter the pool. "I love it here, and the responsibility I have," he said, concluding his remarks. "I know that I have to do it [run Irving Oil] responsibly for the community I'm connected to."

Four months following the Reaching Atlantica speech, on October 5, the Irvings introduced a new face to the community; boyish Kevin Scott emerged as Irving Oil's director of refining growth and the spokesperson for the second refinery project. For some reason, Kenneth and his father Arthur were tidily shaded into the background. Perhaps their absence had to do with the still-lingering bad taste in people's mouths over the LNG controversy, which saw the Irvings get caught up with Saint John city council in a debate over tax relief, or the coming potential controversy over land acquisition in the area of the proposed oil refinery site (landowners had already begun lining up with high expectations about the value of their properties in the face of the refinery's proposed development). Speaking to a packed Saint John business luncheon, Scott proclaimed that the second refinery would pump up to $17 billion into the New Brunswick economy. Experts said the project would instantly up the provincial export quotient by 40 to 50 per cent. Of the current export levels of about $10 billion, it's said that Irving Oil (even without an LNG terminal) represents 80 per cent of the total.

The thing that caught the media's attention wasn't just the impact of the announcement, but the value to labour in the province. With so many skilled Atlantic Canadian tradespeople having been sucked into the Alberta labour trough in recent years, the question uppermost on people's minds was who'd be left to build and operate such a facility. The consensus was that Irving will have to compete with Alberta wages if they hope to pull the project off. Three weeks later, the *Globe and Mail* was still covering the story with a two-page spread headlined "Reversing Fortunes." In the subhead introducing writer Shawna Richer's take on the oil refinery story, the *Globe* wrote that hope was returning to Saint John after years of economic stagnation and the exodus to Alberta. It concluded: "A $7 billion proposal would position the city as an energy hub and help regenerate a lost population." The piece went on to profile native New Brunswickers Jeff and Kim MacDonald, a couple who'd been part of the Alberta exodus but had chosen to return home when Irving Oil headhunted them down.

Kenneth's speech at the Reaching Atlantica conference was more of a watershed moment than anyone knew at the time. Long after the LNG terminal is a reality, after the second oil refinery is a reality, when Kenneth is in his early to mid-sixties and his biography is being written, the author may unearth the Atlantica speech from media archives and reflect upon the key point of what was said: that for the Irvings and Saint John to compete in the oil sector, it's all about "scale." In that context, fifteen to twenty years down the pike, the roar of the LNG tax controversy will sound like a faint echo from the edge of the horizon.

Francis McGuire definitely sees Kenneth Irving as the forthcoming, if not already-arrived, star of the family. If you want to modernize the Irving image, he suggests, Robert or Jim are not the first choice candidates to put in front of a general audience. Kenneth, as evidenced by his Reaching Atlantica appearance and other carefully chosen forums, is truly able to handle and present himself and, perhaps, to present a new Irving image and ideal. The man they put in the forefront of the October 2006 oil refinery announcement, Kevin Scott, is also a buoyant face, having the boyish looks and demeanour that could win nearly any audience's favour.

One New Brunswick journalist thinks Kenneth is the most "cosmopolitan" of the entire family. "He's very polite and calm, and I would say modern." That's probably good for closing deals in New York or Houston, but the downside might be that Kenneth is least like the traditional Irving image of just-folks New Brunswickers. He actually looks like he comes from or belongs in Toronto, Boston, or New York. Except for the absence of the Boston drawl, it's not an overstatement to suggest that he has the air of a young Kennedy. After the Reaching Atlantica address, he was seen departing the Saint John Convention Centre by a set of stairs leading to the underground tunnel connecting the Hilton Hotel and the Market Square underground parking garage (the conference's protestors by this time had been dispersed). There was something remarkable about that fleeting scene. He was accompanied by an entourage of suits and looked like he was en route to something else important requiring his attention, like a meeting in the Oval Office. Kenneth's air and gait looked that day like a cross between a Kennedy and JFK's late confidante and economist John Kenneth Galbraith; it was all a matter of stance, lankiness, and self-assuredness. Or possibly it was just the effect of the suits who were accompanying him.

This persona contrasts with that of his cousin Jim, who, like his father J. K., is happiest playing it low key and near the land. Arthur Sr. also likes the land and the outdoors, as evidenced by his leadership in Ducks Unlimited (saving the land to kill the ducks, one interviewee cracked); his treks to the Northwest Territories for elite guided canoe trips; and, in spite of the obvious risks to his personal safety, self-directed cycling tours of South Africa. But Arthur is just as likely to fly off to New York for a concert or for the theatre. He and his wife Sandra, as is the case with Kenneth and his wife Tasha, are youthful and fashionable and, as one observer put it, "beautiful." Both couples have the ability to draw your eye. This is not to say the other Irvings dress out of vogue or like slobs. They have their nice garb too, but Arthur's side of the family looks more tailored and fashionable. Like his father and his brother, Arthur Jr. also looks younger than his years. One of the things that might be keeping Arthur Sr. youthful is the fact that he's had, at one time, both a daughter and a granddaughter on the same junior high school soccer team. To put it differently, with no intention of sounding mean-spirited, if Kenneth was to be found on a magazine cover, it would be *GQ*, while Jim would be more likely to make his way to the cover of *Canadian Business* or the Canadian Forestry Association's industry newsletter. (Jim's brother Robert would probably be found on the *Moncton Times and Transcript*'s lead sports page because of his ownership of the Moncton Wildcats hockey team.)

It should be noted here, however, that some of the Irving women are increasingly active in a public manner, albeit ever so subtle. Kenneth's wife, Tasha, is said to be responsible for the start-up of a private school that began with six to eight students and in 2006 had an enrolment of approximately seventy. Situated directly across from Rothesay High School, the school is in the old Legion building immediately beside the district school board office, which some might consider pretty in-your-face. She's not only the founder— she's also the principal.

◆

In early 2006, Moosehead's Andrew Oland had the pleasure of getting a personal tour of the Irving Oil refinery with Kenneth himself, the result of an off-hand comment made when they were meeting together over another matter. Oland was surprised when Kenneth offered to spend nearly an hour driving and walking him through the refinery. There was nothing Kenneth didn't know about the refinery, says Oland, adding that his tour guide was "scary knowledgeable" about the intricacies of the plant and its operations. Oland recalls entering the nerve centre of the refinery, the high-tech control room, where Kenneth engaged a senior manager for what turned out to be a five-minute chat. "This individual was very comfortable with Ken. He wanted to tell Ken what was going on and Ken wanted to know what was going on. We leave there and we're just on our way out and Ken says, 'Just a sec. I want to stop here. I'm not sure if my security card's going to work,' but the door opens and we walk through an employee locker room. It's like something just occurred to him and he just walked in there. He wanted to make sure that it was clean. That's the discipline that that organization has."

Oland's take on Kenneth's actions was that he felt pride that the locker room was in fact clean, another basic Irving standard that was being met. Kenneth's brief diversion truly hit home with Oland because it reminded him of something his late grandfather and one-time Moosehead figurehead Philip Oland would have done. "My grandfather used to walk through this plant here [in Saint John] and people would chuckle a bit because he'd see a piece of cardboard or a piece of paper on the floor and he'd pick it up. Because that's his place and if he does that then everyone will follow his leadership. And someone saw Ken go into the locker room, and that would make its way through the employee ranks."

Steve Carson, executive director of Enterprise Saint John, worked in the ranks of Irving Oil for fourteen years, long enough to have a keen sense of what Kenneth's made of (he even recalls him as a kid). He says that Kenneth has developed a style of empowering his senior officials to make decisions. "I think they agree on an overall strategy for where they're going, but the team is certainly much more empowered than when I was there, as far as the process seems to be working now." Carson says this doesn't mean Kenneth works any less than his father. It's just that things are on a much different scale. This is "a time when they really have repositioned the company as a potential major player on the world stage from an energy perspective. And that's a whole different strategy than building service stations and selling pop and chips." Kenneth, of course, gets to ride on the credibility that earlier generations of Irvings have built—a credibility that the company and its people have had the pleasure of enjoying for some time. It's a level—or a scale, as Kenneth himself would say—of credibility that will no doubt attract even more billion-dollar partnerships in the future.

Long-serving Saint John city manager Terry Totten has been to dinner parties with Kenneth and Tasha Irving and describes Kenneth as the antithesis of the corporate "monster" some members of the public might imagine him to be. "If you're sitting down with Kenneth, that's the farthest thing from a monster you'd ever meet," Totten insists. "I recall one time when I was meeting with him and discussing some lands that are owned by Irving companies in the Millidgeville area [of Saint John]. And I said, 'Any interest in developing those lands?' And his comment was, 'Well, yeah, perhaps, but I would only do it or agree to it if we could have quality standards, protection of the environment, and to make sure that we didn't go in and rape the land and the shore. You know, in today's world, we shouldn't be doing those things. We shouldn't be doing those things.'"

◆

Probably more than any of the other sixth-generation Irvings, Jim Irving looks and acts like he's driven to succeed. Some say he works almost too hard, sometimes making himself borderline ill. He is constantly on the road, travelling, selling, and dealing with everything from minor issues to matters as vital as Irving environmental concerns, keeping rural mills operating in a volatile forestry economy, and the lengthy Canada–US softwood lumber dispute. In his mid-fifties, Jim is said to be at work at the Saint John office or mill most mornings shortly after six o'clock. Imagine the impact of that degree of commitment on personnel. His regimen is reminiscent of former New Brunswick premier Frank McKenna, who used to walk to his office and arrive at seven o'clock every morning. All of a sudden, the culture of the provincial civil service at Fredericton's Centennial Building changed. People suddenly began showing up on time. A source who's spent time on the scene describes Jim as a hard-nosed businessman. His persona is less like that of his father, J. K., and more like that of his uncle Arthur. He is friendly enough, but he is also all business.

At first glance, Moncton-based Asssumption Life president Denis Losier doesn't seem a likely candidate for socializing with the Irvings. He's too hip— he's perfectly bilingual, a sharp dresser, fit-looking, friendly, self-deprecating, well versed about fine wines and food, well connected, well liked, approach-able, and a good partier. But he has spent time with some members of the family, including Jim. He concedes that there are times when Jim can come across as being all business, but Losier has also seen another side of the eldest of the sixth-generation cousins. During their work together on the Univer-sity of Moncton funding campaign and in other travels, Losier says he's had fun with Jim, a guy he describes as having no pretensions, like the others in his family. "They're unpretentious people, very ordinary people. We'd go in somewhere and just grab a sandwich. Some people might feel uneasy or hesitant about approaching them, but they're very approachable. They come across just like anybody else."

Losier continues, "I think some people maybe have a mixture of emotions, or maybe they don't know how to approach them, because they have money. But there is never any indication that anyone is less around their circle. It's just not there." Losier insists that Jim is "a lot of fun. He jokes. He's very knowledgeable, he's very quick-minded and he's very funny and very outgo-ing with business people." Part of his seemingly sober demeanour these days might be attributable to the state of the forestry sector, the heart and soul of J. D. Irving Ltd. Things are very tough in forestry these days. You could al-most see it etched in Jim's face as he returned to the private Irving hangar at the Saint John airport one night in October 2006 after a meeting in Halifax, surely one of hundreds of meetings he attends each year.

During the longstanding softwood lumber dispute between Canada and the United States, government bureaucrats like New Brunswick's George Bouchard spent countless days watching paint dry in Washington. At one point during the negotiations, he and government colleague Harry Quinlan spent nearly five weeks in the us capital while commuting home on weekends. For all or much of this time, because of the importance of the file, Jim Irving was also there, a lawyer's office serving as his home base. Bouchard and Quinlan came and went, reporting on the progress—or lack thereof—of the arduous, seemingly endless trade debacle, which was finally resolved by the Stephen Harper government in 2006.

On the Friday night at the end of the second week of the negotiation marathon, meetings dragged on late in the day, forcing Bouchard and Quinlan to miss their commercially scheduled flight from Dulles airport. According to Bouchard, Jim said, "Hey guys, instead of going back tomorrow morning, do you want to go back tonight? You can hop in with me." The leather comfort, spontaneous convenience, and chocolate bar stash of the private Irving plane were, of course, irresistible. Bouchard and Quinlan had already seen enough of Washington, and of their hotel room, to last them a lifetime. "We thought he would go into Saint John, and then have the pilot drop us off in Fredericton," recalls Bouchard. Instead, Jim ordered the pilots to take the plane right into Fredericton. It was us first, then he went on to Saint John. Then he said, 'Guys, Sunday night if you want to come back with us, we'll pick you up.'" Bouchard and Quinlan thanked him for his offer and said they'd meet him at the Saint John airport. Jim insisted on picking them up again in Fredericton.

"So Sunday night he picked us up—him and one of his lawyers and another guy from his organization—and we flew to Washington. When we arrived there was only one taxi." Unlike public areas where taxis line up in succession waiting for customers, this was a private arrivals area at Dulles airport, requiring your own arrangement of ground transport. "So we said, 'You guys go.' Mr. Irving said to the cabbie, 'Would you call for another cab for these guys.' So we said, 'Mr. Irving, go, go.'" Jim jumped into the taxi with his lawyer and Harry Quinlan, leaving Bouchard and the Irving employee to wait out the arrival of a second vehicle. On exiting the sprawling Dulles terminal grounds, about a two-mile drive to the airport's perimeter, Jim noticed that they had not passed the second incoming cab. Before they left the terminal road and hit the highway, Jim turned his taxi around and returned to the private arrivals area where Bouchard and the Irving gentleman were still waiting. "He came back to see if we had a cab and we had none, so he said to the cab driver, 'Call one!' and he didn't leave the place until we had a cab. I'm not joking. True as I'm sitting here," said Bouchard.

Once in their own vehicle, Bouchard recalls expressing to the Irving staffer just how astounded he was at Jim Irving's actions. "And he said, 'Mr. Irving will always make sure that his employees are looked after.'" That said, Bouchard is convinced Jim would have done the same thing for him whether or not there'd been an Irving employee stranded with him at the terminal.

Former *Saint John Telegraph-Journal* columnist Lisa Hrabluk has heard what people tend to say about Jim, that he's tough and hard and seems to lack caring. "But I kind of like him, because he's just who he is, right. He's an incredibly honest man. When I talk to Jim Irving, I do not sense that there are wheels spinning [meaning games] in the back of his head. He is just honest."

Jim does project a basic honesty, straightforwardness, and reliability that are reminiscent of his father, J. K. It's easy to imagine him being schooled by his father and K. C. in the refinements of the career they set out before him. As the oldest of K. C.'s grandchildren, expectations for his performance and delivery must have been higher than anyone else in the sixth generation, including Kenneth. His extreme work ethic and straightforward approach show that he has taken the challenge of running Irving companies very seriously and that the responsibility does not seem to stop at the Irving front door.

For obvious reasons—their power and influence—both Jim and Kenneth have been invited to participate in a very exclusive club that was formed in New Brunswick in 2005. Apparently much to the chagrin of former premier Bernard Lord, the crème-de-la-crème of the business elite in New Brunswick decided to become proactive on the economic development front by forming the New Brunswick Business Council. Others in the influential collective include Allison McCain, Ed Barrett of Woodstock, University of New Brunswick president John MacLaughlan, Gerry Pond, pizza king Bernard Imbault, Moosehead's Derek Oland, Norm Cassie of Imperial Sheet Metal, University of Moncton president Yvon Fontaine, Nancy Mathis of Fredericton's Mathis Instruments, Denis Losier of Assumption Life in Moncton, and David Ganong of Ganong Bros. in St. Stephen.

When I interviewed David Ganong on June 22, 2006, he and his fellow council members had met just the previous day in St. Andrews. As head of St. Stephen's famed and longstanding candy company, Ganong has, like the Irvings, traditions and a family name to uphold when he arrives at the office every day. Giving of his time to the overall betterment of New Brunswick is typical of the Ganongs' commitment to the province. Proportionately speaking, his family's legacy is to St. Stephen what the Irving legacy is to Saint

John. If anything ever happened to the Ganong's plant, St. Stephen would go down like a rock in water.

He says the business council has emerged because New Brunswick has "a very difficult series of economic challenges in front of us." He emphasizes that the council was not formed in response to the Conservative government of Bernard Lord (who was defeated in September 2006 by Shawn Graham and the Liberals), the past governments of Camille Theriault and Frank McKenna, or the next government for that matter. "It's a case of where New Brunswick finds itself in the world economy today," explains Ganong. "We've got a declining population. We've got out-migration of a lot of young people. We've got abysmal education scores, so as employers we see the quality of the people coming into our enterprises is not in many cases what we'd like to have it be. We have the second most obese population in Canada and one of the worst in North America. And that creates an enormous amount of stress on our health care system, creating more stress as we go forward." In fact, at the June 21 council meeting, the members heard from a guest speaker that health care officials are actually seeing a trend toward the use of blood pressure and cholesterol pills for middle school students. On top of all those concerns, there are world economic pressures resulting from the increasing strength of the Canadian dollar and competitors such as India and China, who are beating everybody up in the manufacturing sector. Ganong says the council believes that businesses and citizens cannot legitimately just turn to government and ask them to fix it all. "And so there's an obligation and a responsibility on behalf of the senior leadership in New Brunswick to see what we can do to work cooperatively with all levels of government and to work better ourselves in trying to deal with the issues and create more wealth." One of the threats on the horizon involves the net result of a declining population and increasing age amongst those who remain behind: taxation rates would have to rise. That's not good for business, not good for the average citizen, and not good for the governments that are in power when the taxation wall imposes itself.

One of the things the council has embraced proactively is wellness, which starts with employees and corporate policies toward individual well-being. Ganong says that J.D. Irving Ltd. has adopted some pretty sophisticated wellness initiatives that Jim Irving is prepared to share with the council table. He was prepared to bring his HR people to a future meeting to conduct an information session. If there are techniques and programs others wish to adopt, he's apparently happy to see them do so. Conversely, in such an exchange forum, Jim might hear about new HR initiatives that he might want to adopt back at J.D. Irving Ltd. And so the sharing of ideas and information goes round and around the table. Ganong says that by starting with the wellness of people, the council is starting with a basic social issue. "And the same with education," he says. "What is it we can do to encourage and enhance the education system?" These are the types of broad-based matters the council is pondering.

To be a member of the council, you have to be a CEO or someone of equal or greater stature. (Allison McCain, for example, is the chairperson of McCain Foods, not the CEO.) Moreover, alternates are not permitted at the council and neither are backup staff or entourages. "Never, never. It's not allowed," says Ganong emphatically. "You have to come yourself. You can't delegate it. You can't have a vice president come. You either come yourself or you don't come at all."

Ganong says that when asked to join the business council, Jim and Kenneth Irving had the same response: they couldn't both be there, at least not at the same time. Too much Irving presence would not have gone over well. Not that they actually would have been domineering at the table—that's not what would have troubled them or somebody like Ganong as chair, because they would both have so much to bring to the discussion. It was the public perception of "too much Irving." In a way, this incident is emblematic of the family's public relations predicament as a whole. Kenneth told Ganong that if Jim tired of his participation, he'd be delighted to serve. So that's where it was left. Jim Irving, says Ganong, is not just showing up. He has not missed a single meeting; he has taken on several projects and has brought his "homework" back to the council. His homework has included developing papers based on Irving practices and experiences that would be useful for the province to understand. Some of these have already been passed on to the premier's office for consideration. "It's been done in a very high-quality way," says Ganong. "He is engaged. He's not passive. I think that the moment Jim Irving becomes passive, he just won't show up. If he can't be accomplishing something, he's not interested."

Jim Irving's commitment to the New Brunswick Business Council sounds strikingly similar to the level of commitment K. C. made when he was a member of the board of governors at the University of New Brunswick from the late 1950s to 1968. The 1993 K. C. Irving biography by Douglas How and Ralph Costello provides extensive detail regarding the patriarch's quiet counsel and patient guidance to the university senate and later the board of governors after he was prompted into the role by then chancellor Lord Beaverbrook (Max Aitken). Like Jim at the business council, it's said that K. C. did not dominate or control circumstances at UNB; rather, he played on a team of two dozen other community leaders and business people. They acted as equals.

"There are a number of issues that we're going to address one by one," says Denis Losier of the council. Losier says Jim Irving has joined the council because he truly cares about the future well-being of New Brunswick. "That entire group has a lot of respect for Jim because he comes as an interested participant, as a person, not only as a company. And he does that, I think, because he has a lot of respect for the other people around the table. He's come in as a willing participant to try to help, in his own way, to shape the future of the province." The Irvings, he says, are "very, very passionate about New Brunswick. They're passionate about industry in New Brunswick."

Losier says one of the most interesting things about the council is the involvement of corporations with wildly different scales of operations, the Irvings being by far the largest. He says it shows that big and small companies can work side by side because they share the same passion for the future of New Brunswick. He says that big players like the Irvings might be able to accomplish many of the council's objectives on their own accord, in isolation. "But the fact that they choose to do it with other business leaders in New Brunswick shows that they're open to compromising," even though, as Losier points out, the positions of the business council will inevitably be the result of consensus building and might not necessarily reflect the "Irving position" on a particular matter.

◆

Robert Irving was the first of the family to take root outside Saint John and stay firmly planted. He chose Moncton as his base, today operating a collection of large enterprises that includes Cavendish Farms, Midland Transport, the Majesta tissue plant, and the Personal Care diaper production plant. Several years ago, he spoke to a local Moncton business group in a style and manner that impressed Moncton-based ad man Jean Brousseau.

"He was more effective in seven minutes than most speakers are in thirty minutes," says Brousseau, adding that Robert was direct and to the point, not a waster of words. He knew what he was there to communicate, did it, and got off the podium. It was typical "Irving"—don't mince words, say what you have to say, and get on with other matters.

Like his sister Mary Jean, who is based on Prince Edward Island, Robert is credited with broadening the Irving home base of business to include both the Island, the city of Moncton, and Moncton's sibling city, Dieppe. He has completely integrated himself into the community through actions like chairing the local United Way campaign and the Capital Theatre fundraising campaign and, more than anything, by putting a major junior hockey team—the Moncton Wildcats—front and centre and into the winner's column. On May 14, 2006, the team won the Quebec Major Junior Hockey League (QMJHL)championship, launching the team into the national

Memorial Cup tournament and the city into the national spotlight during the year in which Moncton was already the scheduled host city. Between the community engagements, he's busy overseeing the family's string of very successful Moncton-based enterprises.

How Robert—or the family—decided to make the forays into Moncton and Prince Edward Island is a more interesting and important question than it might appear on the surface. Ever since K.C. outgrew Bouctouche, the Irving world has revolved around Saint John. With brother Jim at the helm of J.D. Irving Ltd., what else could Robert and his sisters have done, given that they also have the chutzpah to run businesses very successfully? It would have been a pretty crowded scene if the younger siblings hadn't ventured out. But did the family make a conscious group decision for this to happen?

Either way, there's no denying the impact they've had on their adopted communities. It was only a few years ago, after all, that Moncton was still a ghost town; today, Main Street is vibrant. Assumption Life president Denis Losier says the Irvings have had a profound impact on Moncton and Dieppe and are certainly part of the resurrection of the city following the devastating closures of several major industries in the 1960s and 1970s, including Canadian National, the Eaton's warehouse, and military installations. Others in the community are to be highly credited—it's by no means an exclusively Irving thing—but the family were and remain an important part of the city's remarkable resurgence and growth. Robert has been the heart and soul of that Irving involvement. Losier says he is truly a part of the community. "Robert is no different than anybody else. I think people almost don't look at him as one of the Irvings. You see him all over the place. You meet him at the arena, you meet him on the street, you meet him at community breakfasts or luncheons."

Which is not to overlook Judith Irving, who acquired Hawk Communications in 2001 from founder David Hawkins, who had moved his agency from Sackville to Moncton during the late 1990s. Judith sold the business in February of 2007 and is currently not active in family business. Hawkins' impression is that Robert and Judith are "kindred spirits" who get along well and support one another. He adds that Judith has a levelling or calming effect on her brother, saying that she brings out the warmer side of a guy who's known to be a hard-nosed businessman.

"You don't have to spend a lot of time with Robert to see his social conscience surface and to understand his sincere and genuine commitment to making the [Moncton and area] community a better place," says Hawkins. Some unnameable people aren't quite so kind about Robert's demeanour, but there's no arguing his success in Greater Moncton. Whatever else he gives to the community through hockey and philanthropic means, his biggest contribution is the running of really excellent businesses. Hawkins says he works hard and he demands a lot from his people, but that "they run world-class businesses."

If you had run into Robert at the Moncton arena in May 2006, you were no doubt caught up in the excitement of his Moncton Wildcats, the team he bought twelve years ago. In those final Memorial Cup tournament games, when the Wildcats came within a desperate breath of taking the trophy, Robert could be seen making his way through the stands shaking hands and cheering like a little kid. For the team's final game against the Quebec Ramparts, J. K. and Jim were there to support their son and brother. They too could be seen in the stands, caught up in the euphoria of the national competition just like everyone else.

Ad man Jean Brousseau has been around the agency game in Greater Moncton for years, and for nearly as long he's been a hockey promoter. In his day job, he's a senior VP at Bristol Communications, one of the region's best and best-known agencies. In 2006, he was also vice-president of the board of directors of the Quebec Major Junior Hockey League and the league's incoming chair. He's been caught up for years in the Quebec league and the Canadian Hockey League as a developer and member of the board of directors.

In 1995, Brousseau left a league governor's meeting in Quebec and boarded a flight to Moncton. It is not the least bit unusual to bump into friends and associates simply by chance on flights to and from relatively small Maritime cities like Moncton, or to see people who seem familiar because they are known locally. Such was the case with Brousseau and Robert aboard that day's flight. There had already been a game plan afoot to convince Robert to buy the Moncton entrant in the league, and Robert was certainly aware of this campaign. The team was in dire straits, to say the least, and its survival was very much in question. It was Brousseau's assignment to enlist Irving's support and salvage the team. Although Brousseau was a longstanding member of the league's board of governors, his reason for being there was linked directly to the hockey interests of Moncton. Oddly, in spite of the intimacy of Moncton's small business community, Brousseau and Robert Irving had never even met. In fact, in the ten years he'd known Robert preceding the 2006 Canada Cup, Brousseau had never done work for any of Irving's businesses. He finally did do a contract related to sponsorship for the Memorial Cup, but that, he says, was a first. Their relationship is about hockey, not business.

On board that Air Canada connector flight through Montreal, the business card tag on Robert's briefcase gave away his identity. He sat near Brousseau in the last row of the aircraft. Brousseau took the cue from the briefcase and decided to ask, "Are you Mr. Irving?" Robert replied in the affirmative. It took no time at all for Robert to level a question that was on both their minds: "Why should I buy that hockey team?" Brousseau's reply? "Well, you'll be the saviour of hockey in Moncton if you do. That's the only reason I could give you." There wasn't much else to say. The business of the team had not been going well at all, with ownership split amongst a group of investors from Ontario and four men in Greater Moncton. Seeming surprised by Brousseau's frank answer, Robert asked if he could make money with the team. "Obviously I'm the wrong guy to ask," Brousseau answered, "because we're losing our shirts." Whatever his motivation, Robert decided to buy the team. Brousseau believes he did so simply because he's passionate about the game of hockey, although he doubts Robert has ever played a game in his life. "He just loves the game," says Brousseau. He thinks Robert played lacrosse and football in his earlier years, but not hockey.

On the heels of Moncton's fleeting moment in the limelight of the 2006 Memorial Cup, Brousseau talked about the team owner and how the famous hands-on, attention-to-detail techniques of the Irvings shone even in this, Robert's business-cum-hobby. He was unequivocal about how Robert's investment and actions definitely set the pace and caused the Memorial Cup to come to Moncton. The result was an overwhelming success, with the city and surrounding areas coming together in support of their joint hockey cause. Brousseau and others also feel it put Moncton squarely on the Canadian hockey map for the first time. As a result of Robert's investment and his ability to attract a high-level coach like Ted Nolan (since returned to the ranks of the NHL), Moncton has arguably gone from being a good hockey town to what Brousseau comfortably calls a great hockey town.

"I'm amazed with this guy," says Brousseau, "how he's so hands-on with everything. He'll be in the room this weekend [June 9–11, 2006] when we do the draft. He'll want to know everything about all the players we're going to draft, he'll want to know their backgrounds. He'll want to know why this guy versus that guy and what this guy's going to be at nineteen or twenty. He'll put the guys [the team's coaches and management] on the spot." It's clear that Robert's interest transcends the mere business aspects of the team. Brousseau says he's one of the most hand-on owners in the league, treating the team as seriously as he treats Cavendish Farms, Majesta, or any of his other businesses.

Brousseau also claims that if Robert asks you something, "you better say it the way it is, because you don't have to lie. You say it the way it is. If you don't know, tell him you don't know. It's easier to say you don't know than going and trying to make up a story." He claims Robert will know right away if you're bluffing or faking it. "You need to know what you're talking about. If he feels that you don't know what you're talking about, I don't think he's going to lose any time on it. You can be guaranteed, after you tell him something, he's going to check other sources." Brousseau says he's certain that in the early stages of their business relationship, Robert checked him out thoroughly.

The dream of a team owner, of course, is to win the Memorial Cup every year. There are fifty-eight teams chasing the same dream, with a projected sixty by 2008, double the line-up for the Stanley Cup, which stands at thirty teams. From the beginning, it was Robert's objective to win the Memorial Cup. It's his objective to win, period. "I think that's his pattern," says Brousseau, adding that Robert is a passionate guy who listens to a lot of people. "He will take the advice of a lot of people to help him make up his mind, but after his mind is made, it's made. And then he's going to go and he's going to make it work." There have been occasions when Brousseau has challenged Robert on hockey personnel matters and Robert has responded, "Yeah, but Johnny, at the end of the day, I'm paying the bill." Brousseau is secure enough now to give right back by saying, "Yeah, but you're still going to pay the bill and we're not going to win." When Robert hears that prospect, he's capable of tuning in and taking stock of the advice being offered to him. Hockey, as has been noted, is an emotional business as well as a high-strung emotional game. All things considered, however, at the end of the day, Robert makes his own decisions.

Robert's passion for Wildcats operations extends from player selection to how the players are doing individually, from marketing to the cleanliness of the washrooms at Moncton Coliseum. "If you go to a hockey game and somebody complains that the washrooms are dirty," says Brousseau, "you can be guaranteed that he will report it to the guy in charge and that they're going to be cleaned. And he's going to make sure it's cleaned. He's so detailed. You rarely see a guy who will pay so much attention to detail." Attention to detail even extends to the guy who pumps up the crowd at Moncton Coliseum. Brousseau says that if Robert gets feedback that the music at Wildcats' games isn't working, he goes to the guy who does the music and asks him to change it. He's even involved in ensuring the quality of equipment. During a previous season, Robert had decided to buy the team a new skate sharpener, so he went to the Wildcats' trainer and asked where he could buy the best one available. The trainer had done his homework and had located one in Rimouski that was only a year old. On the next team trip to Rimouski, Robert asked Brousseau to join him in meeting with the owner of the sharpener to make sure nothing was lost in the French interaction. The price previously discussed between the trainer and the sharpener's owner—$12,000 or so—was taken at face value by Robert.

When the two met, Robert asked, "Okay, is it a good machine?" The guy responded in the affirmative. The two shook hands while the other guy looked at Brousseau. "You've got a deal," Brousseau confirmed in French. The guy looked astounded that the deal had been done so informally, so quickly and efficiently.

Robert demonstrated his irrepressible work habits when in the hometown of a competing Quebec team. Immediately after the game, he would eat and go to bed. The next morning, he would go off to tour a competitor's tissue plant or check out stores carrying his tissue products. And the second the game ends, it's on the plane and back home again. It is not a party scene. Brousseau talks about the difference between Irvings and most other people. Most of society envisions a division between working and living, while to Robert, the two are synonymous. Other people would say, "How can I live if it's all work?" But Brousseau says for them work is life: "You know, some people look at work from nine to five and it's okay. Some look at nine to nine. But work is how those guys live. It's hard to believe, but I think that it's so." Having said all that, they still have a lot of laughs on the road and there was the time when Robert did take a rare break, taking Brousseau and their sons for a day or two of trout fishing at an Irving-owned lodge near Renous, New Brunswick. Brousseau says he could see traces of that desire to be in the outdoors that is so typical of Robert's father, J. K.

The sense of who's who and the mindset of owner-to-employee relationships are never far away, however. Brousseau recalls an instance where the two were in a canoe with a guide. Fishing guides often have a poker face when it comes to interaction with their clients. It's part of their culture. Irving guides or otherwise, they tend to speak when they're spoken to and answer questions; their job is to be wise and fish-smart and tell good stories on request. There are exceptions, but guides are not normally there to joke around and entertain. Being the jovial fellow he is, Brousseau said something funny having to do with his slant on English, which Robert at first did not get—but which made the guide laugh aloud. When Robert looked at the man, the laughter halted. Brousseau repeated the joke and Robert finally laughed. But the preceding effect was clear. The guide, in other words, caught himself out of his traditional role as the professional Irving guide. Brousseau tells the story not to paint Robert as an ogre, but to illustrate that when you're constantly at work like an Irving, it's sometimes hard to separate work and leisure.

Brousseau says Robert's approach to hockey is the same as his—and the other Irvings'—approach to business. "He's not a guy who's going to come back and say, 'Well, that's not really what I mean.' If it's a deal, it's a deal. If it's a bad deal, it's a bad deal," although Brousseau says that very few of Robert

Irvings' deals would be considered bad. He says that when it came to hockey, Robert learned the business, but sometimes struggles between his heart and his mind over decisions because he's a fan and not just a businessman. Nevertheless, "he's a big learner and he learns fast. He knows what's at stake. He's got the guts to risk changing the way that things are done."

When it comes to players, Brousseau says Robert treats them like gold. When player Jonathan Roy was diagnosed with cancer, Robert did everything he could to get Roy to the right treatment centre, including a trip to see Lance Armstrong's doctor. Similarly, between games of the Memorial Cup, a longstanding hockey volunteer from Sault Ste. Marie, Ontario, suffered a heart attack and died on the spot while playing a diversionary round of golf. It was the fifty-nine-year-old victim's eighth time at the Memorial Cup. He was playing in the foursome just ahead of Brousseau and some guests when the incident occurred, giving Brousseau first-hand knowledge of the incident. Later, Robert and other team officials rallied to get the man's wife to Moncton, took care of her on the ground, and returned her home with the volunteer's remains. The team—in other words, Robert Irving—footed the bill without a fleeting thought.

Robert Morrissey, former PEI industry minister and later economic development and tourism minister, recalls dealing with Robert over the Cavendish Farms negotiations. He says that Robert was even more business-focused than his father J.K. or sister Mary Jean. He was "all business, very focused, and not chit-chatty," a "likeable chap," but just not one to make a lot of small talk. Speaking about his business style, the way he would engage in conversation, Morrissey says Robert "wouldn't take his eyes off of you. He would fixate on you."

"Humbility" is the term coined by Mike MacBride, former New Brunswick economic development and tourism project executive, to describe a pleasant one-off encounter with Robert. Its definition, he says, is a combination of "humility" and "ability." MacBride received an invitation to the mid-1990s christening of one of the Canadian navy frigates that the Irving's built at Saint John Shipbuilding, HMCS *Fredericton*. He has no idea how or why he was invited, other than the fact that he was in what was widely perceived as the action department, the get-things-done department during the era of premier Frank McKenna.

It was an elegant midday affair, a lunch served with the fineries at the Saint John Convention Centre. MacBride ended up seated next to Robert, which resulted in an exchange of small talk. The conversation moved from the matter of the launch of the navy's newest frigate—not exactly a little dinghy—to the matter of a nineteen-foot Bayliner cruiser that MacBride kept at his family cottage on South Grand Lake, which borders New Brunswick and Maine. Robert remarked on how nice it was to have a boat like that and then remarked, "That's a big boat, Mike." Given the nature of the event they were attending, with the Irvings launching a mass of steel, technology, and armaments that you couldn't exactly tie up at the cottage wharf, the remark caught MacBride off guard. Nevertheless, MacBride swears that in the moment, in the one-to-one personal exchange they were sharing, Robert seemed sincere and was politely demonstrating genuine interest in his boat. He was a quiet guy, according to MacBride; he didn't exude the charisma of a Ken or Jim Irving. He's wondered ever since the "big boat" encounter whether Robert's low-key approach wasn't perhaps a technique that he purposely uses to disarm people; an aw-shucks ploy to disguise the fact that he is, of course, very astute about business and people, and most probably about boats too. This "humility" might just be Robert Irving's trademark.

◆

J. K.'s eldest daughter Mary-Jean has lived on Prince Edward Island since 1987, when she moved there with her husband, Rev. Stewart Dockendorff, a member of a highly successful blue mussel–farming family from Morell, PEI., and a Baptist minister whose congregation in central North River has flourished under his tutelage. That she has lived on the Island for twenty years and that she married an Islander doesn't matter when it comes to official Island citizenry; she will always be a CFA, a "Come From Away." Islanders have always been of the mind that they are something of a republic. A similar mentality exists on Cape Breton Island and in Newfoundland and Labrador, but on PEI, it is very acutely practised and felt. You can live on the island for years, paying your taxes and all the rest, but you never quite receive your citizenship papers. The longer you stay, the closer you are to being an Islander; but as they say, close only really counts in horseshoes.

Mary Jean started Indian River Farms Inc. in 1991, a time when land use was—as it has been for decades—a major issue in a place that has more finite land resources than any other province in Canada. The nickname "million-acre farm" from the province's long-ago tourism campaigns sounds like a lot of terra firma, but when divided into Island's mix of farms, industrial parks, small urban areas, and tourism and coastal use, the pieces of the pie are pretty quickly chewed up. Mary Jean has adopted a very low profile on the Island since 1990 (and more so since her challenges battling cancer), which is when her rapid acquisition of farmland set off a political firestorm. The acquisitions were focused on the western part of the Island and were estimated by some to have grown to twenty thousand acres at one point. Media, land-use activists and farmers (except those who'd gleefully cashed in their lands for profit) expressed outrage at what was described as an attempt to circumvent the province's property ownership limits. Facing a public mood best reflected by one protestor's placard that read "Prince Irving Island," the government of the day had no choice but to act or lose all confidence behind the standing land ownership legislation. The premier of the day was the late Joe Ghiz. He had plucked Robert Morrissey, MLA for the riding of First Prince, from the ranks of his elected Liberals and rewarded him for his natural, Islandish way with people and the electorate with two successive cabinet portfolios. Morrissey became minister of industry in 1989, and in 1993 was sworn in as minister of economic development and tourism.

Morrissey would ultimately have to contend with the controversy surrounding Mary Jean and Indian River Farms, but he had had previous contact with the family and their businesses. The first was in 1989, a time when the Island was facing what he calls a "desolate economic picture." Among other ongoing economic problems, the closure of CFB Summerside was having a devastating economic and psychological effect on people in nearby communities, especially Summerside and areas to the west.

Morrissey was conscious that one of the key challenges was the Island potato industry's failure to convert itself from what was principally a table product market to a more balanced market mix of table stock and processed product. In the potato business, there are three ways to sell product: as seed potato, as bagged but unprocessed product in the produce section of a supermarket (referred to as table stock), or as value-added, processed product in the form of frozen French fries or hash browns. He called it a "horrible" position to be in for the province's main cash crop. He and his government colleagues had realized as early as 1986 that this over-dependence on the table market did not bode well for the future. A legitimate mix would have been 50/50, but the Island was processing less than 30 per cent of its output and selling the remaining 70 per cent the old fashioned way. This would be analogous to New Brunswick's trees being shipped away for milling instead of going into Irving sawmills and pulpmills for processing. Morrissey could envision the day when Island potatoes would be shipped into New Brunswick plants, with that province reaping the rewards of new processing plant jobs and the spinoffs that would result. He was determined to fix the situation by intervening and by turning the percentages over—having 70 per cent channelled into processing and the balance into traditional table stock. After Morrissey had talked to "everyone in North America" with any remote interest in potato processing, the Irvings emerged as the only people interested in the prospects of turning Island spuds into what would become branded as Cavendish French Fries and spinoff products. Sitting not too far down the Trans-Canada Highway at their massive operation in Florenceville, New Brunswick, Harrison and Wallace McCain and their executives apparently weren't paying close enough attention to the Irvings' manoeuvres into the spud market.

In short order, the Irvings took over the former C. M. MacLean plant in Kensington and within two years doubled its capacity. Former New Brunswick premier Frank McKenna was concurrently trying to convince the Irvings to forget any notions about bringing their interests to the Island and instead to put their plant in Port Elgin, New Brunswick. With the looming cessation of ferry services and related jobs in the district—the result of plans to build the Confederation Bridge—McKenna and local MLA Dr. Marilyn Trenholme had all the more reason to chase down the Irvings and anybody else with an eye toward development in the provincial riding known as Tantramar.

For the purposes of that first deal with the Irvings, even though he was a minister of the crown, Morrissey was asked to sign a confidentiality agreement, a request to which he complied. Satisfied that he was a straight player, the Irvings never again asked for his signature on such a document. Morrissey was more than impressed with his first Irving experience. They knew their numbers inside and out and were prepared to "spill all the beans all the time" about their plans. This was in contrast to Morrissey's experiences dealing with players like Fortis Corporation, Canadian Helicopter, or companies from Ontario that the Island government was attempting to introduce into the local economy, many of which, Morrissey felt, shielded financials and other details from the Island government bureaucracy and elected officials. Many such companies have come and gone from the industrial parks of all four Atlantic provinces, leaving shrapnel deep in the flesh of provincial economic development departments and the Atlantic Canada Opportunities Agency and fuelling attitudes like that expressed in 2006 by Stephen Harper about Atlantic Canadians being dependent on equalization and on handouts.

Over the ensuing years, Cavendish Farms grew, and the McCains angrily followed the Irving lead into the Island market. At one point, even Humpty Dumpty established itself in Slemon Park (site of the former CFB Summerside), an event described by Morrissey as the only emergence of a potato chip plant in North America during that era. He even recalls the date his department closed the Humpty Dumpty deal. It was November 18, 1994, his fortieth birthday. The McCains' anger over the growth of the Cavendish brand name spilled all over the rich red Island soil when McCain official Archie MacLean (who later followed Wallace McCain to Maple Leaf Foods in Toronto) made a most memorable contribution to the CBC Charlottetown television archives when he said it was his company's primary interest to derail Cavendish. Morrissey wanted nothing to do with McCains' game of corporate one-upmanship. Nevertheless, the province did offer the New Brunswick–based company an incentive deal that was similar to the Cavendish package. The Irvings could have packed up in a huff and left their deal in the lurch. But this is where Morrissey says he discovered that the Irvings' word is sacrosanct no matter how tough they might be to negotiate with, or how upset they might be about something. J.K. and son Robert, the principal faces in all of the Cavendish negotiations, would not renege on their pledge to invest in the Island potato-processing sector.

Following these experiences of getting to know the Irvings, Morrissey was the guy who, in one important episode of a dramatic, drawn-out rural soap opera, had to remind Mary Jean in a "rather tense" encounter that her company, Indian River Farms, had exceeded its allowable limit on corporate land holdings and that some of their acquired acreage would have to be sold. Since the 1970s, the Island has had in place various forms of legislation to restrict the amount of land that can be owned by any single landowner if they are non-residents or corporate in nature (with respect to farmland). It was a tough meeting for Morrissey, particularly because the sixty jobs associated with Indian River Farms were in his riding. But "the law is the law," as he still says today, and he wasn't about to back down. His riding or not, he wasn't about to play that kind of political favouritism to protect his political hide.

Predictably, some members of the farming community who'd been crying bloody blue murder over the extraordinary Irving landholdings did a one-eighty and decried the government's decision. At the same time, a Compton potato operation near Morell also wanted to sell huge tracts of farmland to interests other than the Irvings, but the government again stood its ground and said no. Mary Jean and whichever lawyers and family members had been advising her dragged the matter down to the wire, a six-month test of wills that ended just as the province was about to take the Irvings to court. In the fall of 1990 she agreed to sell off some of her acreage. Company literature indicates her firm wound up farming about 2,300 acres, which is within the provincial limits.

Of course, Mary Jean has gone on since then to do business with the PEI government, as reflected in a 1995 government announcement announcing the $14,000,000 expansion of the Master Packaging plant in the community of Borden-Carleton. Although this book is intended not to serve as a list of Irving facts and figures, it's useful to understand that that single act of Irving investment brought about the construction of an additional twenty-five thousand square feet at that facility, as well as the installation of new equipment to expand the company's domestic and international trade markets.

The company currently employs 70 employees, and this latest expansion was intended to bring the total number of employees to 128. The Department of Development and Technology, through Prince Edward Island Business Development Inc., provided the project with a $10,000,000 loan to be repaid in five years. "Master Packaging appreciates this tremendous vote of confidence in our operations from the Province," Mary Jean was quoted as saying in the announcement. As Robert Morrissey can affirm, unlike many other companies the government had enticed to invest on the Island, there was never any question as to the Irvings' intention to satisfy the terms of the loan.

Reviewing the history of Mary Jean's visible business activities is one thing. Getting to know her is quite another. There is a force field around her that seems all the more impenetrable following her challenges with cancer. Source after source came to the brink of speaking off the record but backed off when the interview moment came (no one except Morrissey was prepared to go on the record). One story was told and then retracted, because the proprietary nature of what had happened would reveal that the source demonstrated she has astonishing generosity. So as not to break the confidence, suffice it to say that Mary Jean's connections to Stewart's congregation and her religion in general provide opportunities for this generosity to be wielded, albeit very, very discreetly.

◆

After being nestled into his advertising business in quaint little Sackville, New Brunswick, for nearly twenty years, David Hawkins was asked in the late 1990s to establish a small office in Ottawa at the headquarters of Summa Strategies Canada Inc., a consulting firm owned by the former members of parliament Doug Young (from the riding of Acadie–Bathurst) and Paul Zed (from the riding of Fundy–Royal), who at the time was married to Judith Irving. Liberals Young and Zed had lost their seats in the June 1997 federal election. Young did not return to politics and as of 2006 remained as chairman at Summa, while Zed was re-elected in 2004 and 2006 in the riding of Saint John. Hawkins had known Zed in passing, as did a couple of his employees. He decided to take the leap into Ottawa and spent a fair bit of time with Zed drumming up business in the national capital region.

It's said that on the very same day Judith turned forty, her youngest began her first day of school. For a woman who had held down the family fort and taken care of the kids for years, the house must have seemed empty. But for the daughter of J. K. Irving—patriarch of his generation of Irvings, all of whose children had gone to work—the logical thing would be to get to work. There would be no lazing about for anyone in J. K.'s clan.

At the time, Judith's nephew Jamie, then in his early twenties, was spending a lot of time with Zed, both in Ottawa and in New Brunswick. As a result, Hawkins, Zed, and Jamie hung out together periodically and began talking about business possibilities. During one of those discussions, Zed raised the question of whether Hawkins had ever considered selling Hawk Communications. Hawkins told him it wasn't a top-of-mind thing at the time, but sure, at some juncture it would be something he'd want to do. "Well, we should talk about that," Zed said. "That may be something Judith would be interested in." The topic was floated for several months before Zed raised the acquisition question a second time, and from there the idea gained momentum. According to a popular New Brunswick politician and Irving watcher, J. K. basically bought Hawk Communications for his daughter to run. "Judith had never really run anything," says the source. "But Judith is an Irving. She was always a housewife and all of a sudden she has this corporation to run and she turns tough right away. Right away she corporately knows she has to do things." But although Judith had the personal initiative to pick up the corporate baton and get to work, there is evidence that her father J. K. helped along with her personal and professional transition.

Somewhat ironically, Hawk Communications had done very little work for Irving companies over the years, exceptions being small stints with Irving Oil and a couple of the family's less visible companies in the early 1990s. For many years, Hawk had been much more active on accounts for the McCains. Hawkins believes the Irvings honed in on his company because it was a New Brunswick company and one with a good reputation. There were seventy-five employees at the time, at offices in Moncton, Sackville, Ottawa, Toronto, and Fredericton.

Over the next two years, there were intermittent talks between Hawkins and Zed and Judith, with nephew Jamie in attendance from time to time. The deal was sealed on October 5, 2001. "We were ready for a change," Hawkins says of himself and wife Lorrie. "You know, I was fifty-four, I'd been in the business since I was nineteen years old and I had a long, hard run at it. I'd been working on a succession plan for some years, but these things are very, very difficult to construct and to implement." So for Hawkins, the idea of someone taking over the whole enterprise was "quite appealing" for a variety of business and personal reasons. The negotiations involved many conversations regarding how it might all come together, what the deal would actually include, and what his role might be during the transition. "In many ways, my recollection of it was that I didn't entirely encourage them. I didn't encourage Judith to buy the business. She wanted to be in the business. Jamie was also interested. Paul was interested. They were all interested."

Hawkins says that Judith has a good creative slant to her personality. She'd been a photographer, having taken courses at Charlottetown's Holland College campus. She had a photo studio for years and knew people in the ad business. "I think she was at a point in her personal life where she wanted to get beyond the home and to be in business like other members of the family," Hawkins hypothesizes. "She'd been brought up in a very entrepreneurial family. She had some instincts of her own and interests of her own and this seemed like a business that she had an affinity for and some interest in." Hawkins believes Judith has the same ambitiousness as others in the immediate and extended family who lead enterprises, including, of course, her sister Mary Jean in Charlottetown.

Apart from Mary Jean, Irving women had tended not to be on the frontlines of business. One has to underscore, obviously, the roles Irving women have played through volunteerism and in keeping their families together, as far back as patriarch George's wife Jane. "I think anybody sitting back and observing things would figure this out in a nanosecond," says Hawkins. "I think the Irving family culture had historically been very oriented towards the idea that the men went to work—the men were in business—and the women took care of the home. And then, of course, our entire twentieth century—Canadian and North American culture, the Western world culture—shifted that model during the sixties, seventies, and the eighties, which is when Judith was born and was growing up. So I think Judith really wanted to do more. She wanted to be in business and wanted to join her dad and uncles and brothers and other family members and be in business."

But as much as Hawkins believes Judith was ready to move into the business world, he saw other attributes in her that were even more powerful—and he believes, more important. "I'll give you my first cut on this," says Hawkins, "and I'll be very clear about this. Judith is an excellent mother and if you were to ask me about Judith, I would say that first and foremost Judith is a really, really high-quality mother. And you know, you can't say that about everybody. You'd like to say it about everybody, but you can't say it about everybody. And I'm very, very happy and enthusiastic and proud to say that about her. I also think she's equally competent and capable as a daughter and you can't say that about every daughter either." What Hawkins is driving at is that he sees Judith as a very strong member of the Irving family. "I think she brings a lot of glue to the family. I think she's a very loving family member. I think she works hard to keep the family together and keep the family communicating. I think she supports family members. I think she takes a lead role in that." Hawkins says that if Judith did nothing else with her life but be a good mother, a good daughter, and part of the glue that keeps the family together and communicating, that would be a "huge accomplishment" in and of itself. Hawkins feels that her parents have set a strong example in this regard, but of the kids in the family, Judith would be the best at providing the family glue.

Once in the driver's seat at Hawk Communications, Judith embarked on more than a year of commuting between Saint John and the company offices in Moncton. This involved having breakfast with her still young family, speaking to them during the day on the telephone and trying to get home in time to have evening dinner with them. Periodically, according to Hawkins, she would stay overnight in Moncton, but typically she commuted between the two cities—at least an hour and a half each way—on a daily basis. It was a huge shift in lifestyle and in life perspective for someone who previously had very limited business experience. As she poured her "heart and soul" into the job of leading a thriving ad agency, she sought and accepted advice from family members and others. What Judith brought to the table more than anything, Hawkins says, was sheer determination.

Meanwhile, Hawkins, as had been agreed in the terms of sale, was playing a mentorship role through the transition, a role he had a difficult time working his way through. His twenty-year-old offspring was no longer under his supervision and upbringing. He says that the transition was a difficult situation, one in which he didn't excel. "In fact, I didn't do a very good job at it," he confesses. "I guess to be fair to myself, it was a difficult role. I think they had very distinctive ideas about how they wanted to run the company." He says it wasn't about letting go of the ownership and he didn't feel possessive about Hawk. "In fairness, it was their company and they wanted to do it their way. I just would've gone about it differently. I *had* gone about it differently. I didn't necessarily think they were wrong. It's just not how I would have done it. It was more of a style thing than anything else." The difficulty seemed to rest in trying to convey that the ad business is not just about ledgers; it is very heavily oriented toward relationships—something that is not easily explained because of the art and the nuance of relationship building in the sector. Hawkins says the relationship angle in the ad business is all the more acutely critical in Atlantic Canada.

Hawkins remained in this transitional capacity for sixteen months before taking his leave from having a full-time presence, relaxing into a more casual, consultative role. Four years later, he continued to refer clients to them. Not surprisingly, private-sector clients had been hard to attract because so many potential clients are competitors of other Irving enterprises; for them to do business with Hawk would run afoul of traditional client-agency matters of confidentiality and potential conflicts of interest. Under Judith's control, Hawk Communications became smaller, something Hawkins feels may not have been such a bad thing. Some of the best agencies in Atlantic Canada—if not Canada—are leaner than the old traditional agencies that try to be everything to everybody. Boutique shops are in vogue for many types of clients.

Hawkins summarizes Judith's foray into the ad business and the fact that it was followed by the collapse of her marriage to Paul Zed: "There were some personal challenges that she went through and we've all gone through things like that at one time or another. That was a difficult period. I'm sure it must have been exceedingly difficult, but my observation is that she has come through it very, very well." Says a source other than Hawkins: "If Judith indicated she needed help, J. K. would walk in there with two or three accountants, or whatever: 'Gentlemen, we're going and that's it. It doesn't make any difference what you're working on. We've got to go and help Judith.'" Clearly, although Judith's was the name at the top of the org chart, if there was help needed from time to time, she had lots of backup. But backup or no backup, in February 2007 Judith decided to pack it in at Hawk and sell the company. So after five or six years in the ad game, Judith is a free agent and is probably happy to be liberated from the burden of commuting between the familiarity of Saint John and the stresses and strains of running an ad agency in a less familiar city ninety minutes away.

◆

One of the off-the-record but well-informed and credible interviewees for this book held nothing back. This person has a habit of delivering pinpoint acerbic thoughts no matter the subject, including the Irvings. This person provided rare insights into Jack Irving's son John, a low-key Saint John real estate guy and the only other sixth generation player aside from Kenneth, Arthur Jr., Jim, Robert, Mary Jean, and Judith. To start off, he's a "really, really nice" guy. And as one of only a few New Brunswickers to earn an MBA at Harvard—Andrew Oland among them—he's clearly no dummy. But, says the source, he has a tendency to be overly gregarious, one of those guys with a nuclear power handshake. Apparently, when his name is mentioned to some of the other Irvings of his generation, their reaction suggests that he's not necessarily invited to the family picnic. "Like, you remember that Sesame Street song, 'One of these things is not like the other, one of these things does not belong'"—that, says the source, sums up John.

There is a story that provides a snapshot of John's excessive gregariousness. Standing in line at a McDonalds restaurant, the subject saw John appear at the drive-through window. He tried to carry on an entire conversation through the window and the muddle of employees taking orders, ringing in the cash, and bagging Big Macs and fries. This conversation went well beyond a wave and a "How are you?" It went on in great detail, relaying how a certain meeting had just gone. Another anecdote: at a reception in the Delta Saint John hotel lobby, John once left a small cluster of people to crash through another small cluster of people, unable to contain the need to say hello and to shake hands—atomically, of course. It was apparently noticeable to the people in both groups.

Some say Jack's family might be the most mainstream of the entire Irving clan, perhaps because Jack's expectations of his children haven't been as daunting as those of J. K. and Arthur Sr. Son Colin is off doing his own thing in Toronto; daughter Anne does not participate in the family business; and then there is John, who, like his father, is one of the least visible Irvings amongst those who are active in family business. My source elaborated on one common trait that John and the other Irvings do share—their tendency to ask a question and be genuinely interested in your response. In other words, it ain't all about them. They're said to exhibit genuine interest in other people, what the other person does, and how they're doing at it.

New Brunswick's other Harvard MBA grad, Andrew Oland of Moosehead Breweries Ltd., has an appreciation for John and his openness. In 1994, when Oland was considering attending Harvard, he called John, knowing he'd graduated within the previous five years. Oland was looking for fifteen minutes worth of advice. "I went in, and he was extremely helpful, extremely encouraging," says Oland. "He gave me lots of good feedback and really set me in the right direction in terms of how to approach applying and what sort of things they were looking for. John's done quite a bit of work encouraging young Atlantic Canadians to attend Harvard Business School." That tiny example of helpfulness is one of many things Oland says the Irvings do without taking any credit. There are many things going on that no one knows anything about. Oland makes it clear that the attitude of John Irving and other members of his immediate and extended family has had an impact on how he sees the community he lives in, if not the world.

7. Up-and-Coming Irvings—The Seventh Generation
GEORGE > HERBERT > J.D. > K.C. > J.K., ARTHUR SR., AND JACK > JIM, ROBERT, MARY
JEAN, JUDITH, KENNETH, ARTHUR JR., AND JOHN > JAMIE AND KATE

While K. C.'s grandchildren have adapted for the most part to the Irving ways of doing things, it's the capacity and leadership qualities of his great-grandchildren, the seventh generation, that will determine whether the realm holds together. Most argue that time has run out on the Irvings, that seven generations is simply too much for any business family, no matter how brave, emboldened, and brilliant.

Jim Irving's son Jamie and daughter Kathryn (Kate) are still young, both in their late twenties, and the first of the seventh generation to punch the

Irving time clock. Their cousins are either quite young or not involved in the family business.

As far as the public eye goes, Kate is nearly invisible. All that's known is that she works in sales at the Moncton office of an Irving company called Chandler that can be found in various locations across the Maritimes. Since 1959, Chandler has been one of those perfect building blocks within the Irvings' vertical integration process, offering products and services across a vast spectrum, including such things as work apparel, sanitation supplies, office environments, printing supplies, forms—you name it, Chandler seems to have it. Like Thorne's Hardware in Saint John, Chandler is one of those obscure Irving enterprises, feeding other Irving companies with services and appurtenances while those Irving enterprises feed Thorne's and Chandler with circular Irving money. It appears Kate is working in the trenches, much like her father and grandfather did in their early days.

Jamie already heads up the *Saint John Telegraph-Journal*, one of three Irving-owned daily newspapers in New Brunswick. Together with a plethora of other Irving media holdings, it is often the subject of federal combines investigations and a target of critics who say the Irvings' holdings are too vast and monopolistic. On paper, Jamie is the heir apparent of the responsibilities associated with J. D. Irving Ltd. He attended the Columbia School of Journalism in New York and is said to absolutely love the newspaper business. One bystander with a view on him is Willa Mavis, innkeeper and champion behind the Save Our Shores campaign, a very public battle over the Irving proposal to create a sewage lagoon at pristine Sheldon's Point, near Saint John. With her husband Ross, Mavis operates the award-winning destination Inn on the Cove. The campaign she spearheaded was difficult and hard fought, most of it in confrontation with J. K. and J. D. Irving Ltd. staffers, but Mavis developed a positive attitude about the Irvings once they admitted they were wrong about how to treat the effluent from their Saint John mills and shelved the Sheldon's Point project. Both she and J. K. have since said things in public that illustrate their respect for one another. J. K.'s grandson Jamie, as it turns out, is a neighbour of the Mavises.

Mavis found the young Irving very approachable when they first met at a New Brunswick Museum fundraiser in 2004. She subsequently sent him an e-mail about a negative New Brunswick tourism story that was unfolding around that time, and he responded. After a brief exchange in which she complimented him on the way the paper has turned around, he thanked her, saying, "I'm so used to getting negative comments, it's really nice to get a positive one for a change." This sentiment reflects the impression that for the Irvings, it's lonely at the top and they feel starved for public praise.

David Hawkins, the former ad man, got to know Jamie quite well when the two were spending time together in Ottawa with Paul Zed. In the ripeness of his early twenties, Jamie actually worked at Hawk Communications for a four-month stint before moving to another area within the Irving Group of Companies. Something happened affecting Jamie's very abbreviated sojourn there, the details of which are unclear. "My first observation about Jamie," says Hawkins, "is that he is a very sensitive person. He's a very intelligent person and he's not an industrialist. Most of the people whose last name is Irving, who are in business, have tended to be on the industrial side of things." Jamie, by contrast, is far more interested in the arts, culture, journalism. As publisher of the *Telegraph-Journal*, he's no doubt in the Irving business environment best suited to him for the time being.

Apart from the office, you're more likely to find Jamie at an Alex Colville exhibit in Moncton or the Rodin exhibit in Fredericton than on an Irving woodlot or mill talking to line workers about this piece of machinery or that technique in producing paper efficiently. This characteristic alone sets him apart from the Irving stereotype. He is said to like being in the company of journalists, and, according to Hawkins, he had a good relationship with the likes of the late Dalton Camp and national columnist (and former editor of the *Telegraph-Journal*) Neil Reynolds. One wonders how J.D. Irving Ltd.— truly an industrial monolith—and all the companies associated with J.K. and father Jim's side of the Irving empire, will be managed when Jamie's father Jim retires. One has to wonder whether the family isn't already eyeballing a succession plan that will see senior management come from the outside, or whether J.D. Irving Ltd. and other companies could even go public. It does not appear that Jamie is the right man to run the Irving industrial conglomerate.

Because Jamie's and Kate's business leanings and limitations make them more normal than Irving, and because no other seventh-generation Irvings have come of age, it's impossible to know if anyone will emerge to manage and lead on the scale required by their massively complicated companies. Unless those faces emerge and become clear within the next five to ten years, the stage is set for a dramatic change in the Irving saga. Already having defied the odds by surviving into the fifth and sixth generations, it is almost certain that the retirement of the sixth generation will force the family to make some serious decisions about the future of the Irving Group of Companies. Based on their acumen and true-to-Irving characteristics, the people destined to face this challenge are Jim, brother Robert, sister Mary Jean, and cousin Kenneth. One thing is clear: they are not the band of brothers their respective fathers and Jack Irving have been since the days of the Jim, Art, and Jack Farm nearly seventy years ago. The Irving times, they are a-changing.

PART II

Fixations

8. The Irving School of Business

Everything that twenty-first-century Irvings are has been taught to them. Call them lessons, call them principles, call them ideals, call them traits, call them characteristics, call them strands of the Irving DNA, call them best practices. Some would call them fixations. In general, Irvings have a tendency to be consumed with something whenever they get involved, whether it is directly related to their work, something philanthropic, or something in their personal lives.

There are certain non-negotiable things that it takes to be an Irving and there's a long list of them. Those things, like hard work, entrepreneurship, patience, perseverance, humility, loyalty, respect, attention to detail, and how to cut a deal, are qualities that have been instilled through natural day-to-day interaction between the up-and-comers and their experienced elders, but let there be no mistake: they have also been tactically taught. Some refer loosely to this as the Irving School of Business, and it does seem as though the family has a curriculum of sorts. There's no doubt that in their formative years, up-and-coming family members have been schooled using tried-and-true Irving methodology that is better than any semester spent attending a real business school. Why attend a business school at all when you have your own, with an unbeatable curriculum, right at home? This method of hands-on instruction comes up so frequently with reference to the Irvings that even J. K. discussed it with me.

But there is a key difference between the education received by the twenty-first-century Irvings and that received by previous generations, a difference that, over time, could diminish the true value of their patented approach to doing business. Until the advent of the sixth generation, Irving teachings always came from a single source: George to Herbert, Herbert to J.D., J.D. to K.C., and K.C. to brothers J.K., Arthur Sr., and Jack. The curriculum at Irving U was constant and without dilution. The ways of teaching and learning were very clear. But with the sixth generation, there were four professors, each with his own style, outlook, and emphasis: J.K. teaching Jim, Robert, Mary Jean, and Judith; Arthur Sr. teaching Kenneth and Arthur Jr.; Jack teaching John; and K.C. giving periodic guest lectures. This dilution at Irving U meant that only the offspring of the better teachers and those who spent the most time with their grandfather K.C. could graduate with honours. There was also the sense that each was better at teaching one particular thing: J.K. about being close to and understanding the land; Arthur Sr. about drive and the techniques behind growing a business; and softer-spoken Jack about being kinder to employees. K.C., of course, taught all of these things uniformly in an integrated way.

More than just members of the Irving family have attended the Irving School of Business. Middle and senior managers who've been directly exposed to the Irvings on a daily basis have also been there, although to a lesser degree. Steve Carson, now executive director of Enterprise Saint John and formerly a fourteen-year employee at Irving Oil, jokes that he got his MBA at Irving U and the Irving School of Business. Working at Irving Oil was, for him, the equivalent of attending an exclusive, private university. Irving U taught Carson that even companies on the scale and size of those owned and operated by the Irvings can operate without layer after layer of management and committees. Unlike in government, Irving organizations are flat. Former New Brunswick economic development and tourism deputy minister Francis McGuire tried to emulate this flat administrative approach by structuring his department with only two layers: directors and what he called project executives. This caused a participatory environment of greater equality, minimizing the chain of command.

A source who's done a ton of consulting for Irving companies has crystal clear insights into how things get done using outside consultants. "They're lean and mean," he says. "What I mean is that there aren't huge teams of people. I'm thinking of the J.D. Irving organization. They have really good people. They're very strategic and they're fairly open with us who are on the inside in terms of what the strategy is, what they're trying to achieve and how they're going to manage things, what the goal is." He says that as a consultant, if you perform well and give good advice, then it can almost seem as though you're part of the inner circle for that moment. To achieve that level of trust and status, he says, "you've got to put the Irving underwear on," meaning you have to demonstrate that you know your business. You've got to give them good advice that's reflective and understanding of their business interests. For certain types of projects, the Irvings want consultants to identify risks, categorize those risks, and put in measures to help manage the outcome. "It's not a product like, 'We hire you, you do a study, you give us the study and you go away.' It's kind of like you're part of the team," says the source. But, just as if you were on the inside, you do the work on time and you do it right, or you won't be hearing from them again.

This source has high regard for how sophisticated the Irvings have to be to get the job done and to compete. They're playing, after all, against Exxon, BP, and the other major players on the oil side, and against all of the major wood industry companies on the forestry side. On the oil side, in particular, the source says, "they have a very sophisticated project planning cycle in place because it's a very, very tough business." They have to be organized and tough because on the competitive front, "there's a bunch of bastards in the business with big, deep pockets," not to mention the sheer scale of the competition. This is all the more true in light of the volatility caused by continual crises involving the world's oil-producing nations, such as Venezuela, Iraq, or Iran. In the face of world-scale competition, "they're going to have to be very clever and diversify and integrate their businesses all the more. Hence the LNG terminal, the second oil refinery proposal, and the idea of a regional energy hub centred in Saint John." To some, the Irvings' apparent need to control what's going on at the local level comes across like they're at the helm of a banana republic, like Nestlé in a third-world country. But, says the source, competitiveness is the logic behind their actions.

◆

According to Steve Carson, if something's important, it can get dealt with very quickly in an Irving organization. "The team gets assembled very quickly to make those decisions." Carson learned that in a competitive environment, the Irvings' operational code of immediacy is essential to how they get things done. "There are no discussions around, 'Well, what's this going to do to the stock?' and 'What are shareholders going to think?' You take that whole piece of it away."

In the CBC television documentary *Unlocking the Mystery,* J. K., Arthur Sr., and Jack were asked how the family makes important decisions. An oversized coffee table in the office where the interview took place was sprinkled with old family photographs they'd brought along. In response to the question, J. K. simply reached across the table, cherry-picked one of the images from the pile and showed it to the reporter. It was an image of K. C. and sons sitting and chatting on a park bench. This was a very telling moment, revealing without exaggeration just how the Irvings have managed to conduct business up till the sixth generation. The ability to go sit on a park bench and discuss matters of import amongst the four of them, K. C. and his sons, is emblematic of the family's non-bureaucratic style of decision making. The same park bench meetings cannot be held amongst cousins Jim, Robert, Mary Jean, Judith, Kenneth, Arthur Jr., and John because the family business is now much more complex, and each of the Irvings operates in different spheres.

Carson claims there was an informal indoctrination process of rookies at meetings that wasn't necessarily pre-planned—the situations just happened. If an employee was already in a boardroom finishing another meeting or was in the vicinity, someone would suggest, "You might want to stay here and listen to this." One meeting in particular stands out in Carson's memory. "It was in Arthur's office and there were two rows of chairs. There was a row in front including Arthur and then there was a row behind that, and I was sitting in the row behind. They were talking about a significant project at the refinery, a big project that was being proposed for the refinery. And so the project proponents of the company were there pitching the project. So I was sitting there in the back row and I can't recall who was to my right, but the last available seat, to my left, became occupied by K. C." He wasn't there to be actively involved in the meeting, but neither was he there, as Carson was, to learn the business. It seemed to Carson that K. C. was there almost monitoring things. One can imagine the added nervousness of the meeting's participants in seeing K. C. simply stroll into their meeting.

The project proponents, engineers as Carson recalls, made their pitch, describing what the project was going to cost, what it would achieve, and what the time frames of the installation would be. "And then there was the accounting firm. There were two people representing the firm, responding to the risks associated with this and associated with that and saying why it may not make sense to do this." As the accountants were giving the project proposal a "pretty hard ride," K. C. leaned over to Carson and whispered, "You know, these accountants, you've got to have them around. But don't ever let them run your business." At the end of the discussion, says Carson, the project was approved and went ahead. Having taught his children and grandchildren well, K. C. did not intervene, but merely watched the proceedings unfold, as though he'd scripted the outcome himself.

Carson confirms that the Irving children were treated every bit like rookies, just like any other new employees would be. They too would be invited into certain meetings simply to see how business was done, to observe and absorb. "They were not only brought in to watch," says Carson. "They'd be dispatched to work with the mason putting the stone on a service station. They'd work with the mason for a few days because they should know how that stone goes together so if they're walking through another site in ten or fifteen years and they're seeing some stone being put together, they should pretty much know if it's going together correctly or not." This is reminiscent of how J. K. learned logging the only way you really can, by being in the woods as a member in a logging crew. This direct, hands-on approach to so many practices and trades is sure to build a solid foundation of knowledge that can't be gotten any other way.

Moosehead Breweries' Joel Levesque is among many who recall seeing or hearing of younger Irvings being taken into meetings and other business situations by their fathers. Years ago, a friend of Levesque's was being interviewed for a job by J. K. and his son Jim. Oddly present in a shirt, tie, and blue blazer was Jim's ten-year-old son, Jamie. The younger Irving did not utter a word. He was there solely for the benefit of his own education. This is not unlike how Inuit men are known to teach their sons to be hunters. When they are of age—six or seven years old—Inuit boys are allowed to join their fathers on hunting excursions for seal or caribou. They are not to hunt themselves. They are not to ask questions. They are there solely to watch and learn how the hunting is done.

Francis McGuire, the former economic development minister, recalls being on a three-day industrial tour of several Irving wood-related operations, an opportunity for Jim Irving to show what was happening within J. D. Irving Ltd. Along for the ride once again was son Jamie, by then about fourteen years old. For three days, Jamie never said a word. He was there to observe, to "attend class," and to speak when spoken to. McGuire could see that this established a discipline, a forced attentiveness, and imparted real-life lessons in how adults converse and do business almost without doing business. "I remember if you'd try to talk to the kid, he'd say, 'Yes, sir' or 'No, sir.' That's about all you could get out of him at that point."

Joel Levesque recalls stories of J. K.'s own long-ago induction into the family business. K. C.'s meeting room was often the family's woodlands. "I remember him telling stories," says Levesque, "about working in the woods when he was a young boy, working for his father, K. C. The forests of New Brunswick are their first love, really. You think of pulpmills and paper mills and oil refineries and gas pumps and gas stations, but K. C. Irving loved the forests." So J. K., and probably his brothers too, had many classrooms: the traditional meeting room, the forests, long drives in the car, airplane flights around the Maritimes, warehouses, mills—anyplace where a meeting could be held or a discussion could take place.

Now in their forties or above, Kenneth, Arthur Jr., Jim, Robert, Judith, Mary Jean, and John have evolved from being apprentices to being journeymen and journeywomen and finally to having the responsibility of teaching their own children. One wonders if they still do it the old-fashioned Irving way, or if the changed business world no longer allows the time and discipline required to attend the Irving School of Business. Whether or not seventh-generation family members are getting the full School of Business exposure is unclear. What is clear is that employees still benefit from the Irving ways of teaching. Levesque says just being in their presence does the trick. "If you hang out with them for a couple of years, you've got your master's in business."

McGuire says it's obvious to him now that all of the Irvings (or at least the men) up to Jamie have been through this drill. He describes the unparalleled advantage of being exposed to the dialogue and interaction of real business dealings, a way of learning that is vastly superior to anything to be learned in a classroom or lecture hall. Most people, McGuire says, wouldn't get to participate in high-level business meetings until they're well along in their careers, in relatively senior positions, probably into their early forties. Since Irving children have been present in such situations from their early teen years, it's like they've been given a fifteen- to twenty-year jump on the competition. This strategy makes complete sense to McGuire, a human sponge when it comes to business practices and techniques. He admires how the Irvings have given their children the opportunity to see strategy in action, playing first-hand witness to high-level negotiations. "They're seeing the interpersonal side of business at a very young age."

Fredericton media consultant Arthur Doyle further verifies that there is a de facto Irving School of Business, saying that there are many stories of J. K., Art, and Jack Irving attending meetings with K. C. On the way in, he would reportedly say, "Watch this," and then they would discuss what happened in the car afterward. J. K. has told Doyle on more than one occasion that his father was a wonderful teacher. One need not wonder, then, what percentage of K. C.'s thinking J. K., Arthur, and Jack have brought to their business decisions—his teachings are omnipresent in their way of doing business. As Francis McGuire has said, that all-important continuity, the gradual handing over of responsibility, is a major business advantage, one that the Irvings have used well. McGuire says that as a result of this high degree of continuity, he experienced fewer surprises in dealing with the Irvings than with some other companies that had revolving CEOs or that just didn't understand the value of continuity. He swears that in all his professional dealings—and he's dealt with literally hundreds of companies—he's never experienced anything quite like the Irvings. The closest he could recall was a fisheries company called Blue Cove, where the father and son-in-law had good continuity and the son-in-law eventually became CEO. But there's just no comparing a simple one-generation link to the vast linkage of Irving personalities and the predictable similarity of their practices.

McGuire says it's not enough, however, that the fifth- and sixth-generation Irvings were drilled in the Irving way. He says those that are still making it all happen—referring principally to Kenneth, Jim, Robert, and Mary Jean—also have the talent. "That level of leadership still requires a certain degree of talent and not everybody's up to that. You really need particular skills and I think you have to have that combination of the interest on the part of the individual and the raw intelligence."

It's possible for the necessary attributes—the scope and the breadth, the managerial talent, and the interpersonal leadership skills—to keep recurring within the succession of Irving family members, but what if you expose someone to all the lessons of the Irving School of Business and he or she just doesn't have the interest to play the corporate game? What if Robert had wanted to golf every day? What if Kenneth wanted to spend all his time canoeing in the Arctic? What if Jamie wanted to run off and write instead of continuing in publishing? These are the kinds of scenarios that other business families have experienced when the eventual (and predictable) lack of continuity over the long-term results in a corporate shakedown or a slow dissolve. The only things that seem to have allowed the Irvings to avoid such scenarios so far are their closely knit ranks, and the fact that business lessons have been taught to family members one-on-one from their earliest days.

Another Irving attribute that continually astonishes McGuire is their common abilities in the realm of financial analysis, despite their obviously different personalities and proclivities. Where this comes from in the School of Business curriculum is unclear, but McGuire says it is as common as any of their other capabilities. "It's amazing how all these guys have the ability to work with numbers and systems. And the Irvings have great systems. They all have great reporting systems and a detailed knowledge of the businesses they run." Knowing how to read financial reports and to be on top of their businesses in microscopic ways are other big advantages over competitors. This can only realistically be achieved by keeping their businesses close at hand in the Maritimes. They can physically visit any of their Irving stations, Kent stores, or other enterprises. They hate to be too distant from the businesses they're operating. One exception might be the tankers and the shipping businesses, but as McGuire points out, the tankers and the trucks always return to their Maritime home base. He observes that it's possible the Irvings may not love the region as much as they love their businesses and that they simply may not want to spread themselves too far afield.

The Irving School of Business is in session at all times. There are no semesters, no Christmas, March, or summer breaks, no tenure, and no end to what can be learned. Time spent at the Irving School of Business provides a practicum that is without equal in Atlantic Canada. Perhaps the Irvings should charge tuition.

9. Hard Work and Entrepreneurship

The Irvings are almost always working. And as one frequent Irving consultant put it, "Irvings don't retire." Their lives consist of the constant mission to build stronger and stronger enterprises. They're not big on hobbies—they're big on business. More to the point, business is their hobby. They all have different styles, but hard work and drive are constants.

Moosehead Breweries' Joel Levesque says that people who naturally have a strong work ethic and are exposed to the Irvings end up having nothing but admiration for them. It's instinctively passed down from generation to generation and from employer to employee. Jim, Robert, Mary Jean, Kenneth, Arthur Jr., John, and the rest of the front-line twenty-first-century Irvings may not work in the same ways as their great-great-grandfather Herbert— the nature of work, after all, has changed dramatically over the course of a century—but they still work extremely hard. The commitment and the hours spent at work become addictive, a trait definitely handed down through the generations.

Denis Losier talks about the amazing efficiency he witnessed when working on University of Moncton fundraising campaign pitches with Jim Irving. Losier says that whenever they arrived at a corporate prospect-solicitation meeting, everything was right to the point. The Irvings "don't lose time," as Losier puts it. When there's a 7:30 AM meeting, there's a 7:30 AM meeting. "The meetings are brief and to the point. The request is made, for example, to a corporate representative on behalf of the university—there's chit-chat here and there, but not much. And it's very efficient. Nobody loses their time. And very direct—no beating around the bush." The value of hard work is one of the first things taught at the Irving School of Business.

When people are driven to work as hard as the Irvings, the normal routine of meals and other lifestyle niceties can sometimes go out the door. According to J. K., on family business trips, when K. C. decided he wanted to eat, you ate too, because lunch or dinner might not come until eleven o'clock at night. K. C. might just forget entirely about eating because what he was doing at that moment was of prime importance. He was very focused. So the code became, "You eat when you get the chance." The one saving grace is that you could always have a chocolate bar. That's because there were and always are chocolate bars in the car and on board the Irving aircraft, including K. C.'s favourite, Kit-Kat. (He also had a penchant for cream soda). According to J. K., another

Irving staple is ice cream. They all have a soft spot for ice cream. There's not much doubting what Irvings tend to order for dessert when they sit down in one of their Big Stop restaurants. Of course, while there, they'd be working.

◆

Entrepreneurs like the Irvings don't live and breathe like other human beings. They are obsessed with the challenge of creating new businesses or modifying old ones. Most true entrepreneurs flit from one project to another; some leave a string of successes in their wake, some place successful businesses like building blocks onto one another, and others leave messes and failures in spite of their best efforts and intentions. The Irvings are an entrepreneurial type all their own. In the words of former *Progress* magazine editor David Holt (who's written about hundreds of entrepreneurs), they are "far-sighted risk managers." They look as far as possible into the future; they calculate risk; and then they manage that risk.

Entrepreneurship seldom arrives late in life; its symptoms tend to emerge early. There's a story—one of the humorous Irving myths—that young K. C. kept a flock of ducks in the family garden, the noise of which was provoking complaints from the neighbours. The youthful entrepreneur figured out a way to solve the problem. He butchered and sold them to the very same neighbours, making them the solution of their own problem and bringing in an estimated profit of one hundred dollars.

There's just no questioning that K. C. polished the traits of entrepreneurship inherited from his father and grandfather to a blinding lustre. It took a person with his vision and outlook to see opportunities that no one else in New Brunswick, perhaps in Canada, seemed to recognize at the time. How he grew the family fortune was explained to David Hawkins during one of his afternoon teas at K. C.'s Bermuda home. Much of New Brunswick's woodlands were owned by the railways, he told Hawkins, adding that the railways were controlled by British business interests. By hook or by crook or by extension, that meant that those business interests had control over the woodlands. Some of those British interests had never even seen the lands they controlled and therefore had little appreciation of their value. They saw the New Brunswick properties as just another tract of turf. "So what he saw," says Hawkins, "was a tremendous resource—all of these woodlands that the people who actually owned them didn't treat properly and didn't value. They didn't see anything. They just saw a bunch of scrap wood in a foreign land." As an entrepreneur, K. C. instinctively knew that if he could obtain control of the woodlands, he could do something productive with them. Normal people were blind to this fact.

The rest, of course, is history, starting with the fact that K. C. bought those huge tracts of land for very little money. This is a key point in the Irving story: while there are those who have always complained about the Irving landholdings being too vast, the fact is that those lands were available to anyone in the world to purchase. It just happened that K. C. was entrepreneurial enough to see the value no one else saw. This would seem to support Donald Savoie's theory about critics pounding on the Irvings as an alibi for their own failure or their own lack of entrepreneurialism.

Waxing philosophical, David Hawkins sees a lesson in K. C.'s unique outlook. "I mean, I guess we all have things in our lives that we don't value as much, perhaps, or respect as much as we could or should, and somebody else could turn those things into something more productive." So what Hawkins learned from K. C. and tried to apply in his advertising agency and other businesses was this notion of looking for undervalued things and finding the value in them. "Seeing the opportunity in business is a really valuable thing—recognizing the opportunity, the inherent opportunity. I mean, that's the essence of being an entrepreneur—seeing the opportunity where other people just see nothing."

Hawkins is careful to point out that in no way whatsoever does he compare his own intuitions and ambitions with those of K. C. Irving. What he does share with K. C. is the basic drive to mine otherwise unseen opportunities. "Go back to when they started the oil refinery in 1958 or 1959," says Hawkins. "Who would've dreamed that there would be a need, or that anybody could be so bold as to refine oil in a province like New Brunswick in that era, or that anyone would have the audacity to cut a deal with a California oil company to start a joint venture," which is what K. C. had originally done with Standard Oil. Some would argue that Kenneth's roll of the dice with the planned new LNG terminal and the proposed new second major refinery for Saint John are comparably audacious. Of all K. C.'s grandchildren, it may be Robert who has the entrepreneurial spirit more than his cousins. His brother Jim runs huge businesses; his sister Mary Jean certainly has the bug; and his cousin Kenneth is definitely reinventing Irving Oil all over again. And even though she hasn't retained the business, Judith's innate entrepreneurialism came out in her 2001 acquisition of Hawk Communications. But in terms of breaking out of the traditional Irving business mold, Robert may well take the twenty-first-century prize. He has been the main player behind a new range of businesses (Cavendish Farms, Majesta tissue and Personal Care diapers), he has turned his personal enthusiasm for hockey into a business, and he left the comfort and familiarity of Saint John to venture afield, albeit only as far as Moncton.

Fredericton-based communications specialist Art Doyle says the Irving corporate and entrepreneurial culture is about speed or "high octane." And quality is paramount. They come into an unsatisfactory situation and demand to know who was in charge, with the intention of getting a product or a problem fixed. That's another thing that entrepreneurs do: they fix businesses that are broken or are not meeting their potential. Doyle says the current generations of Irvings understand that dictum as much as they do another K.C. entrepreneurial rule: It's always simple. Don't say something is complicated, because it's not. Even if an Irving wouldn't quite articulate it that way, that attitude and sensibility is embedded in their mindset. It's not even a case of the widely used, "Keep it simple stupid." Says Doyle: "No, not keep it simple. It is simple."

In other words, if an Irving Blue Canoe or Big Stop restaurant is not doing well, it's not a complicated matter. It's as simple as the food not being up to scratch, the staff being impolite, or the washrooms being dirty. If money is being lost at an Irving mill operation, they have the ability to isolate exactly why, be it the cost of electrical power, labour, or raw material. They can do this by following the same daily disciplines, by their common uncanny ability to read a balance sheet, and by teaching their monitoring techniques to their employees. It sounds impossible or unlikely, which is exactly what J.K. admitted to when asked how his father could run major corporations while spending an inordinate amount of time reducing words in a telegram in order to save a few pennies. "That's the way it was. I can't explain it. Whatever job he was doing, he paid attention to it and he worked at it. There was a pleasure for him in getting all of those details right. That was kind of the score card." Yet another Irving dictum says that everything changes and that change is not at all a bad thing. In Doyle's words, "They don't mind tearing a building down and building a new one."

Assumption Life president Denis Losier has a key word that he feels describes the Irvings' entrepreneurial approach. That word is "awakened." That is his way of agreeing that they tend to see opportunities others don't see— that vision trait again. "They're more attuned to opportunities than anybody else because of their big involvement in business," says Losier. An example of this is how part of the forestry side of the business has been adapted to the production of tissue and diapers. These forays into new products happened around the time that the world market for pulp was fluctuating, as was the US dollar. Part of the international onslaught of competition that's occurring, as Losier calls it, is coming from South America, where they can produce cheaper fibre faster. "To grow a tree in New Brunswick, it takes forty years, but in South America, the product is eucalyptus, which takes six to seven years to grow," he explains. Losier says the Irvings compensate for this competitive imbalance by focusing on their vertical integration techniques and creating value-added products. This is perhaps an oversimplification, but what it means is that whenever pulp and other wood-related products shift up and down in domestic or international markets, the Irvings can consider producing more tissue and diapers. "They find solutions," says Losier. "They're vertically and horizontally integrated. And when you start from the seedlings to the paper to the diaper and everything else in between, that's a lot of value for that one little seedling."

Certainly in Atlantic Canada, if not all of Canada, a big part of being an entrepreneur, like it or not, is having to deal with governments. Former economic development deputy minister Francis McGuire recalls that the Irvings have developed a good understanding of how to deal with both bureaucrats and elected politicians. At the same time, the bureaucrats are also astute and are aware of their power and place in the political hierarchy. McGuire says the Irvings are aware that, depending on the strength, knowledge, experience, and political stripe of the elected regime, "sometimes the civil servants have more sway and sometimes they don't."

An example is Robert's handling of his move to have the provincial government modify motor vehicle regulations that, for safety reasons, prohibited transport trucks from hauling two adjoined full-length trailers. McGuire said it was a classic case of the Irvings doing everything right procedurally and communications-wise with the government. Robert went to the department of economic development and explained his business case—that allowing the second trailer would substantially reduce transportation costs between the family-owned pulp mill in Saint John and the tissue processing plant in Moncton. He then demonstrated to the transportation department that the regulatory change would be safe because the only roadways to be affected would be those with four lanes, which removed any concerns about space and vehicular passing. The regulations ended up being changed, having a positive net outcome for the trucking industry throughout, and passing through, New Brunswick.

David Hawkins says one of the key entrepreneurial traits of the Irvings is that they are efficient, that they don't like to waste resources. This would include, of course, not wasting money. "They're not prone to wasting anything," he says. "You have to admire that in a world where—particularly in a world of business—when people do well, they tend to squander a lot of resources. The Irvings don't squander anything knowingly." Hawkins believes the family and their businesses use everything as efficiently and responsibly as they can. "I think K. C. really exemplified that." Hawkins also has a way of putting the Irving scale of things into graphic perspective. When asked to compare the Irvings to Nova Scotia's most noted entrepreneurial family, the Sobeys (next to the McCains the other most dominant business family in Atlantic Canada), Hawkins guffaws. "They [the Irvings] dwarf the Sobeys," he says. "They could buy and sell Sobeys and never think about it. That's a fact. There is no question about that, whatsoever. That's not an exaggeration."

To help put it in perspective—and Hawkins claims to have done his homework on this—85 per cent of all New Brunswick exports come from Irving Oil alone. This does not even include J. D. Irving Ltd., or any of the mass of other Irving-owned enterprises—just Irving Oil. If one can determine the amount of crude imported into New Brunswick, one could figure out the value of the output. Whatever the end number, it's in the billions of dollars. The sheer size of the Irving empire is perhaps the most eloquent testament to their hard work and entrepreneurial spirit.

10. Patience and Perseverance

Classic entrepreneurs do not like to wait for anything. Things have to happen now. The Irvings are no exception; as far as they're concerned, what can be done now should be done now. But their sense of urgency is counterbalanced by a trait that isn't within the makeup of most entrepreneurs: their view of the long term.

David Holt, writer and former editor of *Progress* magazine, says the Irvings remind him of the Japanese, whose stereotypical reputation for having patience and a view toward thinking about the long term is a staple of business school textbooks. Like the Japanese, he says, the Irvings can wait a situation out if necessary, and when they go ahead they make sure that every effort counts. The Japanese business community, of course, is renowned for its discretion and secrecy, much like the Irvings. Holt jokes that maybe the Presbyterian Scots have some kind of philosophical link with the Orient that we know nothing about.

Moosehead Breweries' public affairs chief Joel Levesque provides a more domestic perspective. He says the Irvings know that taking the short-term view of business can negatively affect the people who live in the communities where they tend to build things. If they ponder a mill having to close or worry about their refinery not competing effectively, it's not just their livelihoods that are on the line, it's their community. So they tend to worry more about the future than most business people and certainly more than the average person, Levesque says. "They don't manage for today so much as they manage for the future."

Years ago, Levesque was on a tour of a company woodland operation in northwestern New Brunswick with Jim Irving. They met up with the local

Irving manager and were inspecting the site for a new maintenance garage in the middle of the woods, a building for storing and repairing harvesters and related machinery. The blueprints for the new building were laid on a table, and the manager, Alain Ouellette, began going through details of the plan, when Jim stopped him and said: "I only have one question. Will this location still be the right place for this garage in one hundred years?" There was a pause as Ouellette thought about the nature and intent of the question. Finally he responded: "Yes, Mr. Irving, I think it is." "They take the long view," Levesque adds. "Just like K. C. started planting trees in 1957 knowing he'd never live to see any of them harvested, but now look at the dividends that that decision is paying forty-plus years later."

This kind of thinking has been passed down from Herbert to J. D. to K. C., down to J. K., Arthur, and Jack, then to K. C.'s grandchildren, and now to the great-grandchildren. Irvings can afford to take the long view because they don't have to pay quarterly dividends to stockholders like so many other corporations that have to produce near-instant financial gratification. They don't have to contend with the constraints within which stockholders make other companies think and react.

Even though most of what they want to achieve requires instant action, there are periods when they just take their sweet old time getting something done. This is where their intuitiveness enters in: If purchasing something doesn't really seem useful or necessary, they will defer its purchase until it is—in other words, when it is seen to have a positive impact on productivity or profitability. Levesque recalls a story handed down by his father Charles, a man who spent forty-two years at the Irving-owned Thorne's Hardware in Saint John. They had outgrown a ramshackle old building at the foot of King Street and had built a modern new warehouse on Chestley Drive in the late 1950s. Jack Irving paid Charles a visit: "Charlie, how are things going? Anything you need to do your job better?"

Charles responded with something like, "Well, Mr. Irving, we need racking to put all these pipes and stuff on the wall, to get them off the floor. It would be more efficient use of the space if we had racking."

"Well Charlie, racking's pretty expensive," said Jack. "I tell you what. If we make some money this year, next year we'll buy racking." According to Levesque, they did. Jack Irving did not forget Levesque's suggestion, and the next year they went ahead and bought the racking. The elder Mr. Levesque forgot neither that Jack kept his word nor that he took the advice.

Former provincial bureaucrat George Bouchard concurs that the Irvings are always thinking far, far, far into the future. As he says, "they're not the kind of people that will come to you about a project for tomorrow morning." Believe it or not, some companies actually do; in fact, such is too often the case in provincial economic development circles. Bouchard says the Irvings are thinking fifty to sixty years ahead, emphasizing that it's ingrained in them to do so "and probably it's all injected from K. C. himself, because K. C. was perhaps the first one in New Brunswick to have a [tree] plantation." Bouchard claims that K. C. was leagues ahead of the provincial government when it came to reforestation. A case in point was the Irvings' industry leadership in pursuing with the provincial government a comprehensive report concerning the long-term use of Crown lands for purposes of forestry. Written by an internationally recognized forestry consulting firm, Jaakko Pöyry Consulting, the November 2002 report provides a comprehensive analysis of New Brunswick's crown forests. Although the report carried an industry-wide stamp, Bouchard says the Irvings were the ones who precipitated it. They wanted to know where things would be decades into the future. In their report, Jaakko Pöyry concluded that New Brunswick's conservation strategies should be combined with state-of-the-art tools and the latest available sciences. The consultants also found that significant advances in silviculture could be applied to nearly double the sustainable wood supply in forty to fifty years without negatively affecting New Brunswick's standards of habitat management and conservation. Jaakko Pöyry was also asked to include benchmark policies and practices for forest stewardship and management in comparison with other regions in North America and the Nordic countries. The Irvings wanted to know what was going on internationally, underscoring that the forestry game is an international game subject to worldwide economic conditions.

There are still those who criticize the Irvings for their forestry management practices, accusing them of continuing to cause erosion, affecting rivers, streams, and habitat. Some of the criticisms point to continued clear-cutting, the practice of mechanically crushing leftover woody debris, replanting with a single species of tree, and spraying with herbicides to combat competitive vegetation. But people like Dr. Louis LaPierre and George Bouchard have put their professional integrity on the line by sticking to their guns, saying that the Irvings do practice state-of-the-art forestry management in this day and age.

Bouchard says the long view is just as dominant, if not more so, within the ranks of Irving Oil. He recalls more than a decade ago hearing Arthur Sr. and Kenneth speak in meetings about being in the liquefied natural gas business at some time in their future. There was actually a proposal back in the 1970s involving a Texas company, he recalls, to have liquefied natural gas in the Lorneville Industrial Park. The LNG terminal now in the works is the culmination of an idea the Irvings have been patiently nurturing for a long time.

It seems that there is a similar story for every aspect of the Irving empire. Francis McGuire says that when Robert Irving built the Irving box plant in Moncton, it was clear that he intended to eventually make several more phases of investment and development. What followed were the tissue plant and the diaper plant. However, the fact that the Irvings are so forward visioning can sometimes trip them up, says McGuire. Just because they can envision what's possible over the long term doesn't mean others can. And since they tend not to share what's going on inside their heads, people often don't understand what they're up to. McGuire believes this was a contributing factor in the LNG tax relief controversy. He believes that Kenneth did not foresee the reaction of the angry part of the citizenry in Saint John—those who so deeply resented the tax break given the Irvings and their LNG partner, Repsol. Kenneth and his father could see the long-term benefits of the entire deal, including the potential of Saint John becoming a leading-edge energy hub for northeastern North America, while all the citizenry saw was a miserly tax break.

"They probably thought that people should see the opportunity as well as they do, and understand the difficulties [of gathering investment and establishing the terminal] as well as they do." But of course, that was not the case. "There are two things they don't understand," says McGuire. "First, and it is true of all of them, it has to do with how much information the rest of the world doesn't have. And second, they don't understand how much the other people can't see the future the way they can." McGuire doesn't mean that those outside the Irving ranks are too stupid to see ahead, but that the Irvings are more preoccupied with the future than others. It's simply one of their fixations, this focus on the future. Others would argue that debates over the LNG terminal and other major projects are as much about a clash of values over large-scale development as they are about how to go about it.

As Kenneth Irving suggested during his keynote address at the 2006 Reaching Atlantica conference in Saint John, it's not just about having an LNG terminal, as massive an endeavour as that is. It's really about the even larger endeavour of making Saint John a world-class energy haven. "It's all those other possibilities that make it [the LNG terminal] really exciting," says McGuire. What's interesting here is what was not mentioned during Kenneth's energy hub speech at Reaching Atlantica—namely, the forthcoming announcement of a second multi-billion-dollar oil refinery for Saint John. McGuire believes the Irvings were probably genuinely surprised by the opposition to the LNG tax break and they got into significant PR trouble that may have even thrown a bit of a wedge between Irving Oil and J.D. Irving Ltd., where J.K. is trying to remediate the family's image problems.

The wedge comes in the form of differing points of view between those at the helms of Irving Oil and J.D. Irving regarding public attitudes. The former seems to be saying, "Damn the torpedoes, full speed ahead," while the latter—J.K. in particular—is frustrated that the goodwill built up through their philanthropy and community development efforts are being needlessly squandered. McGuire concludes by saying that the Irvings have consistently underestimated the impact of public opinion.

K.C. grew his way through the Depression, the Second World War, and other times when things weren't exactly rosy for businesses like Irving Oil, such as the late 1970s to mid-1980s, when the company apparently experienced some serious problems that David Hawkins characterizes as "not meeting the break-even point." But in that typical Irving way, K.C. turned that problem period into a fortuitous move, buying out partner Standard Oil when things were in the downturn. "They bought them out when the value was low," says Hawkins. "Just to have the balls to do that. That's perseverance! That's perseverance!" Hawkins also says a lot of business people give up early or shift their focus, whereas the Irvings "persevere in a way that very, very few people do in life." Former *Progress* editor David Holt also harkens back to the Standard Oil buyout, after which the international oil company's president admitted that K.C. was the most prepared counterpart he'd ever dealt with.

While the entire world sometimes seems to be spinning at an increasingly rapid rate, the Irvings have, at least until now, had the patience to look beyond the lure of immediate gratification. And they've had the perseverance to stay with concepts and business approaches that have worked for them in the past.

11. Humility, Loyalty, and Respect

The Irvings pride themselves on three attributes that are inextricably linked: humility, loyalty, and respect. Even their critics cannot help but respect them for these attributes, in spite of whatever other flaws they might have.

The Irvings themselves see loyalty as the underpinning of everything they do. They were taught humility. And when it comes to respect, they're described as treating their employees, their friends, and even their adversaries with respect—and expecting and appreciating the same in return. One Saint John source talks about their trademark style of courtesy, formality, and politeness. "They're polite to a fault almost: 'Oh let me open that door for you.'" This habit of opening doors for people came up time and again during interviews. This style of courtesy is said to be a holdover from K.C.'s personal manner. In return, there is an understood and anticipated formality. The appellation "Mr. Irving" is, for example, standard fare from their employees, regardless of which Mr. Irving they're referring to.

That the Irvings exercise respect even for their competitors and adversaries revealed itself when it came to the tumult that resulted when Wallace and Harrison McCain's personal relationship and corporate interests imploded over matters of succession. It was a messy public spectacle, attributable to the absence of a better succession vision and to the fact that too much wealth was too accessible to too many family members. Even though the Irvings and McCains had been engaged in a public battle over French fries on Prince Edward Island, J. K. in particular was said to be very clear with those surrounding the Irving family that no advantage was to be taken over the McCains while they were experiencing succession problems. Nothing was to be said that would breach that directive.

Moosehead's Joel Levesque has longer ties with the Irvings than most. As noted earlier, he pumped gas for them as a teenager and later worked in public relations for them through his role at Corporate Communications Limited, and his father Charles worked at the Irving-owned Thorne's Hardware for forty-two years. Thorne's is an Irving-owned wholesale hardware distributor in Saint John that still serves the Maritimes and the Gaspé Peninsula. Joel claims they pay back their loyal employees, not just with cash, but with respect. "When my father was sick and was dying, I ran into Jack Irving. 'How's your father,' [said Jack]. He didn't know my father was sick, so I told him he was sick. The next day he's calling my father on the phone to wish him well, best of luck." Jack asked how Charles was feeling, said he heard he was under the weather, and so on. When Charles died six months later, Jack, J. K., and Arthur Sr. all attended the funeral—and this was after Charles had been retired for seven years. Even younger Jim Irving attended visiting hours at the funeral home. "And you can find many, many people who will tell you similar stories," says Levesque. "Sick employees—no question, they're on the company plane down to Boston [i.e., to receive treatment at a private clinic]. Something serious, and off you go." Such stories were repeated many times in the research for this book.

The Irvings are known for surrounding themselves with talented people who are prepared to work as hard as they are and who are as passionate as they are. You won't be seen for long in an Irving office if you're not passionate about the business. Says Assumption Life's Denis Losier: "You don't work for them if you're not putting in one hundred per cent of your effort." But Losier thinks the Irvings have entered a new era and that the approach to their employees has changed. The loyalty in exchange for loyalty has always been there, but subtle shifts have occurred. As times have changed, so has the

Irving attitude regarding how to provide rewards beyond the paycheque and the security of a well-paying job. Ganong Bros. CEO David Ganong describes one of those less visible Irving rewards for employee loyalty. He recalls the day the Ganong candy plant got a call from the Saint John mill on Valentine's Day, ordering hundreds of boxes of chocolates for distribution to company employees—the mill had just hit a production record and the Irvings wanted to mark the occasion.

Speaking about the aftermath of the lengthy and deeply divisive two-year strike at the Saint John oil refinery in the 1990s, Losier says he believes "they empowered a lot of the workers after that in terms of giving them responsibility for certain things that maybe before they thought that management would take care of. I think the attitude towards their workers has changed a lot. The attitude has evolved as society has evolved towards better management of human resources." There are parallels between Losier's take on the contemporization of Irving human resource policies and Dr. Louis LaPierre's thoughts on how the Irvings progressed in terms of the environment (see chapter 18). Both men claim that as the culture has changed, so too have many of the Irvings' business practices. Losier says they give more performance bonuses to employees, they're more into wellness, and they're empowering their employees more than ever before. "Of course, all of those things lead to higher productivity," says Ganong. "Everyone knows if you treat your people well, in return they'll give you more. So there's give and take on both sides." There are surely those who wouldn't see the Irving company-employee relationship situation in the same sanguine light, individuals or groups who feel they've been treated unfairly by the family's tough business practices and tough negotiating style.*

A source who's done a ton of scientific consulting work for most of the Irving companies and who's known and worked for a hoard of their senior project managers says that if you're a loyal Irving person, you're going to be rewarded. He said it's not unusual for senior managers to get a thanks and a perk, a congratulations on a job well done, and a follow-up like, "Here's a ticket for you and your wife to go to Florida." "They do stuff like that. They really do. I know it for a fact, but it's not talked about. I have some good friends who work in their organizations and they've had that kind of a reward after

---

*In an effort to present this point of view, more than a half-dozen attempts were made to schedule an interview with union representative Bob Davidson over the early 1990s Irving Oil refinery strike. Despite considerable efforts on my part to meet with Davidson and despite Davidson's claims that he was prepared to meet, unfortunately, the interview didn't materialize.

a big job." He reaffirms that the Irvings are "exceptionally demanding" and "there's no tolerance for fuck-ups," but if you're loyal and successful, it pays off.

On the other side of the equation, he told of the Saint John mill manager who took a vacation after overseeing the installation of a massive new boiler system. The job came together on budget and on schedule. The manager was a shrewd dude with a solid reputation who ran a tight ship. But when the installation was being commissioned, while it was being started up, somebody messed up, the apparatus got too hot, and "a train wreck" occurred. Even though the manager's troops were the ones who messed up the commissioning, he got the axe. There was no ticket to Florida for him and his wife. Next thing the manager knew, he was working at a mill in Prince Rupert, British Columbia.

University of Moncton professor Donald Savoie was close to the late Louis J. Robichaud, revered former premier of New Brunswick, close enough that Robichaud asked Savoie to organize his funeral. The story on the street has always been that there was a deep-seated acrimony between Robichaud and the Irvings. Whatever truth there might have been to this story went back to the 1960s, when the premier did things he felt he had to do but which may not have conformed with Irving plans at the time. No one's giving details, but that tension apparently lingered between the two parties. Savoie, however, does know one thing first hand: that J.K. and the premier were eventually very close. J.K., in fact, was an honorary pallbearer at Robichaud's funeral. Savoie would not elaborate on the nature of their friendship, which was marked by a particular circumstance or event that occurred shortly before Robichaud died. His refusal to elaborate was out of loyalty to J.K. Part of him seemed to want to tell the story, but Savoie's own loyalty took hold. "I'm not sure he [J.K.] would be upset with me, but the only ones who know—well Louis is dead, J.K. is alive, and there's me. So he'd figure out it couldn't be Louis [revealing the story]." Savoie would only provide a tidbit, a teaser. "A couple of weeks before Louis passed away—we all knew he was going—J.K. did something extremely kind, generous, very touching. I'll leave it at that."

For fourteen years, Steve Carson walked pretty close to his father's footsteps as an Irving employee and could well have become a lifer like his dad if not for an accident of volunteerism. In 1994, Carson left his position in property management, development, and acquisition at Irving Oil to become the executive director for Enterprise Saint John, an economic development agency. Although he's been out of the ranks for thirteen years, he still exudes the crisp, clean-cut, reliable look of an Irving company man. Because of the nature of his role with the company, he knows all too well what many laypeople love to talk about—the fact, which he admits, that when the Irvings buy up a corner for a new service station, it was and remains common practice for them to buy up all four corners if at all possible. It's part of their dominance and competitiveness methodology. They may or may not use the other three corners, but owning them means no one else can.

A rare exception would be the Irving Big Stop at a major Trans-Canada Highway interchange near Salisbury, NB. No sooner was the complex opened following the completion of the highway shortly after the millennium, than an Ultramar station and convenience store opened on the opposite side of the road. They look like David and Goliath, with the Ultramar doing a mere fraction of the Big Stop's sales, but it was surprising to see that the land was available for acquisition by non-Irving interests at all. While with the company, he dealt primarily with Arthur Sr. and Jack, the latter because of his involvement in real estate. Kenneth at that time was still learning the ropes, travelling a lot, and visiting the company's retail outlets, growing into the role his father was designing for him, just as K.C. had designed a role for Arthur.

Carson's father Don worked as sales manager and a branch manager at Commercial Equipment, an Irving-owned automotive industrial supplier, for forty years. Commercial's products found their way into nearly every kind of Irving operation, from service stations to pulpmills to tugboats. Although Steve Carson didn't stay with Irving Oil, he has high regard for their loyalty-for-loyalty proposition. There's certainly no doubt that his father fulfilled his part of the bargain. Saturday mornings were typically work mornings. While Steve was growing up, he would sometimes accompany his father to the office and on sales trips around New Brunswick. During summer months, Mrs. Carson would accompany her husband and their son on the odd in-province business trip, which served as quasi-vacations. Many of these adventures brought Steve into contact with the Irvings, from K.C. on down. Don was one of those Irving people who K.C., J.K., Arthur, and Jack just knew they could call and rely upon to be there for them. Although Don had his line job, he was of even greater value to the Irving family. "Dad was a troubleshooter," says Carson, "involved in any issue going on with any kind of their operations when they needed to find someone that could figure out how to fix it. Dad was an unofficial source when it came to dealing with the three brothers on a regular basis. We'd either be going on site somewhere where a project would be going on or they'd be dropping in [to Commercial Equipment]", says Carson. If his father had work to do in Bouctouche, especially during the summer, he might drop into the compound where K.C. and/or J.K. would be spending time with their families. "From my earliest memories, that's what we did. And I remember going up to Mount Pleasant [in Saint John] to K. C. Irving's house. Mrs. Irving always had a treat and that sort of thing."

Carson says the Irvings were always good to his father, and the fact that he was a hunter and fisherman didn't hurt. Sharing those interests connected him all the more to their way of seeing the world. The sense of dependability, confidence, and reliability that the Irvings associated with Don Carson meant that he had access to the family's prime hunting and fishing places whenever he wanted, especially in the fall. "He would spend a lot of time particularly at Arthur's house," says Carson of his father. Arthur Sr.'s house on Kennebacasis Drive, in Saint John, had a complex swimming pool that was often opened up to the neighbourhood, a place with waterfalls, rocks, footbridges, and a duck pond. Because of the pool's complexity, it often required parts, maintenance, or repairs. While Don would be taking care of those matters, Steve says, "we'd be always welcomed to take a dip." Kenneth and Arthur Jr. would be hanging out. In Steve's adult interactions with Kenneth, mention is still often made of his father, Don. It's no wonder. Because Commercial Equipment was a volume customer for many product manufacturers, the elder Carson was always being provided with promotional aids, some of which were toys. Steve recalls a small battery-operated antique model car that a kid could actually sit in and drive. Problem is, Don didn't bring it home to his son—he made sure young Kenneth got it. Kenneth hasn't forgotten, and still mentions when he sees Steve, that Don Carson went out of his way to be nice to the Irving kids.

The Irvings haven't taken much opportunity to blow their own horn about how they view their employees, except in the 1998 documentary *Unlocking the Mystery*, which found Arthur Sr. expounding on the value and quality of their people. Of all the points he made during the documentary, almost all of them forcefully and with unquestionable conviction, Arthur was perhaps most insistent on this point. "It's just not a buzzword, because every company in the world would tell you, 'Oh, we've got great people and we wear it,' but I tell ya, we really mean it! You can go through this building and you can go through any one of our companies—the culture of our people is different."

Semi-retired New Brunswick provincial bureaucrat and now part-time consultant Jim Scott doesn't disagree with Arthur Sr.'s statement. Scott worked at Irving Oil's head office for a decade, first in an IT capacity at a time when IT was just finding its technological foothold and then later in the company's advertising section. Scott has two stories about Irving loyalty that he says astonished him.

K. B. Reid was one of those dyed-in-the-wool K. C. loyalists, a man who just couldn't bring himself to retire. Rather than put him out to a pasture that

Reid had no desire to go to, K. C. and Arthur Sr. made arrangements to keep him around and keep him happy. Up to the time he was ninety-four years of age, Mr. Reid would arrive by taxi at the Irving Oil Golden Ball building in Saint John and make his way to the office immediately adjacent to Scott's. The elderly gentleman would spend the better part of the morning there, with secretarial staff reading the morning newspaper to him aloud. The reading was done very loud, according to Scott, because Reid had grown hard of hearing. One day Mr. Reid was in his office and then, suddenly, the next he wasn't. He "died in the saddle," says Scott, still amazed years later that the Irvings took care of their long-time employee with such care and respect.

Scott's second yarn involves a young man who began working in the IT section in the late 1970s. He was working there less than six months when he was involved in a serious car accident having nothing to do with his work. The mishap put the individual out of work for a year before he could return to his position. Scott says the man never missed a paycheque.

Ganong Bros. head David Ganong will never forget how the Irvings have demonstrated their humility, loyalty, and respect to his family. The appearance of J. K., Arthur, and Jack fifteen years ago at the official opening of the new Ganong Bros. plant in St. Stephen said a lot to him about how they see the world and their place in it. There wasn't just one brother in attendance to show the Irving flag; all three came out. The three stood in the parking lot to witness the ceremony along with everyone else, and although Ganong recognizes that they had stock in the construction of the new building—Ganong had purchased Irving products and services—he saw their presence there that day as meaning much, much more. "They were there to show support to another New Brunswick enterprise. We're a customer. A lot of the materials that were used in the facility [came from them], but there was a kind of loyalty, perhaps from [these] New Brunswick business owners to [this] New Brunswick business owner." The Irvings were also present and visible when the Ganong family held community events commemorating the eightieth and ninetieth birthdays of David's uncle, Whidden Ganong. K. C. and his sons came to the first event. By Whidden's ninetieth, K. C. had passed away, but all three sons showed up. Ganong believes that these acts make the Irvings the antithesis of a phenomenon he calls Maritime envy, the strange attitude many Maritimers have against anyone who does well. The Irvings, says Ganong, have no such resentment. He believes they were there to genuinely celebrate the Ganong success story. Of course, why wouldn't the Irvings want David Ganong to succeed? The candy producers have got 350 employees, most of whom, for example, probably buy Irving gas. "If the New Brunswick economy sputters," says Ganong, "that's going to impact the fortunes of

Irving because, whether it be their newspapers or their gas stations or the tissue they make in Moncton or the corrugated cartons that they make, [all these things] would affect their businesses. So it's important to them that the New Brunswick economy do well."

The Irvings also have a history of being extremely loyal to one another. As Francis McGuire puts it, they're "like a band of brothers" or like a band of soldiers who never leave a fallen comrade lying in the field. McGuire's not claiming the Irving brothers or their children don't like one another, but even if they didn't, it wouldn't matter much. "It's kind of like, 'I don't have to like you, but you know, we're in the same fox hole together, so, you watch my back, I'll watch yours.' I have no idea if they like each other or not. I have no idea. But they do watch out for one another." But as the family spreads out beyond the true band of three Irving brothers—J. K., Arthur Sr., and Jack— only time will tell how accurate McGuire is in his description and how loyal they all remain to the central cause.

Moosehead public affairs executive Joel Levesque has a clear view on the politeness, courteousness, humility, and respect that members of the family exhibit. He too says they have a habit of holding doors open for people. And if you're at a buffet with them in the woods at one of their various lumber camps, everybody else goes first. They eat last. Such courtesies, he claims, are not just extended on Irving property. As a case in point, throughout his interview in Saint John and Bouctouche, J. K. was constantly ushering onto the airplane and ushering through doorways. "I've been on tours with them and when they're buying dinner, they take a back seat," says Levesque. He adds that they have an air about them, but that it's not rooted in snobbishness. "When you get to meet business people, wealthy business people, or successful people, usually there's big egos involved. And with big egos come ill manners sometimes, a rudeness, a pushiness. There are some people in business you meet that you just don't like being around. But the Irvings are just humble, polite, kind, thoughtful people." It's easy to see how acting this way can be just as disarming as it is charming; this is not to suggest that it's their Machiavellian way of controlling people, but charm can produce certain outcomes. Whether such actions are verbal or physical, like the simple act of holding a door open, there is something amazingly simple and subliminal about how courtesy, humility, and respect can set the tone for everything that follows. The world could use more of this.

Media consultant Arthur Doyle emphasizes that K. C. had the same qualities, no doubt practices he too inherited. In addition to his tough, hard-nosed image as a businessman, Doyle says K. C. was also well known for his polite, soft-spoken demeanour. He argues that demonstrating loyalty, respect, humility, and politeness were and remain holdovers from an old-fashioned New Brunswick country sensibility. "I'm sure it's the Anglophone Scottish of Kent County," he says. He adds that the tendency to say things like "You're looking well" reflects a well-practiced, old-fashioned country manner. "It's enormous the number of funerals and wakes they attend," says Doyle, who suggests that attending wakes and funerals tends to put them on the same level as everyone else. University of Moncton professor and author Donald Savoie, a man from the same sort of rural New Brunswick upbringing as K. C. and his sons, says that none of the Irvings act pretentious. "None of them," he swears. "They're all down-to-earth, Bouctouche-type people."

Former *Saint John Telegraph-Journal* columnist Lisa Hrabluk has a playfully acerbic style when she writes and when she talks. She goes the furthest in describing the Irvings' humble, respectful style, referring to them as "the apologetic billionaires." By this, she means that they want people to treat them like totally normal people, like they're the guys living just around the corner. Yet conflicting with that desire are the trappings of who they really are, of their station in life, and the massive influence and power they hold. It's as though in spite of their fateful inheritances and everything surrounding them, they want to be as ordinary as is humanly possible.

If Kenneth Irving is speaking somewhere, he requests that the front of the room be designed a certain way. Good and experienced speakers tend to prepare for their engagements this way. It's about creating a personal comfort zone for the oft-challenging art of public speaking, a zone that, unwittingly for most audiences, puts the speaker in charge. One of the best techniques, for those who have the capability, is to roam using a wireless lapel microphone instead of being stuck at a fixed podium. Speakers at well-organized conferences are invited in advance to fill out forms detailing their audio-visual and other preferences. Sometimes these details are fulfilled and sometimes they're not; and the results can greatly affect the confidence and delivery behind the presentation. With Kenneth, people listen to his requests and make the necessary arrangements, almost as though the room could be redesigned for him. As mentioned previously, one got the sense at the 2006 Reaching Atlantica conference that the setup for Kenneth's keynote address was tailored to his precise desires. But conversely, Hrabluk says she knows based on her exposure to Kenneth that he genuinely does not want people coming up to him bowing and saying "Yes, Mr. Irving" over this or that. He just wants to say to whoever's making the speaking arrangements, "So Bob, did you go fishing last weekend? Oh my God, wasn't it great?"

Someone in the position of an Irving can more easily make what for others might be an unusual or unreasonable request, and get away with it. But such provisions are not supposed to be acknowledged as being extraordinary. Hrabluk launches into a little skit to reinforce her point: rather than saying "You are so rich and powerful and it is not a problem and we will be very happy to make you comfortable," an Irving really just wants the provider of the service to go, "Yeah, Bob was asking for the same thing yesterday, so it's not a problem. You know, he asked me to make sure that the helicopter landed in that parking lot and not in that one. He's done it a million times." Hrabluk says the Irvings like to keep such matters as understated as though they were asking for two sugar cubes in their coffee instead of just one. She says this is sometimes exhibited by the way they tend to talk to their employees as though they were co-workers instead of underlings.

Former PEI cabinet minister Robert Morrissey dealt with J. K., Robert, and Mary Jean in the era when Cavendish Farms and Master Packaging arrived on the Island economic scene. He describes J. K. as being a particularly "caring" individual who was very proud of the work done by Robert and Mary Jean. He too saw how J. K. treats people with respect and shows his humility. Meeting once in J. K.'s Saint John office, the elder Irving asked if Morrissey was in a rush because he wanted to show him around one of the Irving pulpmills and the Saint John shipyard. As the two strolled up the street to get J. K.'s car, they were met by a succession of people who stopped to talk and shake J. K.'s hand. He seemed to know them all by name. Upon arrival at both the mill and the shipyard, J. K. and his guest were subjected to the very same security scrutiny as would be imposed "on the janitor," according to Morrissey. There was no parking spot marked "Reserved," so J. K. simply wheeled around the lot until he found a spot.

The Irvings are notorious for asking the humblest of questions. They ask it of their employees at all levels, of politicians, of their colleagues, and even of their competitors. It is the basic, fundamental query, "How are we doing?" People say that they use the line for real, that they really mean it. This query is as commonplace as the firmness of an Irving handshake, a practice passed down through the generations like the deed to the Irving ranch. "How are we doing?" So simple and vulnerable a question; and for those who've heard it asked, it always sounds like they really want to know the answer to the question.

In their *Biography of K. C. Irving* (1993), Douglas How and Ralph Costello recount K. C.'s own humble words concerning how proud he was of his achievements: "I wouldn't say proud," he told the authors, "but at least we stirred things up. There is nothing remarkable about it. Plenty of people could have done it." This is the way all latter-day Irvings want to be seen, as though what they do is no different than sweeping the mill floor or driving the Midland truck down the Trans-Canada Highway.

12. Attention to Detail

If the Irvings have proven anything over time, it's that success is derived from following their stringent practices and their winning formula. A cornerstone of that formula is their relentless attention to detail. It's evident in everything they do. One way to verify this is to go to the heart of the Irving enterprise—the customer.

It's a Thursday, the last day of August 2006. At the Lincoln Irving Big Stop outside Fredericton, those few truckers that haven't pulled in for gas, a shower, or sustenance thunder by in their rigs on the nearby Trans-Canada Highway. There are Irving properties like this popping up all along the Trans-Canada as part of the company's dominance strategy. It's a typical evening. Both the truckers' parking lot and the regular parking lot are nearly full, just like always. If this isn't a case of "build it and they will come," then nothing is. The words "Blue Canoe Restaurant" are emblazoned in massive letters on the rooftop, a sign to passersby that comfort food is being served inside. Even though it's an ultramodern service station, there's a tactically crafted rural homeness to the place, including large-scale models of an old-fashioned water tower and farm windmill overlooking the site. After parking the car and heading for the entrance, it's nearly impossible to avoid encountering the hand-carved, oversized sculpture of a goofy-looking, buck-toothed beaver and moose, strategically placed amid the shrubs on the station's well-manicured front lawn. It's a funny conversation piece, with the two beasts paddling a wooden canoe. A plaque says the sculpture was created by Monty MacMillan of Oromocto. The white pine log he worked from is marked as a donation from J. D. Irving Ltd.—of course!

The entire Big Stop (now a part of the Maritime vernacular) has been designed for ease of parking, ease of access to the series of islands housing gas and diesel pumps, and ease of access to the store and adjacent restaurant. The gas islands are the most modern on the market, the kind where you can pay, grab your receipt, and earn rewards without ever encountering a cashier. Good thing, because they're busy as hell ringing in the retail customers inside. The Big Stop store is like a mini Wal-Mart, featuring everything from fresh fruit, snack trays, and groceries to CDs, magazines, toys, and monogrammed trinkets like coffee cups and key chains. Duct tape, cooked hot dogs, Irving hats, and rolls of film round out the plethora of products available in what is really a very small amount of space. The staff are in blue uniforms so crisp you'd think it was the facility's opening day. The washrooms are not like other gas station washrooms: they're astonishingly immaculate, considering that thousands of people traipse in and out of them every single day—yes, thousands. Irving washrooms have a 1-800 number posted, which you can call to register a complaint if conditions are not up to snuff. And it's about more than washrooms. Irving Oil trucks have to be clean; the restaurants have to be clean; the employee locker room at the Irving Oil refinery has to be clean. The Irvings like things just so.

A popular New Brunswick politician who's spent a lot of time in and out of Irving offices says that J. K.'s desk is as clean as a whistle. "That's the style of the Irvings," he says. Whether it's an office desk or an industrial yard, order is the order of things. This carries through to the most micro of circumstances in the overall Irving scheme of things. Long-time Saint John city manager Terry Totten confirms that cleanliness is important to the Irvings. "When you go into their stores, they're spotless. I mean, they look good from the outside, there's a quality. That's what they want to be associated with and they strive for it. I suspect that they would accept nothing less. Proof is in the pudding."

Everything at an Irving Big Stop is well organized—a place for everything and everything in its place. And with every one they build, they learn how to organize things better, leaving no detail undone. Years ago, tourism information literature was isolated on a small rack or two someplace in the store. In the most modern stations, tourism literature has its own properly designed, designated space.

Beside the elaborate New Brunswick visitor information desk and kiosk at the Lincoln Big Stop, there's a framed colour photograph showing the broad, smiling faces of Kenneth Irving, his father Arthur Sr., and brother Arthur Jr., joined by proprietors Linda and Linden Fenety, long-time associates of Irving Oil. The photo was taken during the official opening of the facility a couple of years ago after the Fenetys left their prosperous outlet in a high traffic area of Fredericton. A few feet from the information desk and photo display, a large community bulletin board promotes things like country dance classes and all-terrain vehicles for private sale; half of the scissored tear-away tabs displaying the vendors' telephone numbers are gone. Just steps away is the Blue Canoe, surely one of the only remaining unlicensed restaurants in the world with line-ups of customers waiting to get in at virtually any time of day (late Sunday mornings can be a calamity for travellers colliding with locals intent on their ritualistic family-outing-after-church feed). The daily specials are fixed week to week and are written on blackboards along the wall opposite the long, sweeping, old-style diner counter where lonely commercial travellers prefer to sit. The specials are also strategically posted atop urinals in the men's washrooms, taking total advantage of their captive audience. Seated at the counter, patrons can talk to the waitresses and stare longingly at glass-enclosed desserts topped with either two and a half inches of meringue or a dollop of boiled white icing.

Behind them, there's a sea of booths and wooden chairs and tables that are covered with pre-set condiments, cutlery, and Irving's signature white-and-red gingham-style paper napkins. The ceiling is vaulted cathedral-style, with huge wooden beams that clearly did not come from a Home Depot or Home Hardware. There's an entire section reserved exclusively for truckers behind homey-looking paned windows. Truckers are revered at Irving Big Stops. In one highly visible corner of the restaurant, there's a table prominently identified as the "Blue Canoe Local Charity Table." On a rotational basis, local charities receive about 20 per cent of everything spent at the special table, which is almost always occupied.

The point about the Big Stop is that the Irvings have put thought into every imaginable detail of its design, layout, operation, and level of customer service. Their customers know it; the truckers from as far afield as California know it by word of mouth; and the packed parking lot shows that it works. As simple as it seems, the Big Stop is a masterpiece of retailing.

There are a million stories that illustrate the Irvings' attention to detail, but Steve Carson tells a little gem that only he could possibly know about. One morning in the mid-1980s, during Carson's fourteen-year tenure with Irving Oil, he was rushing up the steel staircase to his office in the Golden Ball Building when he passed K.C. and Arthur Sr., who were exiting the building. He recalls instinctively running faster when he realized who he'd met in the stairwell. The three acknowledged one another as they passed, but when he reached the flight just above his bosses, he suddenly heard Arthur yell, "Carson!" Arthur's brusque voice drew Carson to a halt. "Go down one step!" Arthur yelled from below. Although he had no idea what was on Arthur's mind, Carson complied, taking a single step. "No, jump up and down!" Arthur yelled. Carson didn't know what to do or say, so he spontaneously yelled back, "How high?" Before he could even realize the spontaneous, unintended humour in his retort, Carson was jumping up and down in place in the stairwell. Needless to say, he felt a little silly. Only later did he learn that the treads of the steps, originally inlaid with terrazzo, had a loose tile, which someone in the office had mentioned to the Irvings. When Carson had walked a flight above Arthur and K.C., they'd heard the clatter of the loose tile and wanted to know exactly which one it was. The mystery was solved and the tile no doubt was repaired soon thereafter.

Donald Savoie has witnessed many instances of the Irvings paying personal attention to matters both big and small, and he's heard of many more. Before the construction of the new Moncton International Airport, Savoie ran into J. K. in the waiting area of the old facility. They chatted about several matters, including the fact that Savoie had just returned from Russia, where he observed there to be some amazing opportunities. According to Savoie, J. K. remarked, "Oh, we've looked at it. We've looked at it and I don't think it's for us." What struck Savoie is that he felt it wasn't just an automatic response from J. K. "It wasn't just a flippant answer. He had thought about it. And if he hadn't, somebody had thought about it on his behalf."

Savoie recalls a university-related reception at his house that included among the invitees Robert and J. K. Irving, as well as transportation magnate and legendary Maritime entrepreneur Wes Armour. Within half an hour of their arrival, Robert and J. K. had crossed the room and were quizzing Armour. According to Savoie, the Irvings initiated a discussion about the trucking and transportation industry. "You could see that they had a lot of respect for Wes Armour. You could see it. And they were asking some fairly detailed questions." In a similar vein, when they realized Home Depot was going to be moving into certain Maritime markets, butting right up against their Kent Building Supplies stores, J. K. took it upon himself to conduct some tactical, low-level reconnaissance. He personally went to a string of Home Depot outlets in Florida, asking all kinds of questions about "selling hammers or whatever else," says Savoie. The target of his casual investigation: the unwitting front-line Home Depot staff. Who else but the Irvings would fly all the way to Florida to check out a rival store? Most other corporate executives would send staff out to do this type of reconnaissance.

Being attentive to detail is not a state of mind that can be switched on and off. In the late 1990s, several years after University of Moncton professor emeritus Louis LaPierre had established a professional and personal relationship with J. K. Irving, he was a guest at the Irving fishing camp on the famed Restigouche River in northern New Brunswick. Every afternoon at about three o'clock, J. K. would take his leave from the activity of the moment and place some telephone calls. LaPierre says J. K. was doing his daily check—seven days a week, it seemed—to receive up-to-the-moment status reports on his various businesses. LaPierre got the sense that it was the responsibility of whoever was on the receiving end of those three o'clock telephone calls—someone from Kent, someone from the mills, someone from the shipyards—to have a figure or some form of detail that would indicate to J. K. just where things stood. "So by pulling all of this together," says LaPierre, J. K. would then set out what needed to be done in accordance with where matters stood. "So you could see that there was a whole. All the things fell together in the context of keeping hands on the daily operations. So that when he finished a day, went to bed at night, he knew what everybody had done today." LaPierre believes that by reassuring themselves with up-to-date information in this systematic way, the Irvings can clear their minds of anxiety, and stay fresh enough to push forward so relentlessly day by day.

LaPierre's observance of J. K. is reinforced by others. During a personal tour of a control room at the Irving Saint John pulpmill, J. K. showed former PEI economic development minister Robert Morrissey a computer monitor that told supervisors that they were ahead of the previous day's output of production. Morrissey was astounded that J. K. knew how to read the technical jargon on the monitor, let alone quantify and compare daily outputs. He recalls J. K. congratulating the man sitting before the monitor, patting him on the back for doing a good job. From his several years of dealing with the Irvings, Morrissey says he was always struck by how detailed and prepared they were.

Several years ago, a crew of university students worked their summer jobs at an Irving woodland site near Black Brook, between St. Leonard and St. Quentin in northwestern New Brunswick. Given the remoteness of the site, and in keeping with tradition, the boys were put up at an Irving camp. It's not uncommon for Irvings to simply show up at any company-owned site—anywhere—and see how things are going. One afternoon, J. K. exercised that family prerogative and paid a surprise visit to the camp. He was not happy with what he saw. There were dirty dishes in the kitchen sink and wet clothes from the previous day's rain hanging out all over. The students were diligently working out at the job site, but J. K. was upset enough with the condition of the camp that he told the caretaker the students were to get the heave-ho. The matter didn't affect their employment status, but they were relocated to the nearest motel. At some point after the eviction, J. K. must have thought the situation over and realized why it was that things had been so untidy amongst the students. He reportedly turned around and fixed the camp up, bought some laundry equipment, installed a television, and generally made the place a lot more hospitable. He then had the students reinstated at the camp. The story's source believes J. K. probably knew that he overreacted when he had the students removed and set about in his own quiet, efficient way to right matters. In other words, even when the Irvings' attention to detail gets a little out of hand, their efficiency and sense of fair play can often make up for it.

The practice of showing up unannounced at the most unlikely of company facilities is one that has been handed down through the generations. Just as K. C. pulled into the Saint John Reversing Falls Irving at 11 PM on Christmas Eve 1971, Arthur Sr., Kenneth, or Arthur Jr. are just as likely to drive in unannounced at an Irving station in Sydney, Cape Breton, or Bangor, Maine, today. J. K. or Jim could just as readily show up at a Kent Store in Charlottetown and end up speaking spontaneously to the guy who stacks plywood in the lumberyard about how business is going. When the Irvings make an appearance at one of their businesses, there is no parade, no entourage, no fanfare. They are very much under the radar. They are stealth. This was a K. C. practice that has rubbed off on all of them. "It could happen anywhere, anytime, and they do it," says David Ganong. "And the goal is to satisfy the customer," he adds, not to intimidate employees. "That aspect, in terms of quality and customer satisfaction, is as high at Irving as virtually anybody that I can think of." Ganong says the family knows that's how you beat the competition, which in theory should lead to making money. But he thinks they thrive on the basic principle of beating the competition. Applying attention to detail is a major weapon in their arsenal. "Although we in New Brunswick look at them as being a gigantic enterprise with many arms, they look at themselves as just little guys in a big world." The Irving Oil refinery might be a big deal in New Brunswick, a big deal in Atlantic Canada, and a big deal even in Canadian national terms, but it's still not a big deal compared to the likes of Esso and Shell. "And so they look at the big competition and say, 'We just have to try harder.' And I think they do, the work ethic thing, back to making sure the quality is there, making sure the image branding is there, and," Ganong hesitates, "that the trucks are clean."

Steve Carson says the Irvings' attention to detail is a constant, no matter how many issues are at play. "They would come in and out of meetings with amazing speed and grasp the issues. And they surround themselves with good people who are there to pick up on the details. It's fast paced and quite often there are three or four meetings going on on the floor, and they'll be going in and out to add value where they can along the way." In the greater scheme of things, ensuring that the bathrooms are clean and the plywood is properly stacked might seem like a trivial fixation. But as numerous experiences reveal, this same attention to detail manifests itself throughout the Irvings' business practices, and it's a crucial factor in their success.

13. The Art of the Deal

The ultimate Irving business advantage may be their ability to cut deals and create partnerships. The art of the Irving deal brings into play all of the other skills learned at the Irving School of Business.

Asked if the chorus of politeness about the Irvings doesn't sound almost too one-sided in their favour, too puffy, too pat, Moosehead Breweries' Joel Levesque concedes only that when it comes right down to business, the Irvings are "tough, hard-nosed people. But they have to be. Look at the organizations they're running. So they're no tougher than—well, pick any successful business person, from Donald Trump on down. If you're running an empire of any size, you've got to be tough, you've got to make tough decisions. You have to fire people, you have to have tough negotiations with suppliers." Levesque believes that one of the reasons the Irvings seem to stand out and have developed a reputation for their toughness is because they are in such a relatively small marketplace, where everyone knows one everyone else. "There are just two degrees of separation in the Maritimes, instead of six. So their reputation for being harder than most gets blown out of proportion." Levesque says that with the leagues they play in, if the Irvings weren't tough, the bigger players would steal the shirts right off their backs.

What's at stake—keeping their shirts—is ingrained in Irving family members at a very young age. As a ten-year-old boy, two years before the formation of the Jim, Art, and Jack Farm, J. K. had kept a dozen hens in a small barn behind the family's Mount Pleasant Avenue home in Saint John. He and his brothers dabbled in selling eggs at the time. But when spring rolled around and it was time to head to Irvingdale, the family's Bouctouche-area summer cottage, J. K. had to find a way to liquidate the hens. "So I put a little ad in the paper," he says, "and a fellow showed up with a panel truck. I wanted so much for the hens, but he got the hens in the back of his panel truck and he proceeded to pay me quite a bit less." The future magnate was having none of it. "I got my money. I argued with him. I told him what I thought." Asked where he got the tenacity as a little boy to argue with a grown man, a stranger nonetheless, J. K. responds with absolute, understated, common-sense Irving clarity: "Well, gee, they were my hens."

What followed was the advent of the Jim, Art, and Jack Farm, producing many more fun, memorable chicken stories from J. K.'s boyhood. One involves fowl they'd slaughtered themselves after having raised them in Bouctouche throughout the summer. At the ripe old age of fourteen, with his driver's licence in hand, J. K. headed off to Moncton with his freshly killed chickens in a wooden box that K. C. had helped the boys build to put on the back of a truck. This was during the Second World War, when chickens and eggs were at a premium. He would sell them all around Moncton, including at a grocery store down the street from what was then the Windsor Hotel. The store manager took J. K. into his office. "I had my price and I gave him my price"—something to the order of forty-seven cents per pound. But the man was offering forty-three or forty-four cents. J. K. wouldn't budge, saying he had other calls to make and that he'd be back. "So I went out and up the street to the Windsor Hotel where I sold them all for my price." He returned to the grocery manager to explain that he'd sold all of his product. "That was it. Thank you very much. And I went." Even in those earliest of days under the tutelage of K.C., the Irving School of Busness had instilled in J.K. and his brothers how to stand on their own two feet and how to protect their interests.

In a previous life, Moncton-based Assumption Life president Denis Losier was a key member of former New Brunswick premier Frank McKenna's cabinet, most notably as minister of economic development and tourism. He's had and continues to have many dealings with the Irvings, particularly J.K.'s son Jim. Losier says that when it comes to business, if they're pushed, the politeness can be drained away from a meeting pretty quickly. Jim, apparently, is not afraid to be very straightforward and direct. This can include some forceful banging on the table, he says, but somehow it's "never aggressive towards the person." Forcefulness is used by Jim and other Irvings as a negotiating technique. They don't really lose their cool. Losier says that when you leave a meeting with Jim or any of the other Irvings, there's little doubt as to their position. So is this a matter of intimidation? "Not really," says Losier, "unless you're not used to participating in some high-level meetings where the issues are very tough and very important for the companies and the players involved." Losier harkens back to negotiations between unions and the Irvings. The union reps would negotiate hard and J.K., for example, could dish it right back. When people from the unions or other stakeholders were pushing J.K., he would defend himself and defend himself forcefully. That man in Moncton who wanted to undercut fourteen-year-old J.K. for his chickens knows this all too well. To Losier, J.K.'s style involved the use of some "very tough words, very tough shooting," but that he always respected whomever he was dealing with.

Losier also says that a deal with an Irving is always a deal. If it's negotiated, then it's respected, never mind how tough the negotiations might have gotten. "Their word is as good as anything, and that's the way they've always operated." Losier adds that the word "acrimony" is not in their vocabulary. "They respect people who are just as hard-nosed as they are and when they come to an agreement, then they can celebrate the agreement." He says that in some other circles, you negotiate for a while and people get "pissed off" because you can't agree and it gets personal, and then the fight stays on forever. But with the Irvings, when you finish the negotiation, it's done. "You shake hands and what you've said in the last thirty-six or seventy-two hours during the negotiation…well, it's forgotten." Media consultant Arthur Doyle backs Losier's take on the Irvings' style of toughness, saying that one of the key principles handed down through the generations has been never to pursue revenge, a way of doing things that he links to their Christian perspective on

things. "Now, having said that, it doesn't mean it isn't hard for them to practice it. It doesn't mean that they won't remember for one hundred years."

Credibility and assurance are the things former PEI economic development minister Robert Morrissey associates most with his Irving deal-making
experiences. He says anyone who knows them never worries that an Irving
deal, once negotiated, would ever have to be redone. It just never happens,
Morrissey says. Once the ink is dry or the handshake is performed, there is
something absolute about the deal. Island taxpayers have never had to worry
about writing off an Irving loan. "Irvings never default," he swears. And the
bonus for Morrissey and his premier at the time, the late Joseph Ghiz, was
that "you just knew you weren't going to end up sitting in front of a reporter
trying to explain what you had earlier negotiated for," meaning that the Irvings didn't rape and pillage the PEI public coffers. What was dealt was good
for both parties.

Former New Brunswick deputy minister of economic development and
tourism Francis McGuire recalls a situation in which he was surprised by the
degree of forcefulness used by Jim Irving during a set of negotiations, the
result of a provincial government policy that was likely to impede J. D. Irving
Ltd. "We were dealing with energy costs on pulpmills and we were looking at
some cogeneration opportunities with gas. Arthur Irving (Sr.) came in with
J. K., Jim, and Kenneth. At the time, Jim was barely forty, and Kenneth was
still about thirty-two or thirty-three." J. K. was about two years from entering a form of retirement at the time, and his son Jim spoke quite a bit. In fact,
says McGuire, Jim Irving used an uncharacteristic expletive "because I told
him I was going to give Arthur and Kenneth a deal, which for provincial
policy reasons I couldn't give to him [i.e, J. D. Irving Ltd.]. He was really, really, really mad. It was the first time I'd ever heard an Irving use that word.
He was furious because I was doing a big deal and willing to do it for Irving
Oil." In spite of the exchange, McGuire emphasizes that he and Jim get along
very well. It's reminiscent of what Denis Losier said about the Irvings being
firm but never holding a grudge or being malicious in any way. "He wasn't
mad at me," says McGuire. "He was mad at the situation that I was causing." Throughout the discussion, Kenneth simply sat there and did not utter
a word. Since that time, McGuire has been in meetings where Kenneth has
taken greater command, although he has always remained deferential to his
father, Arthur. This is true of all the sixth-generation Irvings, says McGuire.
"If you get Kenneth or Jim in a meeting, they will say, 'Well, you know, my
father thinks....'"

McGuire says that although K. C.'s grandchildren remain very deferential
to their fathers, they won't necessarily think the same way their fathers have

forever. When they were younger, McGuire said it was as if 80 per cent of their business thinking was in line with what their fathers thought. As they get older, it's more like 50 per cent, and it descends from there. "So there's a nice continuum," says McGuire. "As one generation passes off to the next generation there is change but it is really in a continuous flow."

This matter of flow illustrates McGuire's point made earlier about the importance of having good continuity from one generation to the next and how rare that is in modern corporations whose CEOs come and go. The turnover of CEOs in companies other than those owned by Irvings has always been difficult for governments to contend with because of variations in style and the unpredictability of new personalities. With the Irvings, McGuire says in his wildly animated manner, "There was none of this, 'Jesus! There's a new CEO who's come in, crashing everything. What the hell is this guy all about? What is his business approach all about?'"

Regardless of how badly some of the Irvings might want to develop a softer, gentler public image, with J.K. seeming to lead the charge, they have not morphed into a bunch of pussycats, especially in meetings behind closed doors. Retired New Brunswick bureaucrat George Bouchard says that when they're sticking up for themselves in meetings and negotiations, "they can remind you of what they've brought to New Brunswick. They are very committed to this province. For them, it's where they are from and they want to live here, for which you have to give them credit."

◆

Mike MacBride worked as a project executive for the New Brunswick Department of Economic Development and Tourism during the days of Frank McKenna, and now works as a consultant in related fields. He recalls one remarkably abbreviated meeting in the early 1990s involving himself, then justice minister James Lockyer, Arthur Sr., and Kenneth. A keener for boosting Moncton and for further energizing the emerging and soon-to-be-rebuilt Moncton International Airport, Lockyer was an enthusiastic, hard-working politician who wanted to meet with Arthur and Kenneth to discuss their potential roles with regard to the future of the airport. He was pressing for growth for his own constituency's airport, which, in terms of economic significance, is easily the number two airport in the Maritimes behind Halifax International. As MacBride remembers the meeting, Lockyer laid it on the line with the Irvings about building synergy between their companies and the airport, about making Moncton more of an international fuelling and aircraft repair station. For the first few minutes of the meeting, Lockyer did all the talking, with MacBride nodding in agreement and Arthur and

Kenneth doing all the listening. "They let us go on for about ten or fifteen minutes," says MacBride. "Then Arthur simply took control of the meeting and said, 'When you get the fuel tax and landing fees down, then come and see us,'" to which Kenneth nodded politely in agreement. It was matter-of-fact, short, and to the point. The senior Irving then looked at MacBride and asked, "Do you think that makes sense?" The veteran bureaucrat had no choice but to agree. It did make perfect sense of course. Kenneth did not say a word. "We left with our tails between our legs," says MacBride, having learnt a valuable lesson about how to approach the Irvings. If you're going to make a proposition, you'd better make sure you have a proposition. In other words, you'd better be prepared.

In building their deal-making capacity, the Irvings have even been smart enough to transform retired provincial civil servants into entrepreneurial aids. Former government power brokers like Larry Armstrong and Georgio Gaudet (who like McGuire operated at the deputy minister level in the McKenna government) were hired to provide advice and to attend meetings with them, connecting the dots that traditional Irving employees (or even the Irvings themselves) would have been less likely to connect.

Civil servants who have previously worked with, and often for, the likes of an Armstrong or Gaudet are unable to ignore or escape the nuances and familiarity such individuals bring to the table. Former New Brunswick bureaucrat George Bouchard was involved in several of those interactions with the likes of Armstrong and Gaudet. "Larry [Armstrong] would come to Fredericton just to kind of tell people, 'We're working on this,'" says Bouchard. "And he would tell them [the Irvings], 'You need to do this more.'" "This" refers to any number of tactics, practices, or approaches that the former bureaucrats might see the Irvings as being short on. Bouchard says the Irvings are bringing into play the talents of former insiders like Armstrong and Gaudet more and more. "I think we're seeing a big change between generations. I think this generation (the sixth generation) will not come to government with surprises." On the other hand, Bouchard says they're not about to reveal all their secrets. As Bouchard says, no matter the level of trust, the best entrepreneurs don't give up too much information in negotiations. To do so, he implies, would be a competitive blunder.

The Irvings' tactic of hiring ex-government officials stems in part from the fact that the bureaucrats still inside government are vigilant about public perceptions that the Irvings get too much, too easily from the public sector. Bouchard says they've already got a strike against them when they walk in the door of a government office. Bureaucrats spend part of their time wondering, "How big can we let the Irvings become?" It's not as though people in government could ever stop the Irvings' forward progression, but some of their decisions can give unfair advantage to other companies who receive assistance and who are not established in or committed to Atlantic Canada. "I remember the tone in some departmental meetings, in management meetings for example," says Bouchard, "when quite often it would be said, 'We have to be careful.'" The fear factor, he explains, is that government might be seen to pave the way too readily for the Irvings. He was crystal clear on this point. "Anytime there was an Irving project, there was extra caution. I'm not saying it's about playing against them, but they have more hurdles to go through for the same project that somebody else from outside would normally have."

To counteract that internalized, almost institutionalized government attitude, Bouchard says the Irvings employed and then deployed people like Armstrong and Gaudet, who are better positioned to prepare bureaucrats for the strategies and partnerships the Irvings wish to pursue, to clue the bureaucracies in to the family's long-term visions. Without that type of information, bureaucrats would always look at the short term, the immediate horizon. If this is true with bureaucrats, it's all the more true of politicians who spend all or most of their time preoccupied with today's announcement designed to create tomorrow's good news headline. Bouchard says this improved climate of preparing and informing governments began in the latter years of J. K.'s day-to-day, hands-on involvement. Bouchard says that the contracts they cut with the federal government over the frigate shipbuilding program were a turning point, that they learned a lot through that rigorous negotiation process about prepping people on the other side of the fence.

Of course, the ex-bureaucrats hired by the Irvings have to be people who have not burnt any government bridges, people who have left on good terms, regardless of the political party in power. Former Atlantic Canada Opportunities Agency communications specialist Patrick LaCroix of Fredericton was lured into J. D. Irving Ltd. in early 2007, certainly not just to handle traditional communications matters. He was recruited because his government experience gives him perspectives that differ from those of traditional Irving PR people, including Mary Keith, vice president of communications, who's spent her career in the private sector.

Government people may not like having to tangle with the tough and determined Irvings, but one thing they do appreciate is the family's reliability. Politicians thrive on public job announcements. It's their magic elixir. As a result, many spend their time putting pressure on bureaucrats to assist any and every company that offers a promise of lucrative jobs. Many government-funded and government-controlled job announcements are shaped by politicians, who have a habit of pressuring the companies they're court-ing to project job and investment measureables that are usually founded on guesswork and window-dressing. Many of those promised jobs never ma-terialize. According to George Bouchard, when the Irvings are involved in an announcement about creating ninety jobs in Saint John or Chipman or Kensington or Truro, it's a sure bet those jobs will materialize. "When they're making a commitment," says Bouchard, "you can go to the bank with that commitment." He credits this to the Irvings having their heart in everything they do. CEOs of corporations where shareholders call the shots can't possibly be expected to have the same level of commitment, enthusiasm, or emotional engagement as the Irvings.

David Hawkins agrees with others that although the Irvings can be tough to negotiate with, there are reasons for this. "Over the years, some people have commented to me that they find the Irvings just too tough to do busi-ness with, unnecessarily tough, too demanding, I guess," says Hawkins. "Well, I certainly know what is meant when people say that and have experi-enced that a little. But, overall, in general, I'd say that they are fair. And they do what they say they are going to do. So, they are very credible. It's not easy to operate on the scale that they do and at the same time be as sensitive as everyone might like, including me." Hawkins says one's perspective on the Irvings depends on whether one is buying from them or selling to them. "If you are selling something to them, they may be a touch, or even a lot, tough. But, if you are buying from them, if you are the customer, they are great peo-ple to do business with. They are excellent suppliers and everyone knows this. How else could you build such vibrant and robust businesses? It just would not be possible unless you had very satisfied customers. In my view, the Irv-ings do not get enough credit for being very, very good to work with if you are the customer."

Hawkins makes a point of advising business people that it's a good thing, if you want to succeed in business in New Brunswick, to make a particu-lar point of getting along with the Irvings, "because it probably won't be as great an experience living here if you don't. So make a point of getting along with them." He says that "getting along" is a factor that, if it "clicks in," can influence an awful lot of things. "Any organization or operation with that many tentacles has a lot of influence, so I think people don't want to get on the wrong side of the Irvings. I don't want to get on the wrong side of the Irvings and I have no reason to get on the wrong side of them." They perme-ate so much of New Brunswick and Maritime society that most businesses will inevitably have dealings with one Irving company or another. One never knows when they'll be seated across the table negotiating a deal, either as buyer or as seller. "I mean," continues Hawkins, "have I had beefs with them from time to time? Yeah. I've had beefs with my wife and she's had some with me and quite legitimately." He says you can expect that when you're doing business, beefs are going to emerge. Hawkins says he told Judith Irving outright at the beginning of their negotiations about her buying his company, Hawk Communications, that they were going to encounter difficulties along the way and that they needed to be prepared to handle such events. Hawkins says there were periodic hiccups in transitioning the company, but that he and the Irvings got through them all.

"I don't think you'd have to scratch too hard to find that people have got issues with the Irvings. I think that some people feel they're too powerful, but they'd say that about any organization that powerful. They say that about Mobil Oil, they say that about Wal-Mart, they say that about any organization in a relatively small geographic area with so much influence. They say that about certain politicians—Chrétien, Trudeau, George Bush. So inevitably, if you run a business and you interact with as many people as they interact with—which is millions—then there are going to be issues and challenges. They don't necessarily intend there to be. It's the simple outcome of them doing what they need to do. I think they try to please as many people as they can, but inevitably you can't please everybody."

14. Sobriety

One of the most remarkable lessons passed down through the generations of Irvings is the importance of sobriety. The Irvings are renowned for their avoidance of alcohol, although it is known that one or two who shall remain nameless are capable of having a glass of wine or a cold beer.

Their abstinence is more than likely owed to their Calvinist religious background, which undoubtedly also contributes to the family's work ethic and entrepreneurship. The people with whom they associate, however, are not necessarily teetotallers. We're talking, after all, about a lot of heavy industry personalities, some of whom are notorious partiers, and civil servants, some of whom, it's safe to say, are known to imbibe.

The Irving fishing lodge on the heritage-designated Restigouche River is familiar ground to many of the family's business associates and friends. Down Gulch, as it's called, is just south of the provincial government's oft-criticized Larry's Gulch, where premiers, ministers of the crown and civil servants have been hanging out for decades (from time to time even conducting government business and entertaining clients) at taxpayer expense. You've got to be part of the river culture to appreciate the importance of a "gulch" and of having the privilege of spending time on one: the magnificent

Atlantic salmon floating in privately held pools, the unique culture and personalities of the guides, the chance to nap between excursions on the river, the great food. It's doubtful whether there is another fishing camp or lodge anyplace in New Brunswick where liquor is not on the menu (some places it seems to be the only thing on the menu), but Down Gulch is as dry as it gets.

In the late 1990s, Arthur Sr.'s appreciative colleagues at Ducks Unlimited threw a thank-you fundraising dinner in his honour at the Saint John Convention Centre (he is highly regarded for his dedication to Canada's waterfowl habitat). During the celebratory evening, however, one New York City heavyweight, a cohort, got a playful jab in at Arthur. He drew particular attention to thanking Arthur for a visit the gentleman and other colleagues had experienced at "Dry Gulch." Everyone in the audience knew the customary drill at Down Gulch first-hand or by reputation, so the room broke out in laughter. Arthur was reported to have taken it in stride, enjoying the chuckle along with everyone else.

Long-time Irving associate Louis LaPierre likes a glass of fine wine with his meals. Like most people at his station in life, he's accustomed to it. As he explains elsewhere in this book, the custom is dropped whenever he visits the Irvings' lodge on the Restigouche River for a two- or three-day stay at the invitation of J. K. There is not a drop served. It's all about their discipline, he says.

In *The Biography of K. C. Irving* Douglas How and Ralph Costello relate a revealing exchange between K. C and Lord Beaverbrook (Max Aitken). During the period when Beaverbrook was chancellor of the University of New Brunswick and K. C. was a member of the institution's board of governors, Beaverbrook is reported to have asked his friend: "You don't drink. You don't smoke. You don't wench. What in hell do you do?" K. C. responded with dry humour: "I work."

The presence of liquor, beer, and wine is constant in the circles that Moncton ad man and hockey builder Jean Brousseau travels in. Indeed, before Robert Irving bought the Moncton Wildcats, they were called the Alpines, after the famous New Brunswick beer. But in all of Brousseau's hockey travels with Robert—ten years now and counting—he has never seen Robert swallow even an ounce of alcohol. It's part of what he calls, "the Irving way." Out of respect for "the way," Brousseau does not order a beer if he and Robert are eating together in a restaurant. "I'm not going to change my life, but one thing, by respect, if I'm only with him, I'm not ordering a beer. I don't think it's worth it." Some people would question why he wouldn't order a beer in front of Robert, but Brousseau says it's a simple convention and an easy one to adhere to. If there's a crowd of people around instead of just the two of them, and the crowd is ordering drinks, then Brousseau might conform to his normal tendency.

PART III

Expectations

15. Irvingites

An Irvingite is someone who has attended the Irving School of Business at Irving U, who has spent enough time within one of the Irving corporate cultures to have witnessed, absorbed, and adopted many of the traits, actions, and characteristics of the Irvings themselves. Generally speaking, an Irvingite's personal life and habits have also been altered by the experience. Those who are able to tough it out in the Irving culture (and it's not for everyone) tend to morph into otherworldly beings. The composite Irvingite could be described like this:

- Is passionate about work: completely dedicated to the corporate entity and to the Irving family members; puts work before life; willing to be on call 24/7 without complaint—in fact, with enthusiasm
- Has the ability to contend with ambiguity and frequent strategy changes
- Possesses an untiring work ethic
- Has the creative ability to overcome obstacles to achieve objectives
- Practices clean living
- Possesses the Irving style of humour, always in good taste, not at anyone's expense, not sarcastic
- Has a high degree of integrity and honesty
- Has the confidence to give the Irving family members news or advice they may not like but nevertheless need to know

As well, there are some key words and phrases that define what the Irvings are looking for in an employee:

- Decisive
- Risk-taking
- Fast

· Open to change

· Tough

The bottom line is, you either fit within the Irving culture or you don't. It's really that simple, that black and white. And the Irvings themselves can spot the right people almost right away. "The secret of business, in the end, is people," says J. K. "The people that you get around you and within your organization. You can buy this machine and that machine, but the secret is people. And you've got to have people that you're compatible with, people who, you know, work harmoniously. It all gets back to people." He admits that people-mining is not an exact science. "Sometimes it's a little hard to tell right off, but it doesn't take too long. You have got to have honesty right up front and you've got to have loyal people, and you try to have people who have a great deal of common sense and practicality." It's often said that this person or that person would or wouldn't fit within an Irving organization because they do or don't fit the culture.

Those people with an Irving career background whom Assumption Life President Denis Losier and his firm have hired have always had a lot of good comments about their time there. One thing, he says, is a virtual certainty: when you hire an Irvingite, "you know you're getting a well-trained employee who can work really hard and who doesn't mind spending some time on difficult files. So what I can see from that now is that they've got a well-greased organization in terms of developing their manpower." He adds that the Irvings don't just produce petroleum and forestry products, French fries and toilet paper—they produce good workers. "They're a factory of people. Sure they've been involved in natural resources all their time, but one resource that's very key, is their human resource." David Ganong partly agreed with Losier regarding the quality of Irvingites. But he points out another possible side to that coin. "They also output ones that aren't that good," says Ganong, which of course is a possible reason they're not with the Irvings any longer. "So you've got to do your due diligence on the employee and where they came from [before you hire them]."

◆

At first glance, the late Felix Therrien might not have looked to outsiders like a classic Irving person. After all, he did not learn to read until he was almost fifty. He's a guy who probably never went beyond grade three or four in school but worked his way up to become manager at the Irving sawmill in northwestern New Brunswick. J. K. "discovered" Felix when the latter was hauling logs around in an Irving lumberyard. He and two other fellows piled the lumber in the yard just so. "I'd go down there," says J. K., "and everything was straight. There would never be a piece of lumber on the ground. Every-thing was done right." From that simple observation, he took an interest in Fe-lix, a man who might have spoken up to four words of English, none of which can be repeated in polite company. In those earlier days, when J. K. was over-seeing the logging drives on the St. John River and its tributaries from both Maine and New Brunswick, there would be a crew on the American side and a crew on the Canadian side, with bosses and their teams of men committed to the separate efforts. Felix was given responsibility for the Canadian side. "Felix was full of energy," J. K. recalls. "He'd take a bunch of young fellows and after a couple of weeks, he had them all trained. Felix and his counterpart on the American side, another good man by the name of Leon Morell, were al-ways arguing and involved in a constant game of one-upmanship. They were both good employees, so it was worth J. K.'s trouble to keep the peace between the two. The idea was to keep both crews and their drives going at the same pace and, if difficulties were encountered, to find a way for the Canadian crew to help the American crew and vice versa. It was a highly charged competitive atmosphere. Felix and Leon would not help one another without the right type of coaxing; J. K. had to make it sound to both men through separately held conversations that the other guy needed the help. Only then would each agree to help out. It was all driven by pride and ego.

Eventually, Felix was put in charge of a sawmill. If you were the boss, of course, you had to sign the time cards. Felix, unable to read or write, was at a distinct disadvantage, which he much preferred to keep under wraps. "It was embarrassing to Felix," says J. K. "So I bought him a stamp," which Felix would use to "sign" the time cards. At one point in 1963 or 1964, a new Irving engineer spent several weeks touring Irving-owned mills with an eye toward improvement and efficiency. When the engineer (also a "great fel-low" according to J. K.) returned from the road with his report, Felix did not fare very well. "Mr. Irving, this is hopeless," said the engineer. "Just hopeless. You've got a fellow there managing that mill that can't read or write. You can't have that in this day and age." As the engineer went on, J. K. dug out a spreadsheet that recorded the outputs of all the Irving mills and wood camps. "I said, 'Harry, take a look and tell me which mill is doing the best.' He looked down, looked back, and said, 'Felix's mill. How could that be?' Then the en-gineer said, 'Furthermore, you don't own the mill.' And I said, 'Yeah, what do you mean? I own the mill.'" The engineer went on to describe how he and Felix had an encounter. Felix had put his finger on the engineer's chest and said, "Not Jim Irving's mill, Felix Therrien's mill." J. K. took a good look at the engineer and corrected him. "That's it. It's his mill and that's why he's do-ing so good." From J. K.'s perspective, Felix was right on the money. Things are at their best, he says, "when everybody talks ownership," as though they literally own the operation themselves. This, he believes, is the true sign of dedication and loyalty. He never doubted Felix Therrien's commitment to J. D. Irving Ltd.

"It has nothing to do with the pay cheque," J. K. philosophizes. "It has to do with how they feel about the business. A lot of people are doing good work, but they're not doing their best." It's clear that he feels Felix Therrien did his best. Shortly thereafter, the provincial government came out with a program aimed at improving literacy, an effort that has changed with the times, but is still ongoing in one form or another. Felix was absorbed into the program and eventually learned to read. He was so proud of gaining his literacy that he would purposely sit in a visible office window where employees could see him reading statements and documents. J. K. talks about Felix as a personal point of pride, sharing in the accomplishment of a dedicated employee.

In spite of the traits common to all Irvings, there are those who see cultural differences between Irving Oil people, who are now led by Kenneth, and J. D. Irving people led by Jim. J. D. Irving people are perceived as being a bit more relaxed and having a bit more control over what they do, like their input truly counts for something—they have a bit more freedom. Irving Oil folks, it's claimed, are more automated. One extreme view has it that Irving Oil people are "terrified" at times, although that point of view was never brought forward by former employees such as Steve Carson or Jim Scott. Says one source: "I think they're terrified that they'll say the wrong thing and that it will get back to the family. Everybody [throughout the Irving companies] wants to make sure the company looks good and everything's clean and that it's represented well and everything. But it always seems to be a little more on high alert at Irving Oil. And I think that's more because of Arthur Sr." Asked to explain that observation, the source said, "Well, even Kenneth's on high alert." Arthur Sr.'s overall tendency to be outwardly forceful and emphatic can be an intimidating thing, as was exhibited through his appearance in the CBC television documentary, *Unlocking the Mystery.*

No one can recognize an Irvingite better than an Irving. Fredericton-based consultant Jim Scott learned first-hand from Arthur Sr. that, for some reason, he had the makeup of an Irving man and that his boss had picked that out of him. This was during the latter half of Scott's ten-year stint at the Irving Oil head office in Saint John. He had spent five years working in the company's growing IT section when he was summoned one morning to Arthur's office in the Golden Ball building. It wasn't the best of mornings to be summoned to the boss's office. Scott had been at a hard-drinking conference the night before and was seriously hungover. Sitting nervously in front of the head honcho, thinking his condition was obvious, Scott was certain Arthur was about to say something critical. He braced himself. Instead, Arthur complimented Scott on the work he'd been doing and said he had a new assignment for him. He wanted Scott to "go see the boys" in the advertising department and give them a hand. In spite of Scott's protestations that he had no experience in marketing or advertising, Arthur insisted he would do just fine, thanked him, and sent him on his way. Scott dutifully made his way to the advertising office, located a secretary, and announced that he was there to "give the boys a hand." The lady looked at Scott, meeting his bewilderment with her own, and said, "There are no boys." As Scott tells it, the ad guys hadn't been performing and had all been let go. All of a sudden, he was the only boy in advertising.

The advertising department was not to last much longer for Scott than it had for the ten or so managers who'd taken the job on in the previous ten years. Scott is exaggerating of course, but he says there was definitely something askew about the ad department, which was directly under Arthur Sr.'s control. He went from there back to an IT position and soon after left the company on amicable terms. Since advertising, like public relations, is one of those areas that speaks to the public, it's not much wonder it was a restless area within the company.

Fredericton media consultant Arthur Doyle has worked enough with the Irvings to know that they know what they want when they hire someone. He says they can tell within a day or two whether someone is going to work out or not. You either have the Irvingite characteristics, or you don't. You can practice them diligently and effectively, or screw up and get out of the building. Doyle says one thing most people wouldn't expect of the Irvings is that it's actually okay (as J.K. relates in a previous story), to make a mistake. Risk eventually means mistake, but "if you're afraid to swing a bat because it might hit the ball," as Doyle puts it, then you're not likely to be an Irving player. But Doyle makes a clarification that helps one see things more from an Irving perspective. He claims they don't think about risk the same way normal people do. "What do you mean, it's risky?" is a typical Irving response. "Where did you come from?" What he means, of course, is that everything in the Irving daily diet of decision making is laced with risk. As former *Progress* magazine editor David Holt puts it, the Irvings are "farsighted risk managers."

◆

Lisa Hrabluk is outspoken and outlandishly humorous to such an extent that she does not seem like she could ever work for the Irvings. But somehow she did. Before she became a *Telegraph-Journal* columnist (a post she has since vacated for work with a Saint John communications firm), she was a reporter for the *Standard Freeholder* in Cornwall, Ontario. Cornwall was going through a devastating economic crisis with unemployment hovering at around 25 per cent, one of the worst employment situations west of Cape Breton Island. The paper's editorial executives came up with the idea of doing a series on communities that had rebounded from hard economic times, so Hrabluk was whisked off to Moncton, Saint John, and Yarmouth, Nova Scotia, to investigate comparable circumstances and the ways in which positive momentum had changed those communities for the better. Her interview schedule for Saint John included a visit to the office of Scott Haymen, editor of the *Telegraph-Journal*. During their initial chat, he asked, "So do you like Cornwall?" And she responded, "No, it's a hole." And he said, "Well, you know, we're hiring." Haymen asked if she'd ever worked as a business journalist. "Well, just on businesses that closed," she said acerbically. "I'm working in Cornwall!"

Without much further ado, Hrabluk found herself in a meeting with *Telegraph-Journal* business editor John Morrissey. Suddenly, without prior warning, she found herself taking "the Irving test." The Irving what? "The Irving test. It's a personality test they make all people write. And if you don't pass it, you can't get hired." She says this is the case whether you're going to write for an Irving paper or pump gas at an Irving Mainway outlet. The test has three parts and takes nearly two hours to complete.

"Every human being has to write the Irving test," says Hrabluk. "Oh, it's lovely. The first part is a timed math test, which is great for a journalist, right? I'm sitting there trying to figure out the isosceles triangle angles. And you're not allowed to have a calculator. It's just to see how far you can get." Then there is the adjective test in which you're asked to circle those adjectives, out of a hundred or so, that best describe yourself. The words appear in contrasting pairs, such as "introverted" and "extroverted." Then there's the field containing adjectives you think others would use to describe you. The final part is a booklet containing a series of questions like "Do you like gangster movies?" and "Are you titillated by true crime?" Even though she was primarily a crime reporter for the *Cornwall Standard Freeholder*, she basically lied and wrote, "No" both times. This entire line of questioning requires the "no" answer if you want to get hired, even if you have to lie, like Hrabluk. She says that other questions on the test included "Somebody keeps taking pens from the office. Do you fire them?" and "Some guy's been taking money from petty cash to pay for his kid's education and he's been paying it back. When you discover that he's been doing this, he still owes ninety dollars. What do you do?" Each of these questions requires you to fire the individual involved in order to pass, even if you have to lie about what your real-life action would be. At the end, probably requiring more lying, you have to answer a field of questions involving the use of marijuana and other drugs.

"It goes through every single drug known to man," says Hrabluk. "There were ones on there I'd never even heard of. Have you ever done magic mushrooms? Have you ever been arrested for doing this and that...." The (probably unverifiable) rumour is that even if you're considered a great hire, if you don't pass the Irving test, you're not in.

◆

Terry Small surely passed the Irving test. In fact, he is pretty much the consummate Irving Oil guy. For more than twenty years, he's been the company's manager of marketing, communications, and advertising. In the early 1990s he was approached by a unit at New Brunswick's newly minted tourism directorate (then a division of the Department of Economic Development and Tourism) with a fresh partnership idea in mind. It was the tourism directorate's unique (and daunting) mandate to halt the province's perennial and widely acknowledged "drive-through syndrome." Even more than lowly, flat, dusty, boring Saskatchewan, New Brunswick was dismissively referred to at the time as "Canada's Drive-Through Province," the funnel through which visitors poured en route to "Canada's Ocean Playground" (Nova Scotia) and "One of the World's Great Islands" (Prince Edward Island). New Brunswick was perceived by customers in the target markets as a pylon in the way of the classic Maritime vacation. The challenge was to reverse that perception.

The directorate's combative, multi-pronged strategy included the idea of stopping tourists dead in their tracks. The problem wasn't that there weren't enough visitors to New Brunswick. The problem was that visitors wanted to be in Nova Scotia and Prince Edward Island, destinations that were desirable and well understood by consumers. In addition to the introduction of a new network of diversionary scenic drives and the invention of a vigorous day adventure initiative (a wide and varied menu of new, short-duration travel experiences that would convince transients to stay in New Brunswick), an impactful "point-of-sale" project was mounted. The idea was to catch and hold visitors' attention using new destination and attractions signage, overhauled visitor information centres, and the most obvious of all opportunities: visitor information resources inside Irving's 260 service stations and Mainway stores found in every corner of the province. The premise was simple: go to where the customers already were. In a deal that provided Irving with free visitor guide advertising exposure and other benefits, New Brunswick tourism levered their way into the prominent Irving outlets. Street-front placards announced that official tourism literature could be found in specially designed indoor racks, which varied in size and impact depending on the size and scale of the outlet. The material was well stocked and highly visible. At some locations such as the high-traffic Big Stops, specially trained information ambassadors were placed on site during peak operational periods. Although the information ambassadors are gone, presumably due to funding limitations, the point-of-sale initiative remains in effect as of 2006, a full fourteen years since its inception.

The point is that doing the deal with Terry Small was as simple, as no-nonsense, as win-win as you could ever imagine. Once the decision was made to proceed, the implementation flowed, and Small, in true Irvingite style, seemed to cause things to happen very quickly. Seldom if ever did he seem to have to check things out up the line. Once he'd gotten the green light to establish the relationship with the tourism directorate, he had the authority to make all of the day-to-day decisions. For the tourism directorate folks, accustomed to the slow plodding of bureaucracy, doing the Irving promotion was like dancing with Fred Astaire. Just as surprisingly, although the company's and the government's ad agencies were involved, they were kept at bay, carrying out their assigned tasks but allowing the Irving and government program managers to execute the deals and make the critical decisions.

◆

The November 2003 issue of *Progress* magazine carried a bit about a twenty-three-year-old named Brad McCully, a one-time irrefutable star of the Irving customer service community. McCully is a guy who craved working for the Irvings. He is an individual who, rather than having strong academic leanings, has exceptional PMA (positive mental attitude). By the summer of 2006, having left the Irving fold, McCully was dabbling in community college courses while working for a Truro area car dealership.

Back in 2003, McCully had developed a reputation as the ultimate pump jockey, a customer service wiz extraordinaire. He was so outgoing, hard-working, and responsive to customer needs as he worked the full-service island at the Robie Street Irving in Truro, Nova Scotia, that he caught every customer's attention, big time. The *Progress* story provides a good snapshot of McCully, beginning with the fact that his mother, father, and grandfather had taught him well on the core principle that hard work pays off. Although he'd never met his grandfather Wendell, who died before he was born, McCully knew and was proud of the fact that Wendell had also worked for Irving. He had been a maintenance repairman who travelled across the Maritimes.

Sounding as though it were gleaned from a self-improvement book instead of the real-life lesson his folks had provided him, Brad McCully's mantra was "If you enjoy what you do, you'll never have to work a day."

Following that code, McCully had become, at his level, a star of sorts within the Irving Oil network. Just before publication of the *Progress* story, he had been in the boardroom of a leading Boston-based consulting firm that the Irvings had engaged to conduct a comprehensive customer service review. Irving Oil executives had the wisdom to notice that McCully had scored ten out of ten perfect mystery shops up to that point. Their decision to whisk him off to Beantown showed an understanding that grassroots customer service delivery can be as effective as strategizing consultants and their billable hours. As Irving officials accompanying him looked on, McCully gave the consultants his down-to-earth, simple philosophy: "I use my customers as teachers." He ultimately had so many perfect mystery shop scores, he lost track. He had so many perfect score pins on his Irving tunic that people joked he looked like the proverbial highly decorated "Mexican General." With his reputation and his pins, it seemed that McCully could choose from a very large menu of service-level job offers. Scores of customers had dangled their business cards in front of him in the hopes that he would drop his Irving commitment and go to work for them.

What makes McCully most interesting is that he used hard work and attitude in emulating his employer. He went about his business as though his name was Brad Irving. At the time of the magazine story, he was still bothered by a long-past credit card mix-up he'd caused when the local Coca-Cola representative had stopped in for gas. Once he realized his error, McCully called the rep and provided him with a twenty-dollar Irving gift certificate. The client's response: "There is nobody who does what you do."

McCully left the Irvings in mid-2005, wanting to test his skills in other areas. He wanted to grow professionally. He would have stayed with the Irving organization, he believes, but given his particular aptitude level, there didn't seem to be a move up for him in the organization. You could hear the sentiment and the idealism in his voice, wishing he could have stayed with the Irvings. "They were the best years of my life," he says. "The company did a lot for me and I did a lot for the company. It's like we were working as one." And the company did treat him with respect.

In 1998 Arthur Jr., dressed for summer and "off-duty" (as McCully put it), pulled up to the self-serve pumps at the Robie Street Irving. "I had no idea who he was," says McCully. But as was his custom when the full-serve pumps weren't occupying him, he made his way automatically to help this supposedly average customer. This interaction resulted in a friendship that persists today. The following summer, McCully met Arthur Jr. for a second time at a regional dealer's meeting at what was then the Truro Keddy's Motor Inn. The two talked more extensively there and stayed in contact. McCully would write Arthur letters about new employees who were performing well and Arthur would return the favour with short letters of response. A photo of McCully and Arthur Jr. was taken at that event, a print of which McCully says hangs on Arthur's office wall in Saint John. He saw it there himself when he was given a tour of the city in 2000, accompanied by the Robie Street Irving manager at the time, Tim Haines, and arranged by Irving's Darrell Swicker. Haines has since moved on to a regional role for the Irvings, covering part of Nova Scotia. When they visited Saint John, McCully was given a tour of the lubricant plant and an Irving call centre, and of course, he paid a visit to Arthur's office.

The connectivity between the two does not end there. After the *Progress* article appeared, Arthur had it duplicated, signed it personally, had it framed, and sent it off to McCully. Just weeks before McCully left the company, he and his wife Dineen had a second child, Jenna Mae, sister to Bradley Jr. Arthur Jr. called personally to congratulate him. McCully finally met Arthur Sr. when a handful of Irvings showed up at the Truro funeral of retired, long-time Irving employee Arnold Payson, the individual who had actually supervised McCully's grandfather at one time. All of these events and interactions have had an indelible effect on McCully. "What makes [the Irvings] different is that they can reach out and relate to every individual of the company on every level of the company," he says. "They reach out on a very broad spectrum." The way McCully sees it, most companies' executives (let alone owners) would never do what the Irvings have done when it comes to their personal touch with him as an employee. "There just isn't any comparison." Would he want to work again in an Irving organization? "I would in a heartbeat if I found the right place where I could grow." To put it mildly, McCully misses working for Irving Oil Ltd.

◆

August 31, 2006, is a very average night at the Lincoln Big Stop just off the Trans-Canada Highway near Fredericton. Across the vast parking lot reserved just for eighteen-wheelers, standing by their rigs, there are two random truckers. Jean-Guy Levesque and Louis Branch are engaged in typical trucker banter. Both men are likeable, gregarious, robust, and in their mid-fifties, true veterans of the Canada-us highway grid. The shorter and more robust of the two, Jean-Guy, is from Grand Falls, in northwest New Brunswick. He's retained his dark hair and moustache in spite of his age and he wears dark-rimmed glasses shielding dark brown eyes. He has been driving trucks for more than thirty years. Louis is balding with a grey goatee and bright blue eyes. He's from Bathurst, on New Brunswick's north shore, and has driven for eighteen years.

Both have simple stories to offer up of personal encounters with Irving family members. Jean-Guy once shook hands with Jim Irving at a mill operation near Lake Utopia, in the St. George area, and was impressed with his friendliness. Louis met K. C. while working as a welder at the Saint John dry dock. He swears he actually saw K. C. walk up and give a worker fifty dollars, right out of his pocket, right out of the blue. He can't recall the lead-up, the reason why, but said workers he knew had spoken of it happening before. Surrounded by a sea of trucks of all varieties and brands, the two respond to a string of questions as to what brought them to the Big Stop. They respond without hesitation and with ready answers about the Blue Canoe Restaurant's crowd-pleasing fish and chips (battered fresh on site), the sequestered dining area for those truckers who desire a bit of privacy from other restaurant patrons, the clean washrooms and truckers' showers, and the overall assurance that the lot will be neat as a pin, as well as safe and clear of snow in the winter.

"They're it in the Maritimes," said Jean-Guy. "For now," warning of the encroaching Flying J service station chain that is starting to move eastward through Quebec. Both men said, in unequivocal terms, that no other company in the region can touch the Irvings when it comes to serving truckers' needs. The evidence of this relationship between truckers and the Irvings is inside the sprawling Blue Canoe Restaurant, where, atop a thirty-foot-long, twelve-foot-high shelf overlooking the diner-style stools and service counter, promotional model trucks of many shapes, sizes, colours, and brands are represented. These are a source of pride for drivers who, in keeping with the remarkably tight nature of the trucking culture, can eat their fresh-battered fish and chips, down a coffee, and look up to see a model truck brandishing their own corporate image or those of companies they've hauled for in the past. The collection includes such familiar brand images as Breyer's Ice Cream, Eisener, Arctic Cat, Pole Star, and the familiar yellow and blue of Irving Oil tankers.

It turns out that Jean-Guy also has an Irving connection from long before his trucking days began in the late 1980s. His father, Raoul, was a cook aboard an Irving Saint John River boat that accompanied the same logging crews J. K. used to oversee. The boat was used for accommodating and feeding the hard-working men while they were away from home. Raoul used to tell his son of the day a young J. K. arrived and, with the appropriate boots on, helped men on his crew manoeuvre some logs along the river. Jean-Guy's late brother Albert also worked for Irving, driving a logging truck in the St. Anne area. "Everybody who lives in St. Anne works or has worked for Irving," he said. Asked if he had himself, Jean-Guy's initial response was no, until he recalled that he in fact did once drive truck for Sunbury, an Irving company.

There are tens of thousands of Irvingites in Atlantic Canada, Maine, and Quebec, those who have adapted their lives to adhere to Irving codes of work practice, attitude, and discipline, much of which carries over into their personal lives. Some are like true disciples, completely entrenched in the Irving world. Others, like Louis and Jean-Guy, are on the fringe, happy to work for the Irvings when the opportunity arises and to support their products. Still others, those who are ill-suited to Irving ways or can't live up to the extremes of their practices or values, simply never get hired, or they are hired and leave or are dismissed, never really having been indoctrinated in the first place.

16. The Pride of New Brunswick

Within financial and business circles and at home, the Irvings are as synonymous with New Brunswick and with the Maritimes as maple syrup is with Canada. They're the "pride of New Brunswick." Even those who suffer from the affliction known as "Maritime envy," those who just can't say anything good about the Irvings while they're at home, will boast about knowing them personally whenever the name is brought up while they're away. Tell a Maritimer flying home from their job in the Alberta tar sands that you're writing a book about the Irvings and there's immediate interest, followed by a description of how they're connected to the family. However far-fetched the connection might be, that person sees it as his connection and is proud of it.

The corollary of this is the Irvings' own pride about being in New Brunswick, working in New Brunswick, and making New Brunswick a better, more prosperous place to live and raise a family. Nobody ever argues that point.

"There's no place like home," says J. K., waxing sentimental on the Irvings' commitment to doing business in Saint John, in New Brunswick, and in the Maritimes. And when he says home, he really means home. No one really knows how much of Saint John the Irvings cumulatively hold because there isn't an "Irving" sign or emblem hung on everything. Ocean Steel, Commercial Equipment, and Thorne's Hardware would be just three cases in point. But even beyond the visible storefronts that don't even suggest an Irving presence, much of their real estate holdings are absolutely untraceable.

Terry Totten is roughly the age of Jim Irving and has survived at least three Saint John mayors and God only knows how many controversies as city manager. He's not timid talking about the Irvings where most people in his position would either decline an interview or, at best, go off the record. He's not close to them, but they do have and have had business exchanges and interactions over the years. He has stumbled over them in other ways too. He grew up in the neighbourhood fringing the city's Mount Pleasant Avenue where the Irvings have long had a presence. He doesn't recall any of the sixth generation at his school, but there are vague memories of a number of them being around Rockwood Park and Lily Lake. Over the years there have been purposeful and casual talks and chats about things as diverse as water rates and their impact on the city's pulpmills (with Jim) and being respectful of the city's waterways (with Kenneth). More recently, he's had dealings with Jack's son John because of the Irving-owned Heritage Place real estate project, visible from Totten's city hall office window. But whether he's talking about casual observations or direct business dealings, there's no mistaking about Totten's understanding of the Irvings' impact on the city he works for. "Look," says Totten squarely, "in North America there have been twelve [pulp] mills shut down in the last year [2005–2006] and one has reopened. And I'm thinking, the two in our city didn't shut down and they're working in an international marketplace. They have got to be good operators. Pick up this morning's paper [May 18, 2006] and read about how they've awarded tenders in a joint partnership creating one thousand construction jobs at the LNG terminal."

Totten says he's always meeting people who reside in the city long-term because they originally started working on the frigate-building program or the oil refinery. Just days before the interview, he happened to be on the back deck at Rocky's Tavern and met a big, husky guy with a ball cap on. "Boy, it's nice today," the man in the cap said. "Yeah, it is," Totten replied. Noticing an accent, he asked where the man was from. "Tennessee," he replied. "What would bring you here?" "Oh, I've been here for four weeks now working on those big new turbine units that went into the refinery." That's what goes on all the time, people coming and going working contracts for the Irvings. "There are people in this community being paid good money doing world-class work and we don't even know they're here," says Totten. There was another article that Totten points to in the May 18, 2006 *Telegraph-Journal* morning paper (which of course the Irvings own). It was the story of a tugboat hauling something in the Pacific that had stopped somewhere in Hawaii. The Irvings owned the tugboat. "The issue is, here's an Irving-owned tugboat in Hawaii, long haul, and we in this community don't even know. That's how big they are." Totten uses the same kind of folksy lingo J. K. himself might use, calling the lot of them "darn good operators. They are competent. They're professional. Time is always an issue because the longer things take, the more it costs. And I'm always amazed with respect to [their use of] the word 'quality.'" They talk differently than most other investors Totten encounters because everything is forecasted so far into the future. He agrees with their attitude about quality and about looking at development in the long term. "We have to do it right and it can't be for ten years. It's got to be for fifty years. We've got to make those investments!"

Totten says there are still some in the community of Saint John who believe that the powerful Irving presence has somewhat hindered the development of the city. "My view? You can't turn back the clock. There's two pulpmills, there's a refinery. There was a shipyard. Their head offices are here and my view is, man, when you're fortunate enough to have operators like that here, we should be working with them. Our future, whether some people like it or not, is linked to their success."

The Irving penchant for sticking close to their roots is more than just emotional. It's clearly a matter of longstanding Irving strategy. Francis McGuire wonders whether the Irvings will ever break out of what he calls the thousand-kilometre sphere of operations and influence that has as its epicentre the city of Saint John. Would they ever open up a manufacturing facility in Wisconsin? Would they acquire or build an oil refinery in Louisiana? He thinks not, which is what makes them fundamentally different from the McCains, whose food-processing network is truly global.

Donald Savoie of the University of Moncton says it will never make as much pure economic sense for the Irvings to remain in Saint John with some of their operations as it would in some other more strategic locale. This was true of the first Irving oil refinery and for the new one being proposed. No banker would choose under normal circumstances to build a second massive oil refinery in Saint John, versus elsewhere on the northeast coast of the United States. Only through the insistence of the Irvings would the refinery be built in their home port. To build it elsewhere would have been, as Kenneth said to former New Brunswick Deputy Minister of Economic Development Francis McGuire, "not what my grandfather wanted."

But it's their roots in New Brunswick and the Maritimes that override any temptation to move elsewhere. Savoie says he's certain they've been persuaded at times that they've outgrown the Maritime situation and that they should move on to Toronto's Bay Street or New York's Wall Street. "But you'll never see them leave," he says, adding that it's not rationalization that keeps them in the Maritimes. It's a question of "being here and doing well." He says they all have a deep attachment to K.C., especially. He uses Athur Sr. as an example. "He has a deep, deep, deep attachment to his dad. Very deep, very profound, very real. I don't think they would want to do anything that their dad would not be proud of." Savoie says that the unshakeable emotional linkage to K. C. commits them to staying in the region. In spite of his move to Bermuda, K. C. always said that the place where he was most comfortable was in Bouctouche. "He said that many times around Bouctouche. And K. C. was not one to exaggerate or to lie. He was a Presbyterian."

Savoie says that to find a family that comes even close to having so much singular influence over certain sectors and at the same time over an entire region of a country, you would have to go back to the nineteenth century, to the Morgans, Vanderbilts, and Rockefellers. He is quick to point out that the Irving phenomenon is occurring in a "haveless" region of the continent (not "have-not," as it's often described). He thinks it's doubtful you can find a parallel to the Irvings anywhere today in a growing modern economy. "You might see [this kind of corporate dominance] in parts of Africa where they're making the transition from a rural-based agricultural economy. But to see it in a world that's already established, it's very rare." He adds that in the Maritimes, only the public service dominates more than the Irvings. The Sobeys and the McCains are big, important players, but they can't touch the Irvings in terms of economic impact and value. The reason: the Irvings are just into so many things, some of which, like energy, shipping, and processing mills, are on a massive scale. Hence their position at 129 on the 2007 *Forbes* billionaires list.

You have to look to the likes of a John Pierpoint Morgan to find a personality that, in relative terms, might resemble K. C. It was said of Morgan that when he entered a room, "it was as if a gale had blown through the house." Born in 1837, he was both business genius and philanthropist. Early on he bought railways that were in financial trouble, a process that became known as "Morganization." As the more familiar "J. P. Morgan," he became America's great financier and the CEO of US Steel. One could argue that there is such a thing as "Irvingization" in Maritime society, linked perhaps to the family's practices of vertical integration or dominating the regional market with so many varied products and services. Although Morgan provides an analogy for Irving in terms of dominance, Savoie says that in terms of the family's longevity, one has to turn to the Rockefellers, who eventually turned largely into philanthropists and people involved in public service. "It's not a stretch to make such comparisons," says Savoie, although only time will tell if the Irving name resonates within its sphere of influence as resoundingly and as permanently as those of its American counterparts. In the Canadian context, there is no corporate family that compares to the Irvings, not the Eatons, the Desmarais, or even the Thomsons. The Thomsons, for example, might be richer, but their dominance, in terms of business or philanthropy, will never be the same as what the Irvings do.

One observer draws an interesting comparison between the Irvings and the Thomsons. There was a time when, if you had money and power, no matter what else, then you had influence. But today, you can have influence without necessarily having power. "Power is not the same as influence," the observer said, "and you don't need the former to have the latter. And it's possible not to have influence even when you have power." How does this apply to the Irvings? "I think they're beginning to realize that they have great power but that their influence is actually not where it should be." In other words, the sheer magnitude of the Irvings' wealth should dictate that they could always have their cake and eat it too in terms of getting work, contracts, or approvals for the types of projects they'd like to do themselves, especially in New Brunswick. But there are public policies, regulations, and rules to follow when it comes to economic development, commercialization, and industrialization.

Conversely, the richest folks in Canada, the Thomsons, until recently led by the late newspaper baron Kenneth, may think they have immense influence because of their overwhelming financial resources and perceived associated power. "The Thomsons are wealthier [than the Irvings], but they're non-entities in Toronto." This is because there is so much competing wealth in Canada's largest city, and the public is so jaded, that the Thomsons just aren't that evident day-to-day. The same certainly cannot be said of the twenty-first-century Irvings in Atlantic Canada, whose name and presence is omnipresent in people's lives.

In his article, "Control, Power and Influence: Six Basic Ideas to Consider," C. S. Clarke breaks down what he sees as the elements that link through to power. Clarke says that the person who realizes that he's the only one in control of himself (the Irvings) and acts always upon his own choices becomes very powerful. Not only is he the most free of the influence of others, but he is also most influential upon others. The self-controlled person is admired and sought-after as a leader. He is also intimidating to the insecure (shades of "Maritime envy" and "alibi for failure"). Clarke claims that those who learn the difference between control and influence can find the keys to true power.

There's a story about a former president of the Atlantic Canada Opportunities Agency (ACOA) visiting J.K.'s office in Saint John. ACOA was big on market development in Asia at the time, no doubt an offshoot of a broader federal government policy during the Chrétien era. The ACOA president and his officials sat on one couch and J.K. and son Jim sat on the opposite couch. At one point in the discussion, the ACOA chief made a comment about looking at markets in Japan and other Asian countries. J.K. has pretty large hands. When the offshore market development comment was made, he reportedly placed one of them on the coffee table to make a point, for emphasis, and said: "Why in hell would I want to go over there when I'm sitting beside the biggest, richest market in the world?" The conversation ended abruptly with J. K.'s obvious reference to the United States. It showed his common-sense approach versus jumping on some policy bandwagon that bureaucrats and politicians in Ottawa had drummed or dreamt up. It's reflective of the philosophy of a marketing guru named Barry Smith, a former head of advertising for the Quality Inns chain, who always said, "Kill the easiest duck first." Making headway in Japan is a much tougher enterprise than encroaching a little further south or west into the us or west into Canada.

Former Irvingite Steve Carson, now of Enterprise Saint John, has insights into the reliability of the Irvings as a constant, staying economic force compared to the comings and goings of companies lured to relocate into Atlantic Canada. There are times when the energy and money expended by provinces and cities trying to lure new companies into the region would probably be better spent on building more with the companies they already have. Municipalities and provincial governments practically cannibalize one another, using pots full of federal dollars in the competition to catch the big industrial fish. "We would normally crawl over broken glass to attract companies to our community like those built by the Irvings," says Carson, acknowledging that infrastructure, training, and other incentives are almost always offered to help make corporate relocation and investment numbers work, or at least look more attractive on paper.

If a new company is a million dollars short of a sound business plan, governments do things like alleviate the shortfall by putting utilities and roads to a proposed new plant location. Yet when an existing Irving company expands or a new one is born, people and governments almost take them for granted and often express resentment over incentives being offered by the Atlantic Canada Opportunities Agency, Service Canada, other federal government departments, and local and provincial economic development agencies. Carson says the Irvings not only create equal or greater economic impact than the age-old process of luring new companies into the Maritime economy, they also bring world-class corporate partners with them, such as in the case of the new LNG terminal, which includes a partnership with Spanish-owned Repsol.

Another individual, a senior federal bureaucrat situated in the Maritimes, adds that the Irvings "don't cut and run" no matter what the conditions, a further illustration of their commitment to the region. The forestry sector, with all of its current stresses, strains, and international competitiveness, is a prime example. While other mill owners are abandoning operations and communities such as Nackawic (near Fredericton) and the city of Miramichi, the Irvings are somehow figuring out ways to keep things going and to keep their people employed. Strangely, however, and this is a theme that emerged in several interviews, it's said that the Irvings don't really have an internalized culture of research and development like 3M, for example. When they need to innovate or solve a technological problem of any size, they tend to shop for and buy it.

This is potentially problematic because the time from the discovery of new technology to its implementation, maturity, and obsolescence is getting shorter and shorter. Some people in government say they have encouraged the Irvings to do more to internalize research and development, to the point of discussing potential incentives or partnerships, such as with the University of New Brunswick or the National Research Council. For some reason, R and D is something the Irvings are just not focused on. But when asked if there is one area where he thinks Atlantic Canadian companies—the Irvings included—might improve, Donald Savoie says it's R and D. It's all part of figuring out where the Maritimes are going to be a generation from now. R and D, he says, is an important but historically weaker part of the regional formula for sustainable economic development. Globalization and advancement in places such as China dictate, he says, that both governments and companies like the Irvings' need to do more and more in the R and D field.

Atlantic Canada's municipal, provincial, and federal governments are addicted to making big announcements about companies they've helped attract to the region and into Atlantic Canadian communities with taxpayer-sourced incentives such as infrastructure or training assistance. It's become a non-stop charade in which the three levels of government—but especially the federal and provincial governments—clamour over one another for the in-the-moment exposure associated with the big announcement. Often there seems to be little thought given to the long-term viability of the industries being lured to the region. Assumption Life president Denis Losier says none of the Irving companies are like any other company that strolls into town. The string of wood-industry mill closures occurring in the region (and elsewhere in Canada) early in the millennium is just one example, he says, of how the Irvings deal with market shifts differently. "Some of the companies couldn't care less about closing a mill, but these guys [the Irvings] live here." Instead of picking up and running when markets turn sour, "they re-invest in technology and equipment so they're ready to face the big challenge (and opportunities) on the world market—even though the same tough conditions are impacting them as well." Losier says they're not like other companies that at the slightest hint of trouble just pack up and go.

The citizens of Nackawic know this scenario all too well after the closure of their town's mill, a move that sent the entire community into an economic tailspin that has yet to draw to a halt. The mill closed abruptly on September 14, 2004, leaving more than four hundred employees jobless and jeopardizing the livelihoods of hundreds of supply and service contractors. The mill's owners left millions in unpaid bills, and a trustee has warned workers and other unsecured creditors they may never be paid. Even pensioners who'd sold their lives to the mill were devastated by the actions of us-based Parsons and Whittemore, the company that shut the operation down without warning and then filed for bankruptcy in a Halifax court. The pension fund was unfunded and the matter remains before the courts for resolution. "That's why sometimes it's important to have companies that have roots like [the Irvings] here," says Losier.

Moosehead Breweries public affairs vp Joel Levesque sees it this way too. Even when world markets put a pounding on mill operations, the Irvings react differently than other companies. "What they do is keep things running. They don't shut down a mill. They may temporarily have a shut down, although not very often. Instead, they reinvest. They do something different." They project ahead to what the market shakeout will look like at the end of the troubled period. If the market looks bleak for newsprint, they might look to producing coated magazine paper. As noted earlier, their ability to do this is predicated on their independence, because there is no publicly traded stock or board of directors to answer to.

In the same way that the Irving Oil refinery doesn't really economically belong in Saint John, the Ganong candy factory does not really belong in St. Stephen, New Brunswick. Nor did the McCain orange juice processing plant belong a couple hundred kilometres up the Saint John River from Fredericton in tiny Florenceville. There are many trees, but no orange groves to speak of, in New Brunswick. As Ganong Bros. ceo David Ganong admits, the replacement manufacturing facility his family built fifteen years ago could have been built in many other places and with a lower cost for construction and ongoing operation. One of the biggest reasons for this is the cost of transportation. The need to expand and modernize forced Ganong to admit to himself that he would sacrifice some degree of profit in order to maintain the company's commitment to the community. He openly and fully admits that it was more a matter of emotion than logic. Emotion doesn't factor into decisions in publicly traded companies. Take Ganong Bros. out of St. Stephen and the town would have an economic nightmare on its hands. David Ganong is more humble about it. "It would hurt," he says understatedly. "Our head office is here, so we make a greater contribution to the community than if we were a branch plant." Ganong thinks that many New Brunswickers rarely think about the fact the Irvings are headquartered in their province. As Louis LaPierre puts it, referring to the Irving-owned tissue and diaper plants and how they remain unique in staying committed to the Maritimes, "I don't think Kimberley-Clark would be in Moncton. They'd be in Ontario because that's where the market is bigger."

In the final analysis, it may be that people like David Ganong and the Irvings really just have no desire to live anywhere but where they live. It's a lifestyle choice for them, as much as it is for the workers they employ, who opt to stay in Saint John and St. Stephen rather than join the huge labour exodus to Alberta.

The Irvings' presence in New Brunswick was never more evident to Ganong than the night in June 2006 when he was diverted from a Toronto–Saint John flight to a Toronto–Moncton flight due to thunderstorms in and around Pearson Airport. The Saint John flights were cancelled, leaving Ganong with the choice of staying overnight in Toronto or at least getting closer to home. He chose the latter. After arriving off the flight in Moncton, Ganong was about to book a rental car—his vehicle was parked at the Saint John airport—when John Irving materialized. Having already rented a vehicle and having an extra seat available, John offered Ganong a drive. Given that it was after one in the morning, the guest said he would certainly rather have the company than drive by himself. The other men aboard included the head of Irvings' Sunbury trucking operations and an IBM official who's very much involved in the Saint John Regional Hospital, where John is involved in the supporting foundation.

With John at the wheel, Ganong sat in the back seat and listened as the banter revolved around forestry and the railway, but then shifted to the string of Irving enterprises they unavoidably encountered along the stretch of highway from Moncton to Saint John—a mere ninety-minute drive. They passed Irving stations in Moncton, Salisbury, Sussex, Hampton, Saint John, and other towns in between. They passed, or were passed by, a virtual convoy of Midland and Sunbury trucks, all of which are owned and operated by the Irvings. They were counting trucks the way kids count cows or telephone poles on family excursions. "Sunbury and Midland were the majority of the trucks still on the road at that time of night," says Ganong. Between counting the trucks and listening to John Irving speak, he came to a sudden realization: if the Irvings didn't have so many vast interests in so many sectors, from trucks to railways to ships, probably none of these industries would ever survive on their own in an economy the size of Atlantic Canada's.

Former New Brunswick bureaucrat George Bouchard says that if the Irvings lived anyplace other than the Maritimes, they would not be able to live the down-to-earth lifestyles they do and they would not be as approachable and accessible as they are. Bouchard believes the family is very conscious of the appearance of its lifestyle. "Their style of living is predicated on no flashy cars, no flashy anything, although they could [afford those things]. They are respecting the people that work for them. I think their mentality is, 'If we go above the people working for us, we're probably not going to have their loyalty.' It's ingrained in them that you don't live in a way different from others. I'm sure there's occasions that these people are invited to places that we're not invited, but when they are in New Brunswick with their people, they're very, very conscious of not looking more superior than anybody else."

◆

In spite of the Irvings' dedication to New Brunswick, "there's a great cadre of New Brunswickers who are really not great supporters of success," says David Ganong. "In fact, it's just the opposite. You could argue there's a lot of envy at times in that success. That's a Maritime problem." Ganong knows that in the coffee shops and wherever else you might hear chit-chat about how things are going in New Brunswick, there are a lot of people who'll continue to beat up on the Irvings and their wealth "and how badly they do this and how they do something else and so forth and so on, which is a Maritime characteristic." He says some people feel that if the Irvings are making this or that amount of money, they should be entitled to some of it. Ganong calls this phenomenon "Maritime envy," a term which doesn't leave a very good taste in one's mouth. If the Irvings were in the United States, or even in Ontario or Alberta, Ganong says "there would be applause for their success, entrepreneurship, hard work, making money, growing, expanding." These are attributes, he says, that are embraced by people in other regions who want to accomplish the same things, including improving social structures and the economy in general. Sounding a bit like Stephen Harper in his earliest days as leader of the Conservative Party of Canada, Ganong, although a true and devoted Maritimer, admits that "we're almost too much a dependent society here in the Maritimes" and that negative attitudes about the Irvings perpetuate that over-dependence. Of course Ganong cannot possibly have the same perspective as those in the average Maritime coffee shop. Although he lives in small-town New Brunswick and can relate, to a certain degree, to small-town values, he is probably closer to having the Irving perspective than that of the average Joe. He sits on the New Brunswick Business Council, after all, with Jim Irving. There are no doubt those who are simply envious and embittered, but there are also those who simply disagree over the capitalistic values the Irvings mix with their social values.

Someone who is less of Ganong's ilk and social leaning is Fredericton-based media consultant Arthur Doyle. He agrees with the envy thing, attempting to trace it back to its origin. He says that after K. C. started out in Saint John in the early 1920s, other business people were already jealous of him by 1925. "By 1930, they were sick, they were so jealous. And by 1935, he was the richest one of them all." They'd all been saying he was going to fall on his face—"they still say this about people that do well," says Doyle. But K. C. was going "like lightning," while his competitors were "drifting." The Irvings can't stand drift. "He had the succeeder values and they had the mainstream values and they couldn't take it." If Ganong's and Doyle's "Maritime envy" interpretation is true, then certainly Herbert and J. D. Irving must have been subjected to similar grumblings from people who couldn't stand their success or blamed their own shortcomings on Irving dominance. This goes back to Donald Savoie's argument that those who slam the Irvings are using Irving aggressiveness and success as an "alibi" for their own failures. In the face of this odd opposition to their success, the Irving response of remaining discreet and quiet seems to remain constant. Doyle believes K. C. and those who've followed developed this stance for good reason. You couldn't please the naysayers anyway, so he believed in operating quietly, keeping his head down, and not telling people about his own private business. "And they still have those habits in their bones," says Doyle.

◆

In addition to negative attitudes at home, the Irvings also have to contend with a different kind of negativity in the national arena. Steve Parker, founder and president of Corporate Communications Ltd. (CCL), says that in Canada it's not just what you've done, it's where you're from that dictates one's acceptance in major business or political circles. "Toronto sees B3N on your postal code and it's still an uphill grind." Parker says the Irvings are amongst the few Maritime businesses that seem to have overcome this perceived drawback, earning the respect of Toronto, Montreal, and Calgary in spite of their unfashionable postal code (which, if you're curious, is E2N 4K1). The one single entity most likely to make Maritime postal codes matter more than any other in the future will be Irving Oil. The company—and those in control of its development—are going to be fascinating to watch. For better or for worse, oil is going to loom large in business and in world politics until there just isn't any left.

There are huge challenges ahead for all companies that want to be competitive while remaining in the Maritimes. But there is greater hope on the oil side of the Irving equation than on the wood side, based on world conditions and opportunities in those sectors. This means that although Kenneth has significant challenges ahead as an economic leader and an energy sector visionary, his cousin Jim may have to be even more savvy and resourceful in figuring out what to do with the patchwork of interests (the famous vertical integration and all that), which at one time seemed like a good strategy but in the long run might be a maze. It's not that vertical integration and owning a lot of different companies are no longer fashionable or profitable, but there is something to be said for the sharpness of focus and vision associated with concentrating on a single sector such as energy.

The two Irving futures basically come down to the very foundation of entrepreneurship and the creation of businesses: the single word, demand. As the world becomes more technologically driven, world demand for newsprint is certain to decrease. And as South American interests continue to grow trees cheaper and faster than in Canada, the demand conundrum will be joined by the cost gap for natural resource efficiency and productivity, which will widen, leaving Canada behind the proverbial eight ball. Oil will not last for an eternity, but as Irving Oil Ltd. becomes more of a diversified energy company, as opposed to just an oil company, the sense is that its potential could be limitless.

Of course, the family could just up and sell anything they like anytime they like. With no board and only one another to answer to, it's their free world. David Hawkins and others say that what the Irvings end up doing will matter greatly to New Brunswick. For the time being, the sixth generation will stay to do battle. It can't be imagined any other way. But as Jim, Robert, Mary Jean, Kenneth, Arthur Jr., and John creep toward retirement over the next two decades, who knows what might motivate their actions to protect the family's interests: a seventh generation less prepared, interested or capable of handling the family business affairs, a true collapse in the forestry sector, or yet unforeseen Canadian and world events. Everyone seems to agree that the longer Irving family members remain in charge of their affairs, the better it is for the Maritime economy. In particular, Hawkins says, if Irving companies were sold off to protect the family's money and interests, New Brunswick would lose the centre of gravity it currently enjoys by having Irving head offices directly in its midst. It's important for all companies headquartered in New Brunswick or the Maritimes to remain, but much more is at stake when it comes to the Irvings. Hawkins is careful not to downplay the importance of any other company, but, he says, "the Irvings do more business in the first three hours of the day than Ganong's does in a year." And similar analogies hold true for other companies, even ones the size of Moosehead.

Hawkins adds that there are certain to be emerging sectors that are not even foreseen today. "The world is changing pretty rapidly and so it's hard to know what New Brunswick is going to excel at twenty-five years from now. It may be something quite different, something that we have not much awareness of today. With that said, there's a pretty good chance, given their financial resources, that [the Irvings] will be a partner in whatever that might be." The future is entirely unpredictable and full of opportunities, including everything from mass wind farms to alternative fuels.

The one thing that Maritimers would wish for is that nothing alters the Irving practice of keeping their head offices close to home in Saint John and Moncton. Few would have predicted the decision of Wallace McCain to relocate to Toronto when things shook down at McCain Foods. The minute he did (which was followed by the death of his brother Harrison) things in the head office community of Florenceville ceased to be the same. Technically speaking, McCain head office is still there, but it's just a matter of time before the draining away of the emotion, nostalgia, and loyalty associated with operating from such a completely inconvenient location.

It's said that if you asked the Irvings what it's like to be powerful, they would laugh, that it's just not how they see themselves. Power in the Maritimes, after all, is different from power in a global sense. Arthur Sr. put the concept of power in perspective during his interview for the CBC television documentary *Unlocking the Mystery*: "When the big guys want to roll over on us, we feel it." The point is that everything is relative; the Irvings are frequently viewed as steamrollers bent on flattening their local or regional competition, while they argue they've got to be big enough to compete on a larger stage. As Kenneth said in his speech in the spring of 2006, the oil business today is all about scale.

There are those in Toronto—and the rest of Canada's wealthier regions— who believe that the Irvings got to be so dominant and influential in Atlantic Canada because of some kind of wrong that's been committed. A long-serving federal bureaucrat who's had countless dealings between the Irvings and central Canadian interests, says he still hears undertones of the Upper Canadian attitude that Atlantic Canada is a backwater. The perception is that the backwater status is partly perpetuated by the disproportionate power and influence of this one family, which dominates the region as though it were a little principality they control. He says the region is still not well understood by politicians, federal bureaucrats, and businesspeople. "And it's all with an undertone," he says, "that there's got to be something corrupt here, or how else would they have made it where they have." That view of the Irvings, especially within government, constantly causes questions to arise as to why they should be eligible for anything ever again, while countless unproven companies come and go from the public trough with promises of jobs and investment, only to falter and collapse (or worse still, pack up equipment and leave the region altogether).

The source thinks the media is being perfectly willing to mirror, even promote, such attitudes. What they don't seem to understand, he believes, is that if the Irvings weren't occupying the economic space that they do, in sectors like forestry and energy, huge multinationals undoubtedly would. "And you know, those companies don't have any warm and fuzzy relationship with the region." Those outside multinationals that do occupy economic space in Atlantic Canada's forestry and energy sectors are not the ones typically contributing to the University of Moncton, the University of New Brunswick, and Acadia University, he says. And they're not the ones building civic centres, developing nature parks, and working hands-on at places like Saint John's Prince Charles School (see chapter 19). The multinationals can just walk away at any given time, whereas the Irvings are entrenched—for life.

There have always been those who see the Irvings' philanthropy and other commitments as paternalism. Providing workers with a turkey at Christmastime, holding an annual picnic for the families of employees, and other similar gestures can seem like evidence of a paternalistic attitude. "You can call it paternal instinct, but on the other hand, it's a very caring kind of view," says the same federal bureaucrat, adding that it's better to have that kind of parent, than to have no parent at all, which is what you get when major corporate interests are not engaged in communities the way the Irvings are. "And you might not always like the terms and conditions of life at home with a parent, but nevertheless there has been a parent there." There's currently word that Irving Oil has and will have trouble hanging onto key people because the pay rates for skilled oil workers are so much higher in Alberta. This problem will increase as the new LNG terminal and second oil refinery projects take off, but the Irvings offer more than just wages. It has strong paternalistic overtones, but if the company offers sweet levels of assistance to employees in obtaining a loan or a mortgage, then the company is going to have a hold on those employees for a very long time.

Some would say this kind of paternalism creates dependence on the part of employees—and by extension the community in which they live—that smacks of the old company town phenomenon. But every level of government and every economic development agency in Atlantic Canada is desperate to stop the bleeding of young people from the region, the brain drain as it's referred to. There are a lot of leaders, politicians and others, who would see nothing wrong with companies—Irvings or otherwise—putting in place incentives that convince young people to stay and work in the region, attract ex-patriots home, or attract newcomers and skilled immigrants. It's clear that some other measures tried are not working.

Irving power and dominance in the region, and in and around Saint John and New Brunswick in particular, have been known to cause conflicts in meetings with federal bureaucrats. When the Irvings and their lawyers sit down to discuss terms and conditions of agreements and contracts, they're used to setting the terms. It's usually their show. But in a federal government environment, there are rules to be adhered to, a context that the Irvings and their representatives aren't used to and don't like operating within.

According to the federal bureaucrat: "Their lawyers are used to telling the other party how it's going to be and we [the federal government] just can't accept it that way. Certainly you get the sense that that's the relationship they're in with most of the other businesses in New Brunswick. They get their way. It's an urban legend, or a rural legend, for example, that you ought to get cash from the Irvings because you won't get paid for ninety days." Of course, nobody actually does business in cash these days (unless they're trying to keep things off the books), but many people say there's a lot of truth to that legend. The word on the street, from many suppliers, is that even in the twenty-first century, the Irvings pay on their terms and on their schedule and businesses simply put up with it. In that sense, businesses large and small have provided the Irvings with much of their revolving, short-term financing. This is where the paternalism, if that's what you want to call it, seems to get a little out of control. In a family counselling situation, a therapist might label this cycle as a form of abuse. So why do businesses continue conducting transactions and doing work with and for companies they feel so beholden to and yet often bitter about? That is one of the Irving mysteries. Companies shouldn't be shocked or even surprised at the way things operate in the Irving business world, because it's been that way for so long. Here is where opinions about Irving dominance collide. Dr. Donald Savoie will say that businesses that complain about the Irvings play the dominance card as their alibi for failure.

But for businesses of a certain scale in Saint John and elsewhere throughout the region, the reality is that getting work from the Irvings can literally mean making it in business or not. But if you are going to get work from them, you don't set the terms and conditions—they do. A senior guy at one of Canada's largest specialized consulting firms says there's no such thing as "this net thirty days stuff. If you want to do work with them, get used to being paid in one hundred and twenty, one hundred and thirty days." Why do they follow such terms? The Irvings end up using their suppliers' money to help finance their own businesses. On the other end, they expect and usually get their money fairly pronto. If you've had an Irving gas credit card lately, you know all about this. Cards become dormant rapidly if balances are not kept up to date.

So why do people keep doing work for the Irvings under such dictatorial (or, as my source put it, "ruthless") conditions? There's only one possible answer: they ultimately make money doing it. Financial return is what's in it for them. Nonetheless, he called it a "parasitic relationship." You've got the big organization that has its tentacles into everything. And if you want the work, you put up with it. The federal bureaucrat says people grudgingly recognize that the Irvings are important to their business and to the regional economy.

Back in the proverbial Maritime coffee shop, some Irving employees and contractors verbally bite the hands that feed them, isolating the family further from the community in which they live. Because of the perceptions surrounding Irving power and dominance in Atlantic Canada, the individual family members pay a toll. Of course they don't see themselves as being the calculating, competitive demons they're sometimes made out to be. However, the Irvings' reticence about dealing with the media has not helped matters. By not speaking up for themselves, or by doing so infrequently or erratically, they've arguably contributed to the perpetuation of negative stereotypes. The Irvings, in short, could use a complete media makeover.

17. Media and the Irving Image

When they created him in the early 1960s, writer Stan Lee and artist Steve Ditko surely had no idea that Spiderman and his alterego Peter Parker would serve as an excellent business analogy and that at least one of the lines Lee coined would become a part of international business lexicon. In the Spiderman saga, Parker is told by his uncle Ben that "with great power, there must also come great responsibility." For the Irvings, this sentiment must surely ring true. Saint John journalist and public relations specialist Lisa Hrabluk refers to this as the Irvings' "Peter Parker complex."

Hrabluk points out that New Brunswickers look at the Irvings like they're a de facto government and that, since it's the Canadian way to look to our governments to take care of us, people look to the Irvings in that way as well, whether or not they know it or want to admit it. And just as with governments, she says New Brunswickers have a love-hate relationship with the Irvings. The difference is, the public can't vote the Irvings in or out of power.

Hrabluk covered politics and business extensively in New Brunswick and was always amazed to hear people refer to then premier Bernard Lord and Kenneth Irving in the same tones, as though they both had a responsibility to make sure people were employed. Hrabluk thinks that because of this, the Irvings are sometimes confused by people's reaction to them, which might have contributed to Kenneth's miscalculation over the LNG terminal debacle that erupted when the Saint John city council decided to provide the Irvings and their project partner Repsol with multi-million-dollar tax relief. Making light of the public perception of the Irvings, she jokes that when Kenneth cut the controversial tax relief deal with Saint John mayor Norm McFarlane, Kenneth should have had the courtesy to wear shades so that he couldn't look directly into the mayor's eyes and mesmerize him.

"They're trying to figure out why everyone's mad at them," says Hrabluk. "So now I think they're frightened to make a move. So it's almost like they're in their own glass cage. So I actually feel sorry for them. I remember Jamie [publisher of the *Telegraph-Journal*] told me that when he was a teenager, or when he was in his early twenties, that he felt like the boy in the bubble. He called himself the boy in the bubble."

Hrabluk says she used to cover the Irvings and almost feels sorry for them because everybody starts out so suspicious of their intentions, accusing them of doing everything for money. People always think there's something else to what they're doing—a plot, an ulterior motive, a conspiracy. It can never just simply be, "This makes good economic sense." She rarely wrote about them in her regular political and business column at the Irving-owned *Saint John Telegraph-Journal* because she knew it was a no-win situation: "If I actually agreed with them about a project then I would be vilified." And if she disagreed, she'd get the same reaction but from another camp. Hrabluk says a journalist has only two things: the public trust and his or her own personal reputation. "Once either of those things disappears, then there's no reason to read you."

Hrabluk tells a story to illustrate her predicament. She was covering the First Nations logging dispute back in 1997. One of her pieces prompted a vicious call from "some ornery old guy" who accused her of playing favourites. He was screaming at her, saying she was an "Irving spy" and that he was never going to read her material or the *Telegraph-Journal* again. "I was tired, I was having a bad day, and I said, 'Listen sir, you know what? I am not from here; I'm from Toronto. And you know what? This obsession you guys have with the Irvings is really weird to me and I don't get it. So I don't care what you think but I just find it really weird.'" The man on the telephone drew silent. After a lengthy pause, he finally responded, "You're from Toronto? Well, you're the only journalist I'm ever going to read again." "Why?" she asked. "Because you'll write the truth because you won't be frightened of being fired because if the Irvings don't like what you write and they fire you, you can go home and find a job." "That's retarded," thought Hrabluk at the time. "Because if I could find a job in Toronto, I wouldn't be here."

Many people are puzzled about the Irvings' longstanding reticence about dealing with the media. Fearing litigation or loss of work or contracts, most people generally express great caution and apprehension over the Irvings' individual and corporate reactions to any public information-sharing. In the preparation of this book, the first question asked by every single interview subject except J. K. himself was, "Are the Irvings cooperating with you?" Everyone pondered their position before agreeing to go on tape. In some cases, even people's spouses questioned the wisdom of them going on the record. Some people, of course, declined to be interviewed at all, while others went off the record.

The family simply does not like talking publicly. With public relations fiascos such as the LNG terminal tax debate swirling over their heads, it couldn't possibly hurt them, especially Irving Oil, to play ball with the media more often than at rare events such as the 2006 Reaching Atlantica conference. And there was, after all, proof positive of media fairness and clarity when the fall 2006 announcement came down about a second oil refinery for Saint John. Almost without exception, the story played well locally, regionally, and nationally.

One media practitioner believes the Irvings should assume a stronger public persona, or at least those among them who have the charisma to do it well. Most point to Kenneth as being the most presentable, the one most likely and best equipped to fill this void. As for why they're so terribly mediaphobic, some believe it's simply because they're too busy to bother, that the amount of energy it takes to run multi-billion-dollar corporations is so all-consuming that the media stuff can always wait. According to this interpretation, they might recognize the value of being responsive in the media, but don't get to it because they just don't have the time. Public affairs expert Joel Levesque says that in the last ten to fifteen years, there's been a change in the Irvings' investment in public relations departments—names such as Mary Keith on the woodlands and mills side and Daniel Goodwin on the oil side come to mind. "They're not one hundred per cent successful," says Levesque of the senior Irving PR folks, "but when you represent the kinds of businesses they do as spokespersons, I mean, let's face it, they're smoke-stack industries. They do a better job than most. Look—there are so many issues and they have very capable people." As a lifelong PR practitioner and a leading figure in the Canadian Public Relations Society, Levesque feels that Keith and Goodwin are "extraordinary." Any other company running Canada's largest oil refinery might have a PR staff of eight to ten people, including support, whereas the Irvings, with Goodwin at the helm, have four or five people. And the refinery isn't everything. He's also got the gas stations and stores and Big Stops.

Mary Keith on the other hand heads up public relations for the environmentally controversial forestry operations (a volatile sector on the very best of days), all the community-based sawmills, the weekly newspapers that serve those sawmill communities, the pulpmill, the paper mill, and the tissue mill. Her list of public relations responsibilities just goes on and on and on. In late September 2006, Keith was contending with newscast-leading reports that an Irving forestry operation in New Brunswick might have broken federal law by damaging a migratory great blue heron nesting colony when workers cut a road through to a logging site. Once such a headline is out there, the story is irretrievable; any explanation will dissolve into the airwaves. Keith's explanations of the incident may have been comprehensive and accurate, but she had to know from the get-go that it was a losing PR proposition. People just assumed again that the Irvings were greedy, that they were at fault, and that they probably didn't care about the colony. It's not a hopeless battleground, but it's a daunting one. Also late in 2006, the company spent days trying to manage a story that broke nationally in print, radio, and television, and just wouldn't seem to die down. The CBC broke the story by tracing the circuitous movement of a barge said to contain toxic PCBs and sold by the Irvings to US or offshore interests. The story hit hard on the inference that something illegal (or at least immoral) had taken place surrounding the sale of the vessel. It played for so many successive days, and so negatively, that the public was certain to come away believing the Irvings couldn't care less about destroying the environment.

The media are partly guilty of not giving the Irvings credit for their widening philanthropic investments, their efforts in reforestation and environmental controls, and their ownership of the first refinery in Canada to take the lead and sulphur out of gasoline, which they did well before government regulations required them to do so. On the reforestation front, Levesque says that if you talk to the experts, they say the Irvings do it better than anyone else. "Besides, come on! There's almost no such thing as old-growth forest in Atlantic Canada any more. An old tree in Atlantic Canada is one hundred years old. There might be giant redwoods and Douglas firs in British Columbia that live one thousand years, but an old tree in New Brunswick is one hundred years old. If you don't cut it down, it's going to fall down. So when you talk to the experts, they say 'harvest it correctly.'" Levesque, of course, is a PR guy, not an environmental scientist, forester, or environmental activist, so he speaks from the point of view of someone who has represented Irving

PR interests in a previous life, not from ecological expertise. There are, of course, opposing points of view, put forward by well-informed individuals, people like Dalhousie University professor Martin Willison, who presents a frank yet balanced viewpoint about Irving forestry practices in the chapter "Irving Environmentalism." There, Dr. Willison levels criticisms against the Irvings, while explaining why they tend to do what they do. In a nutshell, they are fundamentally merchants with a "utilitarian business perspective," while their critics lean towards spiritual and scientific perspectives of the natural world. A noted Maritime forester and ecologist who insisted on going off the record goes much further than Willison in his criticism of J. D. Irving Ltd. forestry practices, saying that the most "conspicuous" damage to the landscape results from the company's harvesting practices. These different points of view serve as the stimulus for much of the debate in the media surrounding the Irvings and their environmental practices.

There must be days when Keith and Goodwin wish they could respond to reporters' high-pressure inquisitions with an Irving family member, rather than the efficient but less effective retort of their own voices. A real, authentic Irving who is skilled at communications and is prepared to be the face of the Irving name would certainly do the trick. Even if it's not what they enjoy, even if they don't really have the time, there's a consensus amongst public relations folk that the Irvings should make the move to put one of their own in the forefront.

In that vein, Joel Levesque recalls the oil refinery explosion of 1997, which killed one employee and which rocked the city and the Irving family. The accident occurred around nine or ten o'clock in the morning and was followed before the day was out by an impromptu news conference held by Arthur Sr. at the top of the hill overlooking the refinery. Arthur initially wanted the refinery manager to handle the communications, but he was personally persuaded to do otherwise by Steve Parker of Corporate Communications Ltd., who'd flown in from Halifax immediately after the accident. The media were ready to pounce until Arthur stood front and centre and spoke from his heart, saying, "This is one of the saddest days of my life. We've lost a life here." The fact that Arthur was obviously and truly devastated put an immediate end to the potential backlash that almost certainly would have erupted in the media. There were a few other questions and that was the end of the scrum. For Arthur, it must have harkened back to the day in 1974 when the Reversing Falls Irving station exploded, killing four people. "It really shakes them [the Irvings]," when something tragic or traumatic happens, says a source. "It shakes them and they really look after the families, there's no question. No one ever hears about it. They just look after matters." There's one school of thought that having Arthur stand before the cameras on the morning of the refinery accident was all the more effective because the family members are so very rarely on camera or in the public eye. It was a combination of how he handled himself, the sincerity of his delivery, and the fact that having any Irving step up spontaneously to a cluster of microphones was so unusual. The media must have been in a mild state of shock of their own.

Steve Parker's recollection of that morning is still crystal clear. "It was one of the very first occasions that any of the Irvings walked into the teeth of an aggressive media situation." Arthur's preparation for meeting the media began with a thorough briefing. Parker says Arthur wanted to know everything that was available about what had happened that morning in the refinery, about the victim, about his family. He says the focus was first and foremost on the loss and not the media repercussions. But everyone knew the public would want an explanation. "That's why companies have us hanging around," says Parker, self-deprecating about the value of public relations professionals. "We bring to bear experience in a very narrow field." He admits, however, that when it comes down to a death, the lighter side of PR dissipates awfully quickly.

That experience contained a lesson in public relations that the Irvings may have overlooked. But Parker says he definitely came away with a new lesson learned. "The Irvings showed me that there's more to business and life than just what's going on today," that what gets done today can or should have repercussions for the long term. PR is by its very nature, perhaps mistakenly, the practice of "get them through the day." With the Irvings, however, the long view tends to predominate. He says that some things the Irvings do have warmed him as an individual. By example, he says that when the family goes after a cause, you can consider it "a given" there'll be a positive outcome. Watching them as individuals over the long term, he says what he admires most about the Irvings is their "courage."

◆

The (LNG) terminal controversy of 2005 is a case where there's no doubt the Irvings—with Kenneth at the helm—made a tactical error in seizing tax concessions from the city of Saint John, monies that seem so miniscule compared to the total project cost that they just couldn't have been worth the negative PR they caused. Because of the concession, there is now said to be a permanent citizens' watchdog committee surveying all things Irving when it comes to governments and how, where, and why they provide assistance to the family's various enterprises. Everyone is emphatic that the LNG situation was a total media debacle, that it was poorly handled, in both the lead-up and the aftermath. Even though the worst part of the matter was the way the city council and mayor Norm MacFarlane handled it, the Irvings ended up bearing the brunt of the repercussions. Mayors and councillors come and go, but the Irvings have to live with their public in perpetuity. On the LNG deal, Irving Oil (and every single Irving family member by matter of sheer association) came out looking like money-grubbing capitalists operating under the table at the expense of a citizenry that in many Saint John quarters is not very well off. This served to perpetuate the old mythology that their whole focus is on dominance, money, and power.

The amazing thing about all of this is that at this stage, they do know better, like K. C. telling son J. K. he knew better than to allow the building of a crooked woodlands road. They learned from their woodlands and other mistakes, but less so, it seems, from their media mistakes. They just can't seem to get that media monkey off their backs. The Irvings may have internally moved on from the LNG communications mess, but the public and many observers (and ready defenders) have not. They've gone from having a passive anti-Irving constituency amongst the citizens of Saint John to having a dedicated front of people with a protest mentality. The majority of Saint Johners can't afford to act like this in public because nearly everyone has a brother, a wife, a cousin, or an uncle employed by one of the Irving enterprises. So those who've exposed themselves on the protest front must be a highly disenfranchised and determined lot. So pungent is the waft from the LNG PR mess that it's thought Irving Oil needs an entire public relations makeover in spite of the legitimate, good things they're doing environmentally and at the community level. The makers of Tylenol made the product more acceptable and more famous amongst consumers because of how they handled the Tylenol poisoning scare, proof that even the worst of situations can be managed. In order to relax the citizenry's attitude about the LNG story, a coup would be in order, something momentous on the part of the Irvings . Such a scheme does not appear to be on the minds of Kenneth or the rest of his family. They seem fixed on just keeping their heads down, keeping their noses to the grindstone, and moving forward.

The most visible and damaging public relations and media nightmares for the Irving Group of Companies have arguably been the LNG deal, the sinking of the *Irving Whale* in the Gulf of St. Lawrence, the controversy over K. C.'s will, the conflict with Willa Mavis's Save Our Shores committee, and the lengthy and stressful oil refinery strike. Of the latter, surprisingly, very little was actually written over the two-year period of the strike, according to Dr. Erin Steuter, professor of sociology at Mount Allison University in Sackville, New Brunswick, and author of "The Irvings Cover Themselves: Media

Representations of the Irving Oil Refinery Strike, 1994–1996," a paper published in the *Canadian Journal of Communication* in 1999. Steuter found that, cumulatively, the Canadian newspaper coverage of the strike amounted to less than a three-hundred-page book. Although, that may sound like substantial coverage, she argues that spread over all the available media, this is miniscule. Steuter writes that such a low level of coverage means the public could never really have gotten a detailed account of the central issues and events of the strike. Of course, central to her examination was the monopoly ownership of the New Brunswick media by the Irving Group of Companies, which includes ownership of all of the province's English-language daily newspapers, including the *Moncton Times and Transcript*, the *Saint John Telegraph-Journal*, and the *Fredericton Gleaner*. In her paper she argues that the strike was a unique case in Canadian media, because "the Irving Group, which was in dispute with the workers, is the owner and *de facto* editor of every single English-language daily newspaper in the province." In this connection, she cites the old adage, "freedom of the press is for those who own one."

Steuter's examination also included the *Globe and Mail* and a selection of other newspapers (fourteen in all, from St. John's to Vancouver). She found that the Irving newspapers were not alone in their style of coverage. All were complicit, she claims, in focusing on events related to the strike—"on the effects of the strike rather than the causes and dimensions of the conflict"—or, in other words, avoiding or ignoring the underlying issues and social consequences of what were very painful times for the workers and the businesses affected by the reduction in local consumer buying power, as well as for the Irvings.

"The consequences of this strike extend beyond the lives of the refinery workers in Saint John," Steuter writes. "It can be seen as the first step in a move toward roll back of labour and democratic bargaining rights that may be increasingly eroded." She concludes that corporate-controlled media, in covering the strike and its impact on roll backs in labour rights, make "the unreasonable seem, at first, unavoidable and, ultimately, acceptable." On the other side of the equation, insiders swear that Kenneth for one is known to have truly agonized over the plight of the workers who were on strike for those two long years. It was the family's position that if they didn't get the concessions they were seeking from the union, the company would no longer have been competitive.

One Saint John media observer says it's a shame that Irving Oil in particular is not making better hay out of the good things they're doing on the environmental front. "Irving Oil is actually a very environmentally cognizant company, for an oil company," says this observer. Based on their environmental activities, the observer says the Irvings should take a page out of the story of Lord John Browne, CEO of British Petroleum, who, even though he encountered troubles in April 2007 and was forced to resign, is widely regarded as a corporate environmentalist. "If you read [Browne's] speeches from a few years ago and you read what he's talking about, what oil companies need to do, Irving Oil is doing those things. I remember reading those speeches and thinking, 'Well, Irving Oil has done that.'" And yet, to the people of Saint John and New Brunswick, Irving Oil is still "stinky and gross and destroying our environment," illustrating that a lot more open communication about the good things they're doing would be beneficial for the company.

Joel Levesque at Moosehead says the Irvings are unduly criticized for things like controlling editorial policy at their daily newspapers in Saint John, Moncton, and Fredericton. "I don't care what anybody thinks," says Levesque emphatically. "They do not interfere with their newspapers." When he worked with the Corporate Communications Group, Levesque worked extensively with Irving companies. "I have seen them agonize more over what's being written about them in their own newspapers than in other media." A prime example, he says, is when the *Telegraph-Journal* did extensive coverage on the details of K. C. Irving's will, stories that did not play well at all with the public. The crux of the story was that K. C. was accused of protecting the family's immense wealth from high levels of Canadian taxation beginning in 1971 by shifting his legal domicile to Bermuda, a mid-Atlantic tax haven beyond the reach of Canadian authorities. There control of the Irving companies was vested in a new echelon of Bermuda holding companies. Irving California Co. Ltd., for instance, controlled the trans-shipment of oil destined for his Saint John refinery; the Canadian government unsuccessfully alleged that this allowed Irving to skim another layer of profit from his trade in oil. Unlike many of his contemporaries—those few seriously significant entrepreneurial patriarchs—K. C. was said to have engineered a smooth transition of executive control to his heirs.

Of course there have long been opponents to Levesque's point of view about Irving media control and how they use it to their advantage. The matter of the extreme concentration of Irving media ownership in New Brunswick forms part of an August 2006 article by Kim Kierans written for the journalism ethics program at the University of British Columbia School of Journalism. Kierans, director of the School of Journalism at the University of King's College in Halifax, has spent more than two decades working as a freelance journalist, mostly in the Maritimes.

She wrote that Irvings' media practices have been a matter of debate since 1968 when the family took ownership of all five of the province's English-language daily newspapers, adding to their extensive television broadcast presence. The federal Special Committee on Mass Media examined K. C. and his acquisitions under the microscope, and in 1971, the federal Combines Investigation Branch charged K. C. with breaking competition laws. In 1975, the charges were overturned, calling into play the need to show criminal burden of proof. The matter went all the way to Supreme Court of Canada, which upheld the acquittal on the basis that the existing legislation (since changed to the Competition Act) didn't have enough teeth.

In spite of the acquittal, the family remained in the crosshairs of the federal government and suspicious New Brunswickers who felt that the Irvings controlled too much media. Not much has changed since then, except that their television interests were relinquished in 1994, and Brunswick News Ltd., the family's newspaper division, went on a 2002 "buying spree" as Kierans calls it, acquiring most of the province's French and English community newspapers. That series of moves, according to Kierans' article, leaves the family with all three New Brunswick English dailies, eleven English-language weeklies, seven French-language weeklies, plus radio, Internet, and flyer distribution operations.

It may be that the 2002 move—and previous acquisitions—went unchallenged because of a common feeling that what's done is done and there's no turning back the clock when it comes to concentration of media ownership. This idea is attributed to the former chair of the federal Standing Committee on Transport and Communications, Senator Joan Fraser. Kierans describes how Transcontinental Media Atlantic dominates the print market everywhere in Atlantic Canada outside of New Brunswick. Media acquisitions have for decades been held by common ownership interests: CHUM and other radio networks, Thomson newspapers, Southam, Conrad Black and so on. Fraser doesn't think this situation is irreversible—she advocates stimulating new media ownership to retroactively force the dispersal of existing monopolies: "You have to start somewhere and build for the future," Kierans quotes Senator Fraser as saying.

The consequence of this concentrated ownership, says Kierans, is a narrowing of the variety of opinion before the New Brunswick public. "Irving does not see its newspapers as a marketplace of ideas to help people be better informed citizens in a democracy," she wrote, referring to Brunswick News general manager Victor Miordecki's admission before the 2005 Senate hearings that "newspapers are nice, but it is the distribution systems that are important to me." Kierans' paper goes on to specify ways in which the company does report favourably on stories affecting other Irving companies.

Even if the Irvings do not directly interfere with the media they own and control, says another observer, the public thinks they do, so they can't possibly win. It's a problem for everyone involved: the public, the Irvings, and the journalists who work for them. Some people argue that the Irving-owned papers actually overcompensate for the perception of meddling, by devoting too much attention to negative stories about the Irvings. "If you read the *Telegraph-Journal*," the observer says, "they write about that flare at the oil refinery all the time. And the flare means nothing, right. It's product burning off. It's actually a safety measure. It's a good thing when the flare is going." But to the public, the flare looks evil, like a beacon of air pollution. This observer says the Irvings should just sell the newspapers because they're the least important businesses in the long run.

◆

When he's not providing consulting services, Jim Meek fills the prized back page of the Atlantic Canada business magazine *Progress* with his personal insights into the condition of the region's economic well-being, public policy, and entrepreneurship. Meek's May 2006 column was dedicated to the Irving tendency to remain publicly silent. "Silence is Golden" was the headline. In the piece, he suggested that there is surely wisdom to the Irvings' reluctance to speak publicly. He calls them "hyper-secretive." Like others, Meek suggests that the Irvings are just too busy running their businesses and thinking about the future to "sit down to a conversation with ink-stained wretches like [*Codfathers* author Gordon] Pitts or me." In Meek's view, one silent Irving is worth a dozen scribes writing about them and otherwise trying to analyze and promote concepts like Atlantica. What does he mean? "Inside the family empire, after all, secrecy isn't merely a preference—it's also part of a successful business strategy that has kept thousands of Atlanticans employed over the past fifty years or more." He concludes that silence has, for the Irvings, become their gold standard, and that "maybe the rest of us would be wise to let them shut up and go about their business."

Candy manufacturer David Ganong acknowledges that the Irvings are "very secretive, more secretive than most," about their businesses. Like Meek, Ganong suggests it's certainly their right and probably a good thing that they maintain their code of silence. "It gives them more flexibility to move and I think they just kind of like it that way. And it also doesn't let any information out to the competition."

Meek's and Ganong's argument is interesting, but it's also cemented in the past. Since the Irvings are so heavily credited with looking to the future on every other front, having a forward-looking media management strategy would seem to make better sense than following old techniques. To use their own woodlot analogy, they should find a way to straighten out that media road.

◆

Because they're virtually everywhere in Atlantic Canada and Maine and because of the legendary stories about their business dealings—some no doubt true, many no doubt exaggerated—there are times when, even if the Irvings are right about a project in a given community and there is no land grab or no environmental threat looming in the distance, there is still a backlash based purely on the toxic brew of rumour and emotion.

The family members have all attended public meetings where their integrity has been skewered by people wanting to speak their piece on land use or other matters involving individual or public good. Under such circumstances, it doesn't matter if the Irvings are in the right. There are times when all the logic in the world simply can't contend with an emotional individual or an emotional public collective. Being big and powerful constantly puts them between a rock and a hard place. When they're wrong, they're wrong; and when they're right, they can still be portrayed as wrong. According to an anonymous but reliable source, "all they ever want to do is the right thing. There's no ulterior motives behind what they do. There's no evil master plan. They just want to grow their businesses—they want to bring prosperity to what they do. They want to make sure the businesses are there in fifty or one hundred years from now." But the same individual says that trying to contend with community emotion can be like climbing Mount Everest. "I can't think of a single public relations matter where anyone has ever won over an emotional argument with logic." Part of the problem, of course, has been generated by the Irvings themselves.

When they have been wrong about a land use or environmental matter, they sometimes haven't been quick enough or open enough to rectify the matter. The Save Our Shores public outcry over the Irvings' proposed installation of a sewage treatment plant on the Bay of Fundy shoreline lasted for two years before the company realized or admitted they were in the wrong. Even though J. K. eventually came forward and went to great lengths to repair matters, the collateral damage over that length of time was considerable. In cases like this, they were responsible for their own bad press. Other times, they are victims of reporting. They are media-introverts in a world where being more open, forward, and extroverted with the media is likely, over the long haul, to result in a much better public image. This is not to recommend a Conrad Black approach, where loquaciousness just results in even greater trouble. But if the Irvings are sincere about wanting to be better understood by the public, then they will have to try new strategies. With so much history to evaluate, if they truly want to improve their image, they should return to the drawing board to analyze the public relations traps they sometimes get caught up in.

18. Irving Environmentalism

Most people interviewed for this project agreed that the Irvings are far more philanthropic and involved in community matters than they were fifteen, twenty, or twenty-five years ago, so much so that it must be a clearly thought-out strategy. They've given over millions in contributions to countless interests, from universities to communities, and they've become increasingly focused on issues of corporate reponsibility. Evidence actually shows that from Herbert's, J. D.'s, and K. C.'s days, since as early as the late 1800s, things were always being done for communities and individuals. There are the visible contributions and acts for all to see and the invisible contributions and acts that only the recipients ever know about. In large measure, the Irving's philanthropic and community work has been characterized by the same discretion that drives their dealings with the media. There is a definite irony in that, for if the public was more exposed to the myriad of Irving kindnesses and commitments over the decades, the family might not have such a public image problem. The Irvings undoubtedly do much of their philanthropy and good deeds very much under the surface. One area where they've been quietly but surely making a difference is an area that is absolutely central to their line of business: the environment.

◆

J. K. made a sizeable admission during his October 2006 interview in Bouctouche, saying that he underwent something of a conversion concerning environmental and other social responsibilities when he joined the Premier's Roundtable on Sustainability in the early 1980s. That is when he began to see things differently. He makes it clear that each generation does what it can with the knowledge and technology it possesses. "The knowledge we have today isn't what we'll know tomorrow," he says, which fits businessman David Hawkins's assessment as expressed previously that no man should be judged outside of "his time." Hawkins meant that what constituted standard forestry practices in previous decades is no match for today's more sophisticated sciences and practices.

Earlier, among his loves at the community level, J. K. Irving was completely immersed in a project that was extremely close to his heart, the efforts of the community-based non-profit corporation Bouctouche Bay Ecotour-ism Inc. Chaired by Louis LaPierre, at that time still active as the Irving Chair of Sustainable Development at the University of Moncton (he is now professor emeritus), the corporation was established to undertake an inte-grated development plan for the Bouctouche watershed area. The project list included such initiatives as a marina and a vast trail network, but the gem in the mix was the rejuvenation of the seven-kilometre dune—one of the most significant of its type on the entire eastern seaboard—that stretches across the horizon and naturally harbours Bouctouche Bay. The land was owned by the Irvings but had a history of being abused by all-terrain vehicles, and the "cottages" of a group of longstanding squatters dotted the dune's tip.

It had long been J. K.'s dream to save the dune. Over a span of five years, J. K. never missed the tourism corporation's regular board meetings. Not one. He normally didn't speak unless LaPierre directly asked for his reaction to something on the agenda, but anytime it became obvious that assignments had not been completed by consultants or corporation staff, he did not mince words. He would quietly but with certainty make it clear that things needed to either pick up or alternative means or people would be found to get the job done. There was always the sense that if there had not been a board of direc-tors running the corporation (the community-level equivalent of company stockholders), J. K. would have seen things through much more quickly. It was sometimes obvious, given the pace he was used to keeping, that he was doing a good job of tempering his patience. Not many things are done by committee in the Irving world.

♦

People on the street might still be skeptical, but the twenty-first-century Irv-ings have begun to prove more and more that when there is an environmen-tally sound way to do things, they will do it. Their consciousness has been raised. Retired University of Moncton professor Louis LaPierre was the first to hold the university's Irving Chair of Sustainable Development. In his world, "retired" simply means a shift from the regularity of university life into a life of consulting, as well as plum appointments to committees and panels, such as the committee working to clean up the tar ponds in Sydney, Nova Scotia. In the spring of 2006, he spent nineteen consecutive days participating in hearings for the Sydney project, then turned around and made his contribu-tion to the project's report. It's the kind of work he's done all over the world, clear evidence that his credibility runs high. LaPierre first met J. K. Irving in 1982 as they both arrived at the Premier's Roundtable in New Brunswick, a group of experts and influencers assembled to advise government on how to make the economy and the environment more compatible. "So we sat together in many meetings, had many discussions and then he kind of took a liking to me." The feeling and the respect are mutual to the point that the two have become friends. LaPierre tells the story of J. K. landing his helicopter in LaPierre's yard on the beautiful Northumberland Strait coastal point known as Barachois. En route from Bouctouche to Saint John, he simply had the chopper plopped down to "have a little chat and have an apple."

After the convening of the Premier's Roundtable, the provincial government, J. K., and Ken Cox from NBTel put together enough funding to pay LaPierre's salary and cover his operational costs as his work became more and more focused on sustainable development. The university, meanwhile, had to backfill LaPierre's teaching position at the university. His role would later evolve into the Irving Chair of Sustainable Development. During this time of examining sustainability in forestry and other sectors of the economy, LaPierre really got to know the elder Irving. What soon emerged was the idea of creating model forests, with the Irvings advising the federal government that they would be prepared to support the one proposed for New Brunswick. The model was established in an area from Sussex up the coast to Moncton, the objective being to integrate all of the different viewpoints and objectives on forestry into a single management plan. This action coincided with or followed the international outcry over the clear-cutting practices of major forestry companies, including Greenpeace's activities in London, England, where activists paraded with old stumps to draw attention to the destruction of the world's forests. It was shortly after this episode that J. K. decided to respond to a University of Moncton funding campaign by creating the Irving Chair. J. K. asked LaPierre—he refers to him as "Dr. Louis"—what he thought would be needed to sustain a chair. "A million," was the answer. So the Irvings put in a million, which was followed by other supporters, such as CN, which put in half a million, "and a few other hundred thousand from here and there," according to LaPierre. But it was the relationship between LaPierre and J. K. that got the sustainability ball rolling.

Asked what precipitated a change in environmental consciousness among the Irvings, LaPierre takes a step back in time. He says that once you get to know where the Irvings came from, it becomes clear how and why they would emerge with this consciousness. "Don't forget that the three boys (Jim, Arthur, and Jack) were brought up in Bouctouche, playing in brooks, running on the sand dune, and doing those things as a kid. Those places were ingrained in them." LaPierre talks of J. K.'s times working in New Brunswick lumber camps, learning the business from the forest floor up, so to speak, working log drives down the rivers, running logging crews, and learning lessons from his father about how to cut logging roads. LaPierre and J.K. used to spend time sitting on a porch at the family's fishing lodge on the Restigouche River, chatting about all the new thinking in forestry, where it was all leading and how the Irvings should act in the future. LaPierre's visits sometimes lasted two or three days. Over that amount of time, two men can do an awful lot of chatting. "He has an awful lot of stories," says LaPierre. "Listening to him is like reading a book on the way it was forty years ago. He was very keen in understanding why these issues were moving forward, why you couldn't do this and that."

LaPierre says J.K. was very open to, and respectful of, divergent points of view and new developments in technology. To that end, he's moved away from day-to-day business, and as children Jim, Robert, Mary Jean, and Judith have taken the helm, J.K. has developed a strong interest in new areas, such as wind energy and the development of wind farms, which he thinks have a lot of potential. Thinking toward future business opportunity in that way is not something LaPierre was all that accustomed to. "I don't have any business savvy at all," he admits. "I mean, I'm not a businessperson. I'm not a stupid guy, but I'm not a businessperson. So I found it quite rewarding to be able to discuss some of the ideas that I had with someone who could really make a change. Because really, when [the Irvings] decide there's gonna be a change, they can make it happen quite quickly." LaPierre was much more left-leaning when he first earned his PhD and set about idealistically to change the world in David Suzuki–like fashion. He says he became much more realistic about the need to integrate environment and the economy through his time spent working with the Irvings. Earlier on, he says his attitude was more, "Hey, you've got to stop cutting." What LaPierre learned is that it is possible to integrate the economy and the environment in a managed structure, that you can have a protected, functional environment and still come out with financial gain.

In the past, the Irvings and their contemporaries hadn't considered how things were changing and why certain things were changing. "So I think," says LaPierre, "that J.K.'s time at the Premier's Roundtable and the discussions we had, together with the social pressures at the time, brought about the newer ways of thinking. There was also some political enticement at the time: 'If you do it this way, you can have this.' The bottom line is that J.K. learned that you couldn't cut trees to the brooks and the streams any longer." LaPierre says when J.K. learned such practices hurt the fish, he didn't want to do it anymore. "That's the last thing they'd want to have happen." And it all comes, he believes, from their childhoods. Discussions about growing up formed many of the personal and philosophical chats LaPierre and J.K.

shared with one another. "They were just part of a culture," says LaPierre. "They were part of the culture at the time and they've adapted and changed."

LaPierre believes that through their upbringing, the value of nature is actually ingrained in them, but that subconscious appreciation had to be brought to the surface. Once they learned that they were over-exploiting, they wanted to do something about it. At the same time, they began to learn that, as LaPierre described it, you can increase the take on the forest by 40 per cent of wood fibre per acre by following intensive forestry practices. Intensive forestry includes the mixing of species to avoid monocultures. In addition to higher productivity, this technique also contributes to an increase in wildlife survival rates. Monocultures invite insects to consume trees later down the road. It's great to plant trees, but if they all get eaten, what's the point? What LaPierre says companies like the Irvings need to do is mimic nature by looking at how a natural forest functions, with things like insects, fires, and lightning strikes. Today, fires are suppressed. "So if you want to look at any activity over the landscape that closely mimics widespread forest fires by the clear-cutting of trees, if it's properly done in a spatial way, by understanding fires, you can put in a very interesting spatial management plan. They were quite interested in this objective," says LaPierre. But in earlier days, "they just didn't know how to go about it." He provides other esoteric, technical examples about how forestry practices have changed. Machinery used for cutting can leave deep ruts in forested lands, contributing to the destruction of remaining roots and plant life. But if you move to wider tires with lower pressure—five pounds per square inch versus twenty-eight or thirty-eight pounds per square inch—you can minimize the impacts. If foresters also create road "mats" on the ground using branches from cut trees, there is, again, lessened impact.

LaPierre believes K. C. replanted trees because trees made money. Neither he nor his contemporaries understood in their day what science would later reveal, things like how to cut roads through a forest, how to plant a diverse versus monoculture forest, how to avoid erosion and negative impact on rivers and streams, and how best to condition the forest floor after cutting. LaPierre claims the Irvings now conduct forestry practices based on protected area strategies of their own lands. They've identified special areas and now dedicate and want to protect them. What of the skeptical constituency that sees this kind of talk and activity as window dressing? "From my experience with [the Irvings], I think they're quite sincere. The question is learning how to do things the right way." Sectors competing for land use, such as those in tourism and environmentalists, argue that modern practices or not, the Irvings and other major corporate wood harvesting interests still don't have it right, or that there simply shouldn't be clear-cutting at all, no matter how many trees are replanted. There are business people along the Restigouche River in northern New Brunswick (a Canadian Heritage River designation) who say that Irving harvesting practices are directly and negatively impacting both the quality of the river and its water levels.

But LaPierre insists that once state-of-the-art forestry practices were learned inside J. D. Irving Ltd., they became the internal protocol and then became the foundation of performance criteria for engaging external contractors. "So the guy in the field, if he cut too close to a brook or if he didn't build a road right, he was dinged. If he did it right, then he got bonuses."

There are contemporaries of Dr. LaPierre's who aren't quite so sympathetic with the Irvings or quite so ready to applaud their efforts. One such person is Dr. Martin Willison, a full professor jointly appointed in the Biology Department (the Faculty of Science) and the School for Resource and Environmental Studies (the Faculty of Management) at Dalhousie University in Halifax. In April of 2007, Willison was on sabbatical at a university in China, but in the late 1990s his activities in Canada included membership on the Maritimes Regional Steering Committee of the Forest Stewardship Council (FSC), an organization whose mission is to promote environmentally appropriate, socially beneficial and economically viable management of the world's forests. The Steering Committee produced a report recommending forestry practice standards which were adopted by the FSC International in 2002.

Willison admits to being a "card-carrying Doctor of Philosophy" who generally lives in the ivory tower of academia, so he's aware of the possible accusation that he's a dreamer who doesn't have to deal with the realities of producing jobs and driving the economy. On the other hand, he says, he's sixty-three years old and working in a part of China described as a national poverty area. He says he's doing his best to try and see and understand the world outside the protective walls of the ivory tower and has always done so.

Dr. Willison's perspective on the Irvings goes all the way back to his years as a young university student in Kidderminster, England, a place with a reputation as a one-industry town—the industry being carpet-making. The second largest factory was Brinton's, a family-owned company where Willison worked summers and that is still in operation today. Mr. Brinton lived in a mansion on a landscaped estate with horse paddocks across the street from the Willison family's modest semi-detached home. The schoolmate who arranged for Willison's summer employment there in 1963 is still with the company today.

Willison is reminded of the Brinton factory when he considers that there are many Irving employees who have similarly dedicated their lives in the employ of the various family companies. And he is also reminded of Mr. Brinton in the person of J. K. Irving. He knows there must be differences between the two men, but says there also seem to be parallels. "Mr. Brinton's family were prominent conservatives who mixed business with electoral politics. The Irving family members have shied away from formal politics, but have been highly influenced by means of informal politics within New Brunswick." Willison has worked for Brinton and also spent some time in the forest with J. K. Irving. "When walking in the forest, Jim (J. K.) Irving and I saw things differently. He viewed it through the eyes of a merchant, a utilitarian business perspective; I saw it as one who loves the natural world. Of course, I could glimpse the merchant's perspective and I expect that he could glimpse the naturalist's perspective. He talked knowledgeably and confidently about the company's forest management practices while we walked in a [Irving] plantation. It was clear that he had a good grasp of all aspects of his company's business."

Willison says some people have painted J. D. Irving Ltd. as a "bete noir" among forestry companies and land managers, while the company paints itself as a progressive leader. "I think neither is true. The company has built itself on people management. In the traditional manner of the family company, employees have been drawn into the family and become dedicated to it. The J. D. Irving approach to land management has taken a long-term view, provided this is also compatible with advancement of the family-owned enterprises." Willison says it was clear from his experience spending time with J. K. that although he is a "big fish," he sees himself as "a big fish in a small pond."

"Most people would be more than happy to live in a pond of that size," says Willison, "but he has the restless character of the driven entrepreneur."

When it comes to sustainable forestry practices, Willison sees J. D. Irving Ltd. as being in the middle of the pack in Canada. (Keep in mind that on a global scale, Canada is considered a little ahead of the middle of the pack.) "JDI has been innovative at times," he says, "such as keeping up with advances in forest science." But considering they buy a lot of wood from small contractors, many of whom have low standards of forestry practices, the company's relative overall position tends to drop. In Nova Scotia, where Willison is most knowledgeable, JDI is on par with their competitor, Bowater, whereas Stora "are the medalists with respect to being the most-improved company."

Not only has Willison walked through the woods with J. K., but they have also sat next to one another on a plane while flying over New Brunswick. While looking down at J. D. Irving forests, J. K. pointed also to potato farms that run adjacent and stated "strongly and unequivocally" that his company's forest management practices are far more benign environmentally than potato farming. "Of course, this is true," says Willison, explaining that potato farms exist in soils that are so poor biologically that they offer less than half the value in outcomes (for example, cleaning air and water) compared to forests.

Since companies like J. D. Irving Ltd. replant forests, the biological contribution of trees is restored, except for the period during which trees are being harvested and replanted, which is only for a moment in the grand scheme of things. Because this is what the Irvings do, Willison says that J. K. has a "landscape-scale environmental vision." On the other hand, J. K. claimed that the forest over which they were flying was only slightly modified from its wild state, "which was not true," according to Willison. During the Forestry Stewardship Council analysis, J. K. was "very keen" to win support for his effort to obtain certification for one particular district, but to do so would have required that the forestry operations meet all aspects of the standards being written by the Steering Committee. However, "the majority of the committee were in agreement with his company's representatives with regard to many objectives of the standards process, but there were a few very significant disagreements."

Asked directly what the Irvings could do to improve their forestry practices, Willison says the answer would require a separate book, but there are some pointers. He says that their practices have been improving and so continuing in the direction taken in recent years would be a good move. Obtaining FSC certification of all of their operations would also be a good move and exceeding rather than just meeting FSC standards of practice would also be recommended. Lastly, as many people have come to recognize, Willison says there is the need to develop a new relationship with the earth and this includes more caring relationships with each other as humans. "I think that JDI and the other Irving companies suffer from the aggressive competitive disease which is born of insecurity—the apparent need to beat everyone in a race to the end, where the end is the destruction of our Earthly home."

That race is seen by one long-time Maritime forester, who agreed to speak off the record, as being very detrimental to the environment. This individual has been involved in the same forestry standards assessment process as Dr. Willison, and says he is very knowledgeable about the forestry practices of J. D. Irving Ltd. in both New Brunswick and Nova Scotia.

"My current view," he says, "is that the forestry practices of J. D. Irving Ltd. are far and away the most ecologically destructive of any company now operating in the Maritimes," contradicting those who say the company is making positive changes. "This is not because their practices of clear-cutting, biocide spraying, road building, plantation management, and conversion of natural Acadian forest are worse than those of some other large forestry companies, but because JDI is so much more efficient at forest liquidation and so good at covering up the real story."

He says they are not even close to being able to meet the FSC standards, even though those standards have, in his opinion, recently been diluted. The source is equally disturbed by what he calls the "propaganda" spun by the Irvings. "Unfortunately for the well-being of the natural Acadian forest landscape, JDI is also very efficient at spinning its rationalization for forest exploitation." He went on to say that if this issue is not written about accurately, "it will be a further disservice to the human and non-human beings of this region."

◆

J.K. set out in 1994 to learn a whole lot more about sustainability. He, LaPierre, the federal and provincial governments, and local community interests embarked on a project that in one fell swoop corrected a number of environmental threats and created a model sustainable tourism community. It's no coincidence that that community was Bouctouche. As described earlier, over the next five years, J.K. never missed a single meeting of the board of directors of Bouctouche Bay Eco-Tourism Inc. The board consisted of scientists, bureaucrats (including myself), fishery interests, agricultural and community interests, and tourism operators. The project—really a multitude of projects under one umbrella effort—took J.K. on a sequence of habitat and sustainability learning excursions to such places as Cape Hatteras, North Carolina; Hillsborough College in Tampa, Florida; and St. George Island on Florida's Gulf Coast, a place where endangered sea turtles amble amid the ruins of US army training facilities from the Second World War. By the time the project was over, J.K. had invested more than $2 million (as had the public sector), transforming Bouctouche into a well-managed tourism community boasting a new marina, walking and biking trails, and protection for the oyster fishery, all accompanied by a host of new entrepreneurial tourism opportunities. The centrepiece of the initiative was the Irving Bouctouche Dune, located within a breath of Irvingdale, J.K.'s boyhood family cottage. Two years after the dune was completed, J.K. and LaPierre found themselves winging their way to a black-tie dinner in London, England, to accept a British Airways Sustainable Tourism award. "Number one," says LaPierre, "he was going back to his childhood days and learning a lot of the science that could protect the things he liked."

LaPierre says the attitude has spilled over onto the oil side of the equation as well. The decision to retool the Saint John refinery and produce low-sulphur fuel ahead of the industry curve was the result of smart environmental vision linked squarely to a big future payoff. In 2004 the Irving refinery received the North American Refinery of the Year award from World Fuels, which is cutely referred to as the Stanley Cup of the oil sector. The Saint John facility remains the only one to receive a Clean Air Excellence award from the US Environmental Protection Agency. This gives them bragging rights to being a unique supplier of gasoline in the stringent and environmentally conscious state of California. The company has since moved on to produce ultra-low-sulphur diesel fuel. Certainly part of what triggered this kind of thinking and action was the perpetual negative media exposure criticizing emissions from the Saint John refinery. LaPierre says the Irvings figured, if they were going to clean up air quality, they might as well go all the way, and improve the quality of the products they were putting out. He adds that even in their takeover of shipyards, like the East Isle Shipyard in Georgetown, PEI, cleaning things up became a "special vocation."

On the matter of ships, one albatross around Irving Oil's neck lasted for twenty-seven years: the infamous sinking of the *Irving Whale*, which went down in stormy waters off the PEI north shore, in the Gulf of St. Lawrence, in September 1970. LaPierre says the company got a bad rap over the *Whale*. Ships have always sunk, he says, but when this vessel went down, fishermen and environmentalists were terrified about the possibility of the ship's cargo of 4,200 tonnes of bunker C oil ruining the sea bottom, the Island coastline, and the vast resources associated with both. "You know, when it sunk out there, they were told the best thing to do was to leave it there. But when the [oil] started leaking out, well, they didn't know any better [what to do] than anybody else." LaPierre says there was nowhere for the Irvings to go for an answer. No one knew at the time how to raise the vessel without the risk of it breaking up and causing a marine disaster. Even when the *Whale* was raised, on July 30, 1996, the company took a substantial rap on the knuckles for the amount of Canadian taxpayers' money that brought about the undertaking. They were definitely the bad guys of the *Whale* saga. As LaPierre argues that "there are many ships which have sunk and not one of them garnished the time and press that the *Irving Whale* did," suggesting the company got a long-term bad rap.

◆

Willa Mavis wasn't always an advocate of the Irvings and their stance on business and the environment. Her father, Arthur Gorham, was of the same generation as K. C. Irving. He was a fish exporter who, like most of the public, was an observer of K. C.'s amazing business progression. Also like many others, he was not terribly enthusiastic about some of K. C.'s business tactics. So like a lot of other New Brunswickers, Mavis admittedly had a bit of an attitude about the Irvings.

In 1992, just after she and husband Ross had opened their dream business, the popular Inn on the Cove on Sand Cove Road in Saint John, she found herself on a media collision course that occupied her time and New Brunswick's news headlines for nearly two years. Although the inn has earned its place as a fixture in Saint John, it appeared for a time that the couple's site selection for their enterprise might have been a bad choice. Willa and Ross are two hard-working individuals who had a vision for an upscale inn overlooking the Bay of Fundy tides. In person, she comes across as both smart and a sharp dresser, someone who's super organized, with a good eye for design and detail. He's as amiable as Al Waxman, a guy who can cook up a storm and whose ultimate desire is to put a smile on the face of the guests who walk through the front door of their establishment. So the two were well-suited to the tourism business, a sector that demands a diversity of talent, creativity, and entrepreneurial savvy. The couple had just moved to Saint John from western Canada, scraping together for the business every penny they had, including the cash from their RRSPs and a sum of money borrowed by their son.

Then just two weeks into their operation—after months of investment, construction, and preparation—an Irving official unexpectedly knocked on their door. It wasn't a room for the night that he was interested in. His name was Bill Borland, the Irving pulpmill's environmental officer. He was there to explain about plans to build what he termed "waste water treatment facilities" on the property immediately adjacent to the newly minted tourism enterprise. The treatment facilities were intended to make the Irving pulpmill compliant with environmental regulations. She and husband Ross had a different description of the proposed facilities. "We called them toxic waste lagoons, because that's really what they were." The day Borland came to the door with the news (it was a legal requirement that the adjacent residents be officially notified of a scheduled public meeting), Ross arrived home from the day job he then held as head of the Saint John United Way and it just happened their son Greg was home on a break from his Great Lakes shipping job. When they got through "the double speak," as they call it, and with the wind completely knocked out of them, the Mavises realized the proposal meant there would be a four-foot-diameter pipeline running by their place carrying effluent from the two local Irving mills to adjacent Sheldon Point, where the treatment facilities would cleanse the mill's waste water. "It was like somebody kicked me right in the chest," she says fourteen years after the fact. From the dining room of the inn, you can almost touch Sheldon's Point. For a tourism enterprise whose entire cachet was founded on the beautiful Bay of Fundy and its natural surroundings, it truly was an investment nightmare in the making. Oddly, Mavis says she didn't really see it as a fight with the Irvings. She saw it as a matter of dealing with a major company that had simply chosen the wrong way to solve a problem they were faced with—and they'd chosen one of the worse possible locations.

A former stringer for CBC radio in Saint John and for the weekly *Kings County Record*, Mavis knew exactly what she had to do. It didn't hurt that husband Ross had once owned a weekly paper in British Columbia. When the public meeting took place, a pre-event telephone campaign she embarked on achieved its desired effect. At that initial meeting, it was standing-room-only, including a pack of media representatives. Out of that meeting came a coalition that she formed and led, known as the Save Our Shores committee. "SOS" as set to become a familiar phrase in the New Brunswick legislature and in New Brunswick households. The committee set to work: they got their hands on the environmental assessments; they held an open house; and they conducted an open public walk of Sheldon's Point "so that people could see exactly the land that was in jeopardy." At that walk, the Mavises met Gary Presser, an individual from Red Head, New Brunswick, with a strong background in environmental matters. Over the following weeks, Willa and Presser spent twelve hours per day together on the phone. Willa and Presser did most of the committee's legwork, bulldozing their way ahead in an effort to stop the company's plans. As Mavis explains, "We gave the impression that we had a huge, huge team behind us—and there were several other people on the committee—but it was really Gary and I."

Her conspicuous absence from a brand spanking new hospitality business put a lot of stress on the venture, but with their life's investment at stake, the Mavises really didn't have a choice but to fight the Irving plan. Some suggested they should just sell their property to the Irvings and be done with it. "But I said, 'That's not the solution at all. I wouldn't do that to my neighbours,'" says Mavis. "You know, I mean it was the wrong thing to do on the Bay of Fundy, and our goal was to convince them that it was the wrong thing to do."

So for two full years, Willa was on radio, on television, and in the papers—"so much so there were people who thought I was an elected official, yet they couldn't remember having voted for me." It was a tough time for lots of reasons, including people having both purposeful and passive opposition to her stand. Some Saint Johners defended the Irvings with comments like, "Where would we be without the Irvings?" and, "You shouldn't be doing that."

"I mean," Mavis recalls, "[then mayor] Elsie Wayne was saying, 'How dare you pick on those poor boys!' Yeah, the little innkeeper who's totally broke is picking on those multi-billionaires." Wayne is known across Canada for her antiquated style of politics. (It must have given Jean Charest shivers the day after the 1993 federal election when he awoke to find it was only the two of them who remained as Progressive Conservatives in the new Canadian parliament.) She clings to that old way of doing business that the Irvings, in earlier times, became associated with. Wayne shunned Mavis and refused to even speak with her.

Mavis couldn't quite grasp this notion of "where would Saint John be without the Irvings." "Let's turn it around the other way," she says. "There's always people to fill a void. If the Inn on the Cove wasn't here, something else would be here. I mean, let's not have that kind of an ego that we feel that, 'My goodness, if it wasn't for Willa Mavis.' I just don't have an ego like that. So if K. C. Irving hadn't moved here in 1927 or whatever, somebody else would have. Somebody else would have seen some value in the city somewhere. What makes Moncton tick? What makes other areas tick? I think we have to be pleased that they've stayed here. And kudos to them because they're setting the example. They're saying, 'We can live here and we can have fabulous homes and lifestyles in Saint John.'" But ultimately, Mavis says the Irvings have to be kept in some kind of reasonable perspective.

In his efforts to defend the Sheldon's Point plan, Bill Borland had made several public references to a facility near Terrace Bay, Ontario, on which the Sheldon's Point project would supposedly be modelled. According to Willa, he'd said it would look like a small man-made lake where people would picnic on Sundays. So Greg Mavis took off for Terrace Bay in his Honda with his camera in hand. For starters, the facility was ten miles out of town, so no wonder it didn't affect anyone. Greg ended up being kicked off the property, but by then he had captured what he went there for—photographs. The images he took showed a lagoon with fog rising from the water's surface and foam "oozing over the sides," not quite the idyllic little lake described by Borland.

That same summer, the second summer of the ordeal, the Mavises were sailing with friends on nearby Grand Bay when a worker from the inn called Greg's cell phone saying J. K. wanted to meet with Willa at two o'clock that afternoon. They sped off the bay and returned to the inn to shower. "I said to Greg, 'Put on your Acadia shirt,'" which he did. The Irvings of course are alumni of the Wolfville-based university. With his Acadia shirt, sincere, honest face, blonde hair, and tall frame, he had the right look. She put on a skirt and a crisp blouse, "because I knew they were people like that. We were fighting fire with fire." When J. K. walked into the Ocean Room of the inn for the first time, he reacted the same way everyone does when they see the view. "I just stood there to see what the reaction would be," says Willa. It didn't hurt that it was a perfect August day, complete with blue sky and clouds so fluffy and nice they looked like props. J.K. is a fairly big man, but so was Greg's grandfather, her previous father-in-law, who was six-foot-four, so she wasn't about to be intimidated. "'Mrs. Mavis,'" she remembers him saying, "'if I could just turn you around to my way of thinking.' And I looked him right in the eye and I said, 'Mr. Irving, if I could just turn you around to my way of thinking.'" To this day, Willa believes J.K. was being misled by the company's planners and engineers. He was shown Greg's "clandestine" photographs and admitted to her he wouldn't want to live beside anything remotely like the Terrace Bay facility. J.K.'s eyes were opened, but a tipping point in the public debate occurred with the airing of an episode of CBC's now-defunct regional news magazine show, *Land and Sea*. The producer put the show together in a way that juxtaposes Borland speaking of the idyllic lake with the camera panning the photos Greg took in Terrace Bay. It was a humiliating media moment for the Irvings.

Throughout the two years, Willa had been obsessively stalking politicians at events and openings. Along came a Sunday afternoon function at the old New Brunswick Museum that she knew then premier Frank McKenna and then provincial environment minister Jane Barry would be attending. "So Sunday afternoon I get all dressed up and I go to the old museum. And I'm sitting on the aisle, on the left hand side, and that's the side that Mr. McKenna was coming down. Pushy thing that I am, I jumped up and said, 'Mr. McKenna, I don't know whether you remember me.'"

McKenna jumped in and said: "Of course I do. You're the woman who wants to save our shores."

Willa responded with a simple, "Yes."

And he replied, "And you have."

To which Willa responded, "Pardon me?"

"You have," he repeated. "I met with the Irvings earlier this week and they are going to do this magnificent treatment facility [at the mill site] and so you've won."

"Mr. McKenna, would it be appropriate to give you a hug."

"By all means."

As she hugged the premier, Willa could not believe the turn of events. The technology the Irvings ended up implementing made them world leaders in treating pulpmill effluent. There came a day when J.K. called Willa, introduced himself, and thanked her for "making us do this the right way." When the Irvings' public announcement about the new plan finally came, the Mavises were thirty thousand feet in the air en route to a Florida vacation. But later, for the official launch of the new facility, Willa Mavis went alone. That afternoon, she was helped with her coat and in finding a chair by none other than Jim Irving, who acknowledged her presence during his remarks. But J. K., in his remarks, went much further: "None of us would be here today if it hadn't been for Willa Mavis." She was truly blown away. He went on to say to her, in front of the assembled crowd, that if there was anything she thought the Irvings should be doing, "you let me know." Did he really mean what he was saying? "He meant it," Mavis is convinced. She goes on to say that J. K. Irving is a very sincere guy. She adds that you don't have to always be right in the beginning, so long as you're morally right in the end, which she feels he was.

Today, at a site within view of Sheldon's Point is the Irving Nature Park, the iconic gift from the Irvings to the people of Saint John and everyone else who cares to visit. The park is a six-hundred-acre site that the Irvings describe as having been saved from the threat of environmental decline. Since the conclusion of the Save Our Shores campaign, the Mavises have become good friends with Kelly Honeyman, who's a neighbour and who manages the nature park. The Irvings also planted all the trees along Sand Cove Road leading to the park. J. K.'s wife Jean has seen to it that daffodils are planted along the route. It's all a far, far cry from where the lagoon would have taken them.

Mavis later received an invitation to speak to the city's environment committee about how one person can get things done. She told the entire story, including the part about J. K.'s call. "He's a real gentleman," she told the assembled group, not realizing that J. K. was sitting discreetly at the back of the room. When the committee proceedings were concluded, the chair invited comments from the gallery. J. K. stood and reportedly said, "I just want to say that if you've got any projects around here that you want done, you just ask Willa and me and we'll get it done." She never did take him up on his offer to call. "He's a busy man and I'm busy as well," she says. The ultimate irony for the Mavises came in the form of an award. The Tourism Industry Association of New Brunswick inaugurated a K. C. Irving award for excellence. It was presented to them personally at the podium by Kenneth, in honour of his grandfather.

◆

Former New Brunswick bureaucrat George Bouchard says the heightened Irving consciousness about public relations and the environment comes partly from the problem that they've already got a strike against them whenever they start a new project, due to public attitudes and perception. The reason is both simple and understandable: "In New Brunswick, a lot of people think they're taking too much space." Having to override such attitudes and perceptions is "pushing" the twenty-first-century Irvings to counteract some of the old Irving ways. So serious is Jim Irving about counteracting the old ways that Bouchard recalls him several years ago spending every Monday during the summer with groups of thirty to forty teachers at the Iriving operation in Juniper, illustrating and speaking about how the company was treating the forests. This was a precursor to having programs in New Brunswick's schools, which evolved in 1996 into the J.D. Irving Limited Forest Discovery Box, a professionally developed, curriculum-based product that features hands-on forest materials like "tree cookies" (slices of tree trunks showing rings), tree pollen, forest maps, and magnifying glasses. Six videos were produced to take forest operations and issues into the classrooms. All the materials are available in both French and English. Teachers and students helped design the box and its contents in partnership with the company's foresters. Its arrival in classrooms across New Brunswick was greeted with overwhelming enthusiasm. Over one thousand Forest Discovery Boxes are now in use in schools in New Brunswick, Nova Scotia, and Maine.

To help make sure the project happened, Jim invited a group of senior provincial bureaucrats to the Irvings' Restigouche River fishing lodge to discuss the school program before it took shape. The group included Bouchard, Jack Syroid, Tim Andrew, and Claire Morris. According to Bouchard, an avid fly fisherman and registered fishing guide, Jim had said, "We're going to have dinner at the lodge and then we'll go fishing before going back to Fredericton." But when dinner ended, the bureaucrats were looking at one another surreptitiously and wondering, "When are we going to go fishing?" Knowing Bouchard, he must have been chomping at the bit to get on the river. Jim, however, was less enthusiastic about fishing than he was about talking through the schools program idea. The group did eventually get to go fishing, but not until Jim was finished tapping their minds.

◆

There was a time when most New Brunswickers and Maritimers would not have associated the word "environment" with the name "Irving." But some say that is changing. One of Canada's top environmental scientists thinks the Irvings' interest in being good corporate environmental citizens is legitimate. "It's legit and in such interesting ways," he said. "There's no question that they're world leaders in sustainable forest management. It's not bullshit. It's real." The facts speak for themselves, he said, like the fact that K.C.

was planting trees and investing in the future before any other company in Canada. It wasn't just responsible. It was smart on K. C.'s part, an individual with an old-school outlook, one that is attached to the land. The source said that as far as the environment goes, the Irvings hire the best experts to advise them. "So they're as good or better than anybody else in New Brunswick in that regard."

Asked if the Irvings are following government regulatory processes, the source said the environment is an area where they will pay for what's required to get the best job done. "They don't cheap out on that. When they get documents that are produced for their regulatory processes, you'll see that they're as rigorous as anyone's—or more." "Land is important and valuable," said the source, adding that contrary to much public opinion about K. C., "He was sort of a husband to the land."

19. The Interactive Philanthropists

As mentioned earlier, the Irivngs have tended to treat philanthropy as a private and unostentatious matter. Even as they've become increasingly active as philanthropists, they have not sought the limelight. Assumption Life president Denis Losier and others tell of the Irvings lending the company jet to assist families needing access to specialized hospitals in the United States or elsewhere. Losier says they wouldn't want any publicity for such acts "because it's not their way of doing things. They know they can do that and they do it, but they don't want people to know about it."

A similar Irving initiative that is visible is Irving Oil's Fuel the Care program, an initiative providing Irving gift certificates to assist families needing to travel long distances for serious family health care matters. According to the company's own literature, Fuel the Care has provided assistance to nearly seven thousand families from Atlantic Canada and New England. Interestingly, to apply for the program, you don't call Irving Oil. The company has entrusted evaluation of the candidates to the hospital facilities themselves, notably those specializing in medical care for kids, including the IWK Health Centre in Halifax, Saint John Regional Hospital, and the Janeway Child Health and Rehabilitation Centre in St. John's. There's a similar network in the United States coordinated through the Children's Miracle Network of Eastern Maine Healthcare Systems.

Losier is almost awed by the impact the Irvings have on social development in their region. "It's just incredible," he says. "All around Atlantic Canada they're making their contribution in communities wherever they have some employees. They're reinvesting back some of their money into health care, education, and in schools." And when it comes to the Irvings, there is no investment dividing line, Losier suggests, between anglophone and francophone people and communities. Nor do they discriminate based on size. They're into sponsoring things big and small, an endless stream of sponsorships at the urging of every team and organization that believes they should be the apple of the Irvings' eye.

In the summer of 2006, author and University of Moncton professor Donald Savoie had just attended a meeting of the Trudeau Foundation held in Wolfville, Nova Scotia. The trip to the Annapolis Valley town included a visit to the K. C. Irving Environmental Science Centre, a gift from the Irving family to Acadia University in 2002. A member of the foundation, Savoie had urged the board to meet there because they'd met in every other region of Canada except the Maritimes. Everyone associated with the foundation was blown away with what the Irvings' contributions have wrought at their most common alma mater. "It's really remarkable," says Savoie, which speaks loudly from a man who spends much of his time these days at Oxford University. "I usually stop to buy gas at an Irving," Savoie explains. "The reason I do—and I don't know anything about gas. I have no idea whether they have better or worse gas, but I'll tell you one thing: that whatever they get for a gallon, whatever they get for a litre, if they're going to invest it anywhere, it's going to be in my region. If I buy Imperial Oil, well it's for Stanford—bye, bye. Stanford will be the endowment. So I have a certain bias."

According to Acadia's website, the environmental science centre was created to encourage the cross-fertilization of ideas among students, faculty, and community, a place where students can study, professors can hold seminars and give presentations, and the university community can host readings, artistic performances, and formal scholarly gatherings. Its design and the materials used, especially the selection of wood finishes, fulfil the family desire that the centre be infused with the natural world. The gift included facilities for botanical and environmental research, six acres of public gardens (the Harriett Irving Botanical Gardens) representing native plant communities of the Acadia Forest Region, a glassed-in winter garden, a garden of medicinal and food plants, plus fully wired conferencing and educational facilities. The science centre not only dramatically enhanced the already prestigious Acadia campus, but is also now a major attraction throughout the region serving as a catalyst to the Academy for the Environment. The Irvings, especially Arthur Sr., were involved in every aspect of the centre's development. After all, it has his father's name on it.

Savoie also points to the level of personal commitment J. K. and son Jim gave to the University of Moncton's most recent fundraising campaign, which by all accounts was a highly successful venture. "I have to tell you, they rolled up their sleeves and did the work. They didn't just co-chair this to be co-chair. They made their calls and so on." This echoes Denis Losier's description of doing fundraising calls for the university with Jim. They would do their business and be on their way with very little muss, fuss, or small talk.

There's no arguing that as the Irvings' resources have grown, so has their philanthropic order of magnitude and its impact on both the people and communities of Atlantic Canada. Savoie mostly credits J. K. and Arthur Sr. with this growing momentum. There's also the possibility, he believes, that Arthur's second wife, Sandra, might have contributed to the change, as has J. K.'s wife Jean. "Sandra Irving is very much a community-minded person," says Savoie. "She gives a lot to the community, is involved in all kinds of activities, and has got a big generous heart. I think she might have pushed Arthur there a bit." He adds that a lot of people are curious about the growing emergence of the Irvings in community circles. "The answer why, I don't know. What I do know is that they have really moved and they're very much a part of the community."

◆

Steve Carson, Irving veteran and executive director of Enterprise Saint John, knows all about the family's community-mindedness. His story illustrates how sometimes it's been Irving employees, in addition to the family members themselves, who've perhaps kept community-support activity out of the media spotlight. As a native Saint Johner, Carson was always active in the community, involved to one degree or another in the transitions that were positively affecting the city. His story took place in the mid-1980s, a fairly exciting time for the city. Carson had recently bought a Victorian row house on Orange Street and was involved in the city's Heritage Trust and related initiatives involving preservation of the city's heritage. One day, there was an intervention on the part of one of the senior Irving management people, one of the stalwarts who had a reputation for keeping other employees in line. "He was the eyes and ears kind of guy" when the Irvings were out of the building, explains Carson. This was part of the company's culture. "He took me aside one day and he was always very good to me, but he said, 'You're involved in some organizations out there and you might just want to be careful not to get too active or too high a profile because sometimes around here, you know, you've got to stick to your work.'" Carson says the man was trying to do him a favour by being frank. What he meant, of course, was that if the perception built that Carson had too much time on his hands, then maybe, just maybe, people would start to think he wasn't pulling his weight at the office. "That was a pretty strong message," says Carson. He recalls shortly thereafter being asked to chair some organization in the city and deciding to decline the opportunity. "Maybe that's not what I want to be doing right now," he told the askers.

What the elder Irving statesman, the friendly advice-giver, was perhaps not completely in touch with, was how the Irvings themselves were getting more and more involved in the community. Shortly after the exchange, Arthur Sr. stopped Carson in the office hallway one day and said, "I notice you're involved in some of the heritage work going on in the community." Carson froze, believing he might be in for a lecture about putting work before other commitments. He quickly scoured his mind for an explanation that would characterize his involvement as being minimal, something like referring to the restoration of his own Victorian row house on Orange Street. But that's not where Arthur's head was at. "There's some really good initiatives there," he said to Carson. "If you ever need a hand, let me know." Carson breathed a sigh of relief and realized on reflection that the "old guard" within the Irving business culture was gradually being ushered out the door. He says that in hindsight, the experience with Arthur coincided with a new emerging sense that being involved in the community was the right page to be on.

"The company's still transitioning today," he says, "with employees [getting] more involved in the community. We're seeing a lot more of that, much more of that now. I think a lot of it has been driven by the senior Irvings, the three brothers, because they're at a point where they've got time and an able organization under them and sons and daughters that are very capable, that they now have the opportunity to take a few steps out of the organization, take that business experience they have and address things in the community." Although there are a myriad of things they're involved in, from universities to sustainable tourism projects to civic buildings to who knows what else, Carson hones in on J. K.'s personal contribution of time and money to the anti-poverty initiative at Prince Charles School in Saint John, discussed below. Carson says the initiative began with J. K. not just sending money, but asking probing questions and saying, "We need to understand this." The result was a study commissioned on behalf of the school to come to grips with the issues causing poverty in and around the school. Carson says the last thing the Irvings want to do is get involved in something just by writing a cheque. "Many people are looking [to the Irvings] for donations to do things, but I can't think of too many examples where they've contributed significantly to something and not wanted to add value other than just a dollar amount. When they take something on, they take it on with the same approach and passion that they do with their business." That's the kind of involvement that saw Arthur Sr. head up Ducks Unlimited nationally for a period of time. Carson says each one of them seems to go wherever their interests lie. "I don't imagine they sit around on a Saturday morning and say, 'You know, you should do this and I should do that.'"

Enterprise Saint John first emerged in 1994 when the business community decided it was time to fold the city economic office in favour of a private sector–led organization that would have fewer layers and less bureaucracy. While initially Carson was involved in the recruitment of an individual to head the new operation, the executive search eventually fell through and Carson began to consider the job himself. In spite of his curiosity about the job, there was a something nagging at Carson's mind about economic development and overall picture of business in Saint John—what he calls the "two agendas in the community." The two agendas were the community agenda and the perceived or real Irving agenda. The issue was that the Irvings were big and resourceful enough unto themselves that they could basically do whatever they wanted. "They just continued to build and evolve and grow," he says, saying even ahead of the October 2006 oil refinery announcement that there was no end in sight to that potential for growth.

In those days, the Irvings were so busy, says Carson, they really didn't seem to have much time for community economic development that wasn't directly under their purview. Meanwhile, the community understood that most of what the Irvings did was basically good for the community in one way or another, while also believing that the Irvings didn't care about the well-being of other businesses and wanted to own everything, run everything, and buy from no one but themselves. He says there might have been a time when this was more the case, in the 1960s and early 1970s—the era when K.C. was expanding the business to such gigantic proportions. But from his perspective within Irving Oil, he honestly didn't think this was the case any longer.

The only person able to help Carson clear his mind and make a decision was Arthur Sr. himself. Saturday mornings were traditionally a good time (and reportedly still are) for Irving Oil executives to deal with a lot of the weekday issues that were "leaking" from the week previous. Carson says there was always a group in the office on Saturday mornings. It was also a good time to "get people's ear on things," including Arthur Sr.'s. He wound up one particular Saturday morning in Arthur's office and the two went over a few Irving Oil matters before the conversation turned to what was really crowding Carson's mind. Much to Carson's surprise and satisfaction, they had a very open and frank conversation about the supposed two agendas. Carson didn't directly reference the anti-Irving sentiment that existed throughout the community, but Arthur did. And he told Carson that he was "sick and tired of people saying that we're not encouraging new business, that we don't want business to come here. That's the only way our business is going to grow, is if that happens." Carson says Arthur told him that if he chose to accept the job at Enterprise Saint John, any time there was a new business looking at Saint John that believed the Irvings would not be supportive, "I want you to tell me. I'll talk to them." Carson comments, "I don't know if it was a good thing or a bad thing that he didn't try to convince me to stay." In the end, he took his leave from Irving Oil with Arthur's blessing, took the Enterprise Saint John position, and claims that what Arthur offered and promised that Saturday morning has happened, not only with Arthur himself, but also with J. K. and his son Jim.

Two years after Carson went to Enterprise Saint John, there was an opportunity to court an operation linked to what he described as one of the "biggest logos in the world." Part of the training he received at Irving Oil, what he calls his "Irving MBA," including that unmistakable Irving attention to detail, rubbed off on Carson. Part of the preparation for wooing that client to Saint John involved placing a call to J. K. to seek a favour. He asked J. K. to consider making a call to a key individual from the prospect company whom Carson knew was a friend of his, someone with whom he was known to have a good working relationship. J. K. thanked Carson for including him in the process and, although he downplayed whatever role he might be able to play in the pitch, said he'd be happy to have such a discussion if the opportunity arose. Two days later, J. K. called Carson to advise that he'd made the call, adding, "I don't know if I'm any help or not" and opining that "building businesses and growing businesses in this community is what we all need to work on together." J. K. wound up the conversation by thanking Carson for asking him in the first place. A few weeks later, the client made a commitment to invest in a Saint John operation. Carson says J. K.'s action in that instance is just one example of the many things the Irvings have done over the years that refute the widely held perceptions of their extreme competitiveness.

◆

Philanthropy has a history of well-resourced people dropping off nice fat cheques and disappearing back into their castles. This doesn't diminish their good intentions or the positive effect of what they do. But the Irvings have shown that when they choose a cause, they love getting involved with the same degree of vigour and enthusiasm that they apply to their own businesses. It may be philosophical or it could be that they just can't help themselves: once obsessive-compulsive, always obsessive-compulsive. As mentioned earlier, when the Bouctouche dune plan began in 1996, J. K. was addicted to the intricacies of the project, never missing a meeting of the board that directed the initiative. He had a couple of million bucks on the table, but employees could have seen to it that his interests were protected. Rather, he was there every step of the way, never missing a beat. When the dilapidated Loyalist Burial Grounds in downtown Saint John were being restored, J. K., Arthur, and Jack were on it like they were redoing their own backyards.

But the most striking case has been the previously mentioned Prince Charles School initiative in Saint John, which is evolving as a philanthropic model. The project sprang from the awareness that poverty was having a devastating effect on many families connected to what was generally regarded as one of the poorer schools in the city, an institution that could literally be seen from the Irving corporate offices. J. D. Irving Ltd. worked with the school and hired professional management consultants to conduct an assessment of the root causes of the continuing cycle of poverty and associated afflictions, such as a high rate of teenage pregnancy, unwed mothers, and kids getting into trouble. The study was clear on one critical point: get a clutch on the situation before kids reach grade eight and you'll be likely to make positive change in their lives.

In 1994 the company seconded Moncton teacher Debbie Fisher, who'd worked on the Irving-sponsored Forest Discovery Boxes, to take the lead on the Prince Charles School project. Through her continuing involvement, today an estimated 140 J. D. Irving employees are involved as one-on-one mentors in various school subjects, as sports coaches, and in various other roles, helping to improve the fortunes of the children. Most contribute two hours per week on company time, cumulatively providing a total of ten thousand hours since the project began in earnest in 1994. Because the initiative began more than a decade ago, the project overseers have been able to track the progress of students under its purview. The first group of students are now in grades eleven and twelve in the Saint John area, and for many of them there is light at the end of the tunnel. They are the first group of alumni.

"We're winning," says J. K. of the program's effect on Saint John's inner-city youth, but emphasizes that the province of New Brunswick still needs to fund urban schools in disadvantaged neighbourhoods to a greater degree. He argues that it makes social and economic sense to do so, citing a bill of $66 million per year for the provision of social services helping the Saint John area. "We've got to flatten the curve," he says. "Personally, I'm interested in the results." He believes that as the New Brunswick public becomes more aware of the project's outputs, they're going to demand that similar efforts be made everywhere there's a need. In the short term, other companies have begun to follow the Prince Charles School model, including Irving Oil, Aliant, and the Atlantic Health Sciences Centre.

J. K. says very matter-of-factly that this work is "necessary" to the same extent as the family's environmental work. What's interesting about J. K. in this discussion is that he now grows more excited speaking about his philanthropic projects than he does speaking about his businesses, which are becoming more like proud reminiscences. His mindset, his attitude, the way he now sees the world, is every bit the archetype for the twenty-first-century Irvings: kinder, gentler, human, sentimental, open, proud, giving, and involved—all while still exhibiting the classic Irving traits.

20. Inheritances

The twenty-first-century Irvings stand to inherit much in material terms when J. K., Arthur Sr., and Jack pass away, although it will take a battalion of lawyers and accountants to figure out where it's all supposed to go. It's a daunting task if you can believe *Forbes* magazine, which puts the family's current worth at $5.9 billion US. Exactly who is in charge of doling all this out is unclear. Although there can be no doubt that the three brothers worry about it, there is a consensus amongst Irving watchers that the Irvings aren't really motivated by money in the way most people would think. For the Irvings, it's more about maintaining the family ideal and the business momentum. (Then again, isn't it always the people with money who have the luxury of saying it's not their fixation?) More to the point, their relationship to money seems to be about understanding how money can get business things done. Arthur Sr. alludes to the functional use of money during the CBC documentary *Unlocking the Mystery*. He says it's great to have money if you want to buy a hamburger now and then—an analogy for being able to live well, if not take care of one's self and one's family. His point was that money is merely an instrument for obtaining what you need.

The lesson about the value of money was always taught by K. C., perhaps as a way to ease his sons into understanding the value and purpose of their forthcoming inheritances. There's a story that when K. C.'s grandchildren used to visit him in Bermuda, they would go out to dinner. He would dole out to each of them just enough to get by for the occasion. But he made it clear they would have to make choices from the menu, and if a soft drink put them over their allocation, they would have to drink water. And after the meal, they were apparently to return to their grandfather what they hadn't spent. Completely accurate or not—and the source was credible—the story speaks to the kinds of simple, real-life lessons K. C. liked to provide to his children and grandchildren.

Moosehead's Joel Levesque says that the Irvings don't focus on money and inheritance the way people think they do. Growth, he says, is what drives them. "Growth, growth, growth. If you're not growing, then you're going backwards. I think that's what drives them, and they certainly are driven. But they're not driven by money. They really don't care about it in that way. Yes, their businesses have to be profitable or why would you be in it? But that's not what drives them. It's growth. I think they're probably like many people who have been entrusted with a great deal of wealth or a great deal of capital investment. They worry more than you or I, but about the future, because the weight of all these enterprises is on their shoulders and what happens to all the people who work for them and their livelihoods, and so on."

There aren't enough Midland and Sunbury transport trucks in existence to haul all the cash the Irvings would have if they liquidated their assets. But the truest, most valuable inheritance the sixth- and seventh-generation Irvings will acquire isn't really money in and of itself; it's all those lessons and principles taught to them at The Irving School of Business, a means to making more things happen, to generating more prosperity.

◆

The failure of many business families to plan and manage their futures well is centred around what Thane Stenner calls "affluenza," which can be defined as a lack of ambition brought on by a life of wealth and privilege. It's sometimes also called "living in Cannes," a reference to young jet-setters who use family money they did not earn to fashion a fabulous lifestyle. Stenner, first vice president and investment advisor of the T. Stenner Group of CIBC Wood Gundy in Vancouver, says that having wealth can make it difficult to instill humility in children, to teach them respect and a good work ethic. "Wealth can sap a child's initiative, independence and drive to succeed," he says. "Wealth can also create a good deal of conflict within a family, creating stark divisions between the older and younger generations and rivalry between siblings and amongst the extended family." However, he reassures that with vigilance, education, and early intervention, parents can inoculate their children against the dreaded affluenza.

J.K., Arthur Sr., and Jack Irving certainly did not "live in Cannes" and they have followed practices to prevent the spread of affluenza to their children. This is the legacy of personal teachings handed down to them from Herbert to J.D. to K.C. They've all ensured their children get out to work at an early age; they've exposed them to meetings and situations through which they can see first-hand how business works; and they've discouraged the acquisition of things like flashy cars and huge homes. It's said that young

Irvings don't have ready access to tons of cash. They have to get out and start earning a living. In J.K., Arthur Sr., and Jack's earliest days, this meant raising and selling chickens and eggs. When J.K. left the roost, he worked his heart out in the New Brunswick woods. In the twenty-first-century context, the newcomers have had to get out and earn an education and then learn how the littlest and largest things are done within the company.

David Ganong did not "live in Cannes" either. As a young man, he worked in Ontario, at Dupont and at Molson's Brewery, which was a good move in terms of his family business future. "In our case, we're a smaller enterprise," he explains. "On my watch, we had to grow up and become a Maritime company exporting to the rest of Canada. That's something that involves competing more effectively against the world. And the world doesn't exist in Saint John or St. Stephen. It exists in Toronto and New York and elsewhere. And so it was very important to get a broader business background for somebody like me." But the Irvings, he says, are already engaged in sizeable, world-level enterprise because of the very nature of their businesses; therefore, up-and-coming family members don't need to leave and work elsewhere. "They're buying oil in the Middle East or in Venezuela or wherever it may be that they're choosing to buy today and they're transporting it on their own ships," says Ganong to illustrate his point.

By contrast, some McCain family members did end up "living in Cannes," the consequences of which were catastrophic. The lifestyles of some second-generation McCains did not bode well for their capacity to run a large corporation, which led to a split between brothers Wallace and the late Harrison McCain over whose children were best suited to carry on running their highly successful businesses. When all was said and done, Wallace was in Toronto focused on the acquisition and operation of Maple Leaf Foods, Harrison was destined for heart failure, and the McCain cousins were not exactly the best of buddies. The larger threat to the McCain situation as it relates to New Brunswick is that the family's shaky succession plan will ultimately see their head office in tiny Florenceville relocated to a major urban centre like Toronto.

One of the insights of author and professor John Ward, an expert in family business succession, is the simple notion that children of the business wealthy need to learn that their wealth was the result of determined effort, that prosperity didn't just materialize out of thin air. This could not be truer than in the case of the Irvings, whose work ethic and discipline have driven their success. Some say that the real Irving turn-on—their zeal for competition and entrepreneurship—negates the desire for money for money's sake or for the sake of having a jet-set lifestyle. In other words, they've become addicted to the gamesmanship of business, not to the money. That experience has been true until now, but there are no guarantees for the future. Beyond six or seven generations, as the genetic immunity breaks down, the Irvings will become more and more susceptible to the disease. The affluenza antibodies were infused in J.K., Arthur Sr., and Jack because of the way K.C. spent personal time with them, teaching them the ways of business and the world. The brothers were also successful in transferring the antibodies to their children. In order for the transfer to continue, Jim, Kenneth, Robert, and all the other sixth-generation Irvings have to ensure that they pass on the K.C. treatment, a treatment that most probably extends all the way back to Herbert in the late nineteenth century.

On another note, Stenner says having a passion for managing corporate wealth doesn't always translate into a passion for managing personal wealth. The problem with personal wealth management in medium to large family businesses is that behind each detail is more detail, requiring patience, tolerance, and understanding amongst the family members about what's going on with their assets and money. "As wealth grows, complexity grows," says Stenner. But by following a well-managed succession plan—"a wealth map," as Stenner calls it—family business owners can avoid having to spend too much time on the wealth management stuff, freeing them up to pursue their true passions in life. And when those on the periphery of the business (such as spouses and the extended family) are included in the picture and provided with a constant flow of up-to-date information, "they find relief." Personal or business wealth couldn't be much more complicated than it is for the Irvings. The reasons: they have so many companies and there are so many Irvings. They can't all be involved in planning the future, which means somebody has to communicate what's going on through the ranks. Here's hoping that communication within the family ranks remains better than Irving communications in the public forum.

21. Succession

In business, as in literature and in life, there is a closing chapter to everything. Products and companies come and go; business leaders come and go. So it is with the Irvings, in spite of the fact it seems like they've been around forever and always will be. But George, Herbert, J.D., and K.C. are gone and others will follow. Because they have already defied all of the odds of family business longevity, it becomes increasingly probable that as K.C.'s sons pass from the scene and the sixth generation retires over the next two decades, serious and significant measures have to be put in play in order to protect the family's money and their integrity. More than any other complex business they've managed before, the complex business of succession is at hand.

Since the days of the Morgans, Vanderbilts, Rockefellers, Eatons, and even the McCains, family business planning and succession have become an industry unto themselves. There are now individuals, companies, and institutions that specialize in these fields, the development of which the Irvings must surely be acutely aware. One of these individuals is David C. Bentall, a man who experienced both frustration and satisfaction as a central figure in his family's three business succession episodes. He learned enough before he turned forty-five to help create an elective at the University of British Columbia Business Families Centre, an initiative of the university's Sauder School of Business. The elective is titled "Working in the Family Business."

Bentall knows the new UBC program will not just provide family business owners with theories behind succession; it will be a legitimate, scientific field of study with applications for today and long into the future. Bentall himself is living proof that families with investments big and small can rise or crumble depending on who in the family does what to whom and when. The Bentalls weren't on the scale of the Irvings, but they weren't running a corner store either. The story begins with a company formed nearly one hundred years ago by Charles Bentall, an entrepreneurial K.C. type of guy who ran Dominion Construction in Vancouver from 1915 to 1955—forty years of building things with no lack of vision or success. David Bentall says his grandfather was an engineer who had a particular knack for the qualities of efficiency and aesthetic design. He created for Dominion what David calls a "design-builder reputation."

Today, things aren't what they once were, meaning that the "family" in his family's former business has all but evaporated. Dominion eventually became Bentall Capital, whose website brims with projects, ideas, and visions for various endeavours in real estate development. The company showpiece, the landmark Bentall Centre in downtown Vancouver was built between 1967 and 1981. Consisting of four office towers and an underground shopping complex, it was at the time the largest integrated facility of its kind in British Columbia, with more than 1.2 million square feet of space. A fifth tower, Bentall 5, opened in 2002 with twenty-one floors and is now being expanded to thirty-four floors, adding another 600,000 square feet to the bulging spatial equation.

The Bentall story explains how easily things can become unravelled in a large family business, where emotions run high and both love and logic can be lost almost overnight. Charles had a succession plan to make his son Harold president, but what unfolded within the next generations was far less predictable. Three main events occurred, including a destructive split between David's father, Harold, and Harold's two brothers, over who should succeed him as company president. The long story short is that a succession of disputes caused irreversible acrimony between the three Bentall brothers with unavoidable peripheral impact on their children. In the end, family members ended up cashing in their chips and outside management was brought in. It was complicated, stressful, and devastatingly hurtful. For David Bentall personally, "it was emotional because it was my identity." In the absence of a truly orderly succession plan, this series of events could happen to any large business family, no matter how well intentioned they might be. As new generations emerge, ideals and priorities can change.

Today, Bentall speaks publicly on a regular basis about being both witness and participant in the three succession scenarios that so dramatically affected his family's relationships and future. The speaking began informally with an invitation to address the British Columbia law society, where people told him they found the information helpful. What's followed is a new business focused on family business lectures and counselling. He has a stock presentation of twenty-three core slides built around a simple lesson: plan, plan, plan. In his presentation he stresses the importance of developing processes and structures for the three primary elements of family business planning: family, business, and ownership. Each of these, in Bentall's view, should have a formal structure, including the outside board, the family council and the owners' assembly. Using his first-hand experience, Bentall is positively evangelical about being proactive in building family unity, creating comfortable forums for issues to be discussed, introducing a universally trusted third-party facilitator to the process, having a code of conduct to guide interactions, and keeping spouses and non-active members informed.

Working alongside Bentall is previously-mentioned associate Thane Stenner, of the T. Stenner Group of CIBC Wood Gundy in Vancouver. Stenner's group is a leading group of professional advisors striving to be the global leader in family business and wealth counselling; they use what he calls a "private family office" model to assist in integrating and managing the financial affairs of businesses, charitable organizations, and families with a net worth of $10 million or more (the wealthiest in the stable is slightly above $1 billion). Stenner is also co-author, with James Dolan, of *True Wealth: An Expert Guide for High-Net-Worth Individuals (and their Advisors)*. Stenner has found a niche that is important to the Canadian economy and he is intent on occupying a large space within it. In 2006 he and his associates were providing professional assistance to thirty-three families and had a five-year goal of reaching fifty-five to sixty families and capping it there. There is a ceiling because the services they provide are personal and very hands-on. As part of a "private family office" they become directly engaged in private family matters.

He claims that business families generate an estimated 80 per cent of Canada's gross domestic product and typically have a higher rate of growth and much higher commitment levels than hired CEOs and other managers. But with such overwhelming commitment comes a high level of emotion. Piled on top of emotion is the matter of pride. "Some successful business families think they don't need help because they're successful," says Stenner. This misconception, says Stenner, is a classic mistake that even America's famed and all-powerful Rockefellers were smart enough to avoid sixty years ago when they became pioneers in the science of family succession. Effective succession is, clearly, not a new thing. Some European families have been managing succession successfully for many generations.

With two sons in the famed beer company's ranks, the chairman of Moosehead Breweries in Saint John, Derek Oland, has spent considerable time and mental capital getting his head around the matter of succession. Oland cites John L. Ward's book *Perpetuating the Family Business: 50 Lessons From Long-Lasting, Successful Families in Business* as a good guide to family succession. Ward is a professor and co-director at the Kellogg School Centre of Family Enterprises at Northwestern University, as well as founder of the Family Business Consulting Group International. His book explains a series of family codes, including "The Owner-Managed Business," "The Sibling Partnership," and "The Cousin Collaboration." He presents "The Five Insights" to family business planning and succession:

- Respect the Challenge
- Predictable Family Business Issues
- Communication Is Indispensable
- Planning Is Essential to Continuity
- Commitment Is Required of Us

Ward also works with a set of four P's:

- Policies Before the Need
- Sense of Purpose
- Process
- Parenting

He goes on to provide a series of fifty lessons under such titles as "Irrevocable Retirement," "Non-Family Executives," "Family 1st—Business 1st," and "Wealth Is Neutral." The latter subject is one of the most interesting. It speaks to the fact that money in and of itself does not make people better or evil. But there is historical evidence that as wealth grows, the inherent tendencies and personalities of individuals can become amplified. Alcoholics, by way of analogy, are only problematic when they have access to too much alcohol. Alcohol is neutral in the way that wealth is neutral, until either or both are experienced beyond moderation. And alcohol, as it known, can bring out the best and the worst in people.

As a distant "student" of Ward's, Derek Oland has actually been asked to speak on the matter of succession at the University of Alberta. His message is a simple one: family succession in business takes a lot of continuous, ongoing planning in the areas of finance, management, and the attempt to ensure the ongoing success of the business itself. "You don't always have the royal jelly to have the right person to make the tough decisions," says Oland, meaning that just because someone has your DNA, doesn't necessarily mean they have the intellect, the acumen, the leadership, or the desire to run a large company. As with the Irvings, there's been a good batch or two of royal jelly in the Oland family—Oland is the fifth generation in the business since it first took root in Dartmouth, Nova Scotia, in 1867. After a lengthy history of product and market development, the sons of matriarch Susannah Oland eventually built a brewery in Saint John. The Oland family business story is nearly as enduring as that of the Irvings, but the complexity of sorting out finances and assets with an eye toward succession is much more complicated with the Irvings.

In later-generation business families, if it's apparent the royal jelly is no longer jelling, it's often important that the family members have the wisdom, maturity, and foresight to simply step aside from the running of the business and play the role of shareholder, not day-to-day decision maker. "If it becomes an ego game as to who runs the company," says Oland, "the ego may not be the right person at the right time. You've also got to manage the financial side of it because with all the implications of tax and capital gains tax, a company's got to buy themselves out every generation. When a person's got three or four children, it's pretty hard. You've got to start early to be able to accumulate enough cash to pay the taxes, but also pay off those who are not (going to be) involved." Some companies, he adds, are meant to be run for the long-term, some are made to be sold off, and some just shouldn't continue at all because their products are no longer relevant or in demand. "If there's an expertise in buggy whips, as they say, unless you can turn it into something completely different, [the market and demand] won't be there."

One way to help determine the capacity of children to assume the reins of corporate control is to have them work summer jobs and other entry-level jobs. Moosehead even encourages the sons and daughters of all of their employees to work for the summer if there are opportunities available. Oland's sons Andrew (thirty-eight in 2006) and Patrick (thirty-six) had to acquire experience elsewhere. Among his experiences, Andrew spent time as a junior foreman in the steel shop at Halifax Dartmouth Industries Ltd. ("if you can run welders, you can run almost anything," says Derek) and Patrick worked at Christie Brown and Beatrice Foods and stayed in Toronto in pursuit of his Chartered Accountant accreditation. Only then did he return to Saint John and a role within the family business. Third son Matthew got his MBA from Queen's University, worked at H. J. Heinz and Colgate Palmolive, and is now a senior marketer at Smucker Foods of Canada in Markham. Fourth son Giles is a Halifax-based entrepreneur in the wireless setup business. But they all worked summer jobs at Moosehead. As important as the summer stints have been for his sons, working in other corporate cultures gives them a chance to "flex their wings so they can learn how to function in a non-friendly environment, in a classic business environment," as Derek puts it. Two of the benefits of working away from the family business are that it's possible both to make mistakes and to quit. Children of family business owners can have a very hard time if they live by the belief that they can get away with any number of errors or blunders. Oland says no one wants their children walking down the hallways of the company with the other employees talking behind their backs about having it cushy.

Oland has a warm way of humanizing it all, providing a ready escape for his children should they choose it. "I'm getting into a little bit of philosophy here," he says, "but as parents, Jackie and I both have the idea for our children that we want them to be happy and productive. If they can satisfy that answer for themselves, then you've done your job as a parent. That's the job before you worry about the company. You've got to do your job as a parent because I see an awful lot of organizations where they haven't done a good job and the kids never really stand up on their own feet." Oland's own pathway into running the company wasn't completely orthodox. After completing high school in Saint John, he attended McGill University but flunked out by Christmas. Agriculture was the focus of his studies, but his heart wasn't in it. With his father Philip (P. W. for short) upset over his son's premature departure from McGill, Oland wasn't about to show up immediately back in Saint John. Instead, he used his contacts through the Canadian Brewers Association and landed a string of jobs at Molson: two months in engineering, two months in the lab, and two months in the bottle shop. Oland went on to get a degree at the University of New Brunswick and, after another short period in Montreal, approached his father about a job. The rest of Oland's story is one of running a successful business whose products are considered staples of the Maritime culture and are also recognized around the globe.

Oland said he believes his sons will eventually run the company one day, "unless they screw up."

J. K. agrees with Derek Oland that it is more important for individuals to be content than to be in the family business. "The most important thing is that they do something that they're going to be happy with in life, and if that happens to be in the business, so well and dandy," he says. On that point, he swears he had the freedom to choose his own path in life, hence his decision not to finish his degree at Acadia University in Wolfville and to rough it in the woods during his early twenties rather than leap into a more traditional business role with one or more of his father's companies. Even if there were expectations that, as an Irving male, he would ultimately be in the family business, things have changed. "I believe that for kids growing up, it's different today than it was years ago and that they should all be happy in what they do and enjoy it and do the best they can in what they're doing. That's what it's all about. And so there's no grandiose plan that they're going to do this or that. If the duck can swim...." Here, J. K.'s candour hints at what may already be known by he and his brothers and their children: that some or several of the seventh generation may either choose careers outside the company or not have the capacity to make a valuable contribution.

As for those among J. K.'s offspring who've chosen to be in the business— Jim, Robert, Mary Jean, Judith (until recently), and grandchildren Jamie and Kate—he says: "I am very happy with them and we have a great time. And that's what all the fun is about." His daughters Mary Jean and Judith and his granddaughter Kate were the first women to enter the family business. One wonders, had there been a sister to the three brothers, whether or not she would have entered the fray. J. K. says he actually felt sorry for his mother, having to raise three boys, especially in the face of K. C.'s business-driven absenteeism. "My mother must've had an awful time when I look back at it. I feel sorry for her, really. If we had had a sister, it would've been good for the outfit." What he seemed to imply is that a sister might have softened the edge on the lot of them. Mary Jean was the first Irving woman who "showed up" in the business. J. K.'s eldest daughter continues to operate Master Packaging and her own potato farms on Prince Edward Island. "Mary Jean has got a real business sense," he says. "You know, either you have it or you don't have it sometimes. She's got the right instincts. She has a heart. With her health [it is widely know that Mary Jean has battled cancer over the years] she has a problem and she handles that. But she does all right."

◆

K. C. Irving wasn't just an industrial and entrepreneurial visionary; he was also a succession visionary. It seems he knew that the key to keeping the coming generations in line was to ensure they had to work. K. C. obviously never heard the term "affluenza," but he instinctively knew how to avoid that affliction. "[The family members] have no serious money on an individual, personal basis," says one interviewee. The point is that the sixth generation just wouldn't have gotten paid for anything unless they'd worked. Although the details are of course private, the way K. C. arranged trusts and inheritances seems to have been structured to keep family members earning their keep. As a result, twenty-first-century Irvings can't spend their days golfing or "living in Cannes." K. C.'s intent was that they all had to keep going to work. He seemed to know instinctively that ready access to too much wealth can wreck a family.

In too many wealthy families, there is too much accessible wealth floating around. K. C. transferred his businesses, his ideals, and his discipline to his three sons and his grandchildren, but he did not really transfer the wealth the way most people might imagine he did. It's said that according to K. C.'s will, because they were in Canada and not in Bermuda, sons J. K., Arthur Sr., and Jack, could not even act as trustees. This is not to say he thought his sons were incapable of executing his estate. He just knew how to protect their interests.

One source says many wealthy people tend to be hard on their children and more relaxed with their grandchildren, explaining why the third generation are more likely to end up "living in Cannes." With the Irvings, though, its only in the past ten years or so that observers have begun to see a shift in the lifestyles—more elaborate homes, for example—on the part of the sixth-generation cousins. Kenneth, it's rumoured, would love to have a Challenger jet all to himself, but Arthur really wouldn't allow it. Instead, Irving aircraft are pooled. The vehicles they've driven have essentially been modest (reminiscent of K. C.'s practical blue Meteor) in contrast to the elite car culture that some other business families buy into.

◆

The pressure on K. C.'s grandchildren and great-grandchildren (for the moment focused on Jamie and Kate) is possibly even greater than it was on J. K., Arthur Sr., and Jack. This is because the legacy has now grown so large, it's as though twenty-first-century Irvings aren't just working to run good businesses; they're accountable for the very dignity of the family. The responsibility might be shared and spread out over a number of people, but individually they probably wake up mornings feeling like they're in it alone. Asked if the twenty-first-century Irvings are "toeing the line" in terms of following the family formula, Moosehead's Joel Levesque said it is not a matter of toeing the line. "It's more like carrying the torch. It's an awesome responsibility that's been handed down from generation to generation and I would say that it's probably one of the most stressful jobs in Canada—being an Irving family member—because you have this legacy of K.C. Irving, the famous K.C. Irving, one of the most successful entrepreneurs in the history of Canada." One of the reasons the grandchildren and possibly K.C.'s great-grandchildren, feel the responsibility so deeply is because of the expectations of their grandfather and the fact that, according to Levesque, they worshipped him. "They spent a lot of time as youngsters with their grandfather and I've heard them tell the stories. And if you go into their offices, you see the pictures on the walls. They absolutely loved their grandfather," the man who, in spite of his mammoth workload, took the time to walk them through the New Brunswick woods, and taught them how to shake hands properly.

A popular, long-serving New Brunswick politician says there is an invisible transition of responsibility and decision making taking place from the ranks of K.C.'s sons to their children. The politician tells of meeting with J.K. about the future of a piece of land in Saint John. J.K. said he had to check with his son Jim over the matter. The politician and J.K. went downstairs together to the doorway of a boardroom where Jim was in a meeting. J.K. motioned for his son's attention. When Jim came out of the room, J.K. explained the nature of the request and said, "I should have talked to you about this. Are you okay with that." Jim responded, "Oh yeah Dad." And the matter was instantly settled.

◆

There are signs that the Irvings, notwithstanding the collegiality of brothers J.K., Arthur, and Jack, are not necessarily engaged in an orderly process of succession across the family divides. Where brothers and sisters are concerned, things may be on the up and up. But where cousins enter the fray, there might be "trouble in the Highlands" as one observant and knowledgeable Saint John source put it. For people on the ground in the port city, there are clear indications of things going "east-west" (in different directions) between the cousins (essentially between J.K.'s and Arthur's children). First and foremost are rumours of a corporate divide in things as basic as where their offices will be situated within the city of Saint John. Currently, their buildings sit side by side. Second, conditions in the wood side of the family (J.D. Irving Ltd.) are a struggle. Being in the wood business at this moment in time is tough, while in the oil patch, profits are said to be soaring. In oil, there is no way down. In wood, there seems, for the moment, to be no way up. One of the last *Saint John Telegraph-Journal* front-page banner headlines in 2006 decried the decline of the forestry sector in New Brunswick. You can almost see this reality etched across the face of Jim Irving, perhaps the one person in New Brunswick most determined to get through the muddle and turmoil of the wood sector.

These contrasting highs and lows are not a good recipe for keeping things warm and fuzzy among a family of business keeners who are highly competitive and proud. Aside from when they're jockeying for access to aircraft at their private airport hangar, the Irving cousins don't necessarily need to be bumping into one other everywhere they venture; the business community of New Brunswick isn't that small. Nevertheless, there are signs that the divide is more serious. During Judith's time running Hawk Communications, for example, it's said she did not attract any business from the oil side of the family business, which has a fairly hefty advertising account. That's not exactly in keeping with the Irving formula of vertical integration.

While their fathers are said to remain extremely close, Jim and Kenneth are described as being "warm" and "cordial" with one another. What will transpire after the passing of their parents is on many people's minds. There are good, logical reasons for them to be moving in different directions. It's the nature of what their businesses are and what they do. On Jim's side, virtually everything about the business has a domestic focus: pulp- and sawmills, trucking, and, until recently, buses. Not all of his businesses operate solely in the Atlantic region, or even solely in Canada, but the emphasis is definitely domestic. In Kenneth's oil world, virtually everything is international in scope: they buy foreign oil, mill it through their colossal Saint John refinery, and then sell the end products to a combined domestic and international customer base. Where Jim's brother Robert fits here is unclear.

"I don't like half of my cousins," said another observer, making the point that just because they're related doesn't mean it's natural that Jim, Kenneth, Arthur Jr., Robert, Mary Jean, Judith, and John should be pals. The suggestion has even been made that Kenneth thinks Jim is "uncouth" while Jim sees Kenneth as "a spoiled little rich boy." The public, of course, enjoys conjecture like the notion that the twenty-first-century Irvings aren't getting along. It's akin to David Ganong's theory about "Maritime envy," the tendency of Maritimers to criticize people who do better than themselves. Who knows? As expressed earlier, Jim and Kenneth might find such observations humorous as hell.

Certainly when the brothers Harrison and Wallace McCain parted ways personally and professional in the 1990s, some people and the media thrived on their strife. People loved having a made-at-home, true-to-life New Brunswick corporate soap opera. Human nature being what it is, some in the public would likely enjoy another corporate family battle to keep themselves entertained.

The New Brunswick politician who says that there is "trouble in the Highlands" cites a turn in the road that he says many people noticed. A dinner was held in the spring of 2006 to honour J. K.'s wife, Jean—a tribute to her volunteerism and community work over the years. It was done in association with the Salvation Army, who presented her with the highest award given by that organization. It was also one of the largest events of its type ever held at the Saint John Convention Centre, with approximately 1200 people in attendance. Some were even bused in from Bouctouche. "What was interesting," he says, "is that there was a whole side of the Irvings missing from the dinner. Irving Oil never showed up. No one. The word 'boycott' wouldn't be right, but they weren't there. It was kind of obvious that that would be unheard of seven, eight, nine, or ten years ago." This politician predicts that the divisions between the leadership at Irving Oil and J. D. Irving will become more pronounced over the next year or two. He suggests this will take the form of new office arrangements being considered for J. D. Irving, perhaps on Pugsley Wharf in Saint John, and in a land trade deal being worked out with the city in the Loch Lomond Mall area for Irving Oil. He says the growing distance between those two main organizations and individuals has to do with the two moving apart culturally and the belief that the oil company is making huge profits while the forestry-related companies are suffering along with the rest of that sector across North America. He says normally there would not be the sense of a power struggle within the Irving ranks, "but Kenneth is the new guy, no question; he's the guy"—meaning he is the star that shines brightest for the families' future. He suggests that it can't be easy for Jim to be both in a tougher corporate climate while Kenneth is receiving this sort of notice. Kenneth's rising stature was a point raised again and again during interviews for this book.

The politician believes that J. K., Arthur, and Jack are still tight, but that their children are not necessarily on the same page. If there are any stresses at all between J. K. and Arthur Sr., he supposes, it probably has to do with the LNG tax deal, a public circus that he says was a major, unnecessary blow to the family name and image. "My sense is that, corporately, J. K. was really upset that this tax deal drug the name of the Irvings down."

The source says the negativity of the LNG story is why the name "Irving" resonates negatively—again, despite their substantial philanthropic efforts in so many projects, institutions, and communities. It turned into the kind of unnecessary series of headlines that adds strain to the normal stresses that can potentially occur between cousins operating such totally different companies while sharing the same brand name.

As one who has witnessed and is living the challenges of succession in a longstanding family business, Ganong Bros. CEO David Ganong has a very practical outlook on the Irving circumstance. He says there's a possibility that for the first time in the Irving story, there may be a bit of divide and conquer going on. If you fast-forward fifteen or more years, the "glue" of J. K., Arthur, and Jack will no longer be present. And with the public pro-files that each of their kids has developed—Jim, Kenneth, and Robert in par-ticular—things could look very different down the road. "Whether cousins have the same bonding as brothers will remain to be seen," he says. Ganong believes that cohesiveness and good succession planning for the future are very important things. It will affect the entire family. "Because the moment you've got a minority shareholder in an enterprise that isn't actively involved in that enterprise, then sooner or later you run into a situation where some-body says, 'I think I'd rather have my cash.' And if there isn't a willingness on behalf of the other minority shareholders to acquire that position, then that position [figuratively speaking] goes to General Foods." What Ganong means is that as the future generations move in and stake out their posi-tions, the chances of going to the public market increase, followed by head office moving to Toronto and New Brunswick becoming a mere branch plant operation. Once you're in Toronto with fifteen different branch plants in dif-ferent locations, New Brunswick becomes just a dot on the Irving corporate map instead of the epicentre.

A widely respected Maritime businessman says he does not want to be presumptuous about the Irvings. What they do is their business, he insists. "I have the greatest respect for the Irvings and I don't want to ever give any impression in the book that I don't have a lot of respect for them. And you're going to get an awful lot of people that are gonna sing their praises. And they do a wonderful job. But you have got to sort the wheat from the chaff." The source said that with seven generations, it just gets naturally tougher and tougher. "Some of them are going to have to evolve to being professional shareholders rather than frontline managers, because in certain cases, you're going to have to be tough about who plays what roles inside and outside the companies." This person suggested that all looks well on the surface at Irving Oil and J. D. Irving, but that some "dumb decisions" have been made recent-ly—the LNG tax fiasco as a case in point. It's as though, he said, twenty-five years of hard-earned community goodwill built up by the family through their philanthropy was burned up instantly. "I mean, anybody will tell you that that was dumb." And he says it was even dumber because, relatively speaking, it was for "chump change." He said he imagined that it was Arthur Irving Sr., not Kenneth, who pushed the LNG tax relief deal with the City of Saint John with an aggressive thrust. He admits that the Irvings have enjoyed an impressive run of steady progression, but this doesn't mean they're infallible. "They're so confident of their own capabilities that they don't really use the professionals [to the degree they probably should]," he says. Nor do they seem to surround themselves with outside board members and influencers. Even Power Corporation of Montreal has outside board members and professional management, in spite of the fact that the Desmarais are one of the smartest, most powerful business families in Canada. This businessman was insistent that the Irvings need to be careful they don't tip from confidence to over-confidence.

Enterprise Saint John's Steve Carson has a more optimistic view about the twenty-first-century Irvings and the differences between them. He thinks that by not being the same, they might, in the long run, bring even more to the table. It's an interesting hypothesis: more diversity in the talent pool, innovative thinkers who challenge one another, and the possibility of healthy competition. "Why would that be such a bad thing?" he asks.

David Ganong thinks the Irvings have done a good job on the succession front up to now. He believes it's a by-product of how K.C. ingeniously set things up and the fact that succession planning is always taking place at one level or another within the empire. "But," he says, "the bigger part of that is, how do you manage the various family individuals, especially as the pyramid gets bigger?" A previous generation within the Ganong family had some troubled dealings—it wasn't as messy as the McCain affair, but the Ganongs did end up in court. The family and the enterprise have survived intact, but to get there one brother moved on, leaving the challenges and possibilities for the future with David. It wasn't the way the family would have wanted it.

Ganong's point about how his family would have wanted things to turn out is reminiscent of Kenneth Irving's response to Francis McGuire concerning why he would continue developing the oil company interests in Saint John versus a potentially more profitable location such as Louisiana. It was simply and succinctly not what his grandfather wanted.

◆

As the years pass and Herbert Irving's three great-grandsons complete their productive lives, the sixth-generation business leaders—Jim, Robert, Mary Jean, Judith, Kenneth, Arthur Jr., and John—will face two frontiers involving some very serious decisions. The first involves how they should go about extricating themselves from their businesses as they enter retirement, while at the same time guaranteeing the ongoing security of what Herbert began building in the mid-1850s.

The second is how best to continue their respective fathers' uniquely interactive philanthropy. How they tackle the latter will be just as important as the former, because it is through their actions in helping build strong communities that the Irvings will be known and regarded over the long term. These are not communities strengthened solely by expanding enterprise, additional bricks and mortar, and more job creation, but communities where the underpinnings—the social and educational pillars that could certainly use philanthropic investment—are made secure. Businesses, after all, come and go—they merge or they get bought out—while communities are constant and perpetual.

As interactive philanthropists, the Irvings have the resources and the power to continue helping Atlantic Canadian communities to reach a higher level and to offer a higher quality of life. The current generation of twenty-first-century Irvings—the sixth generation—will be posed with making choices unheard of in the Irving journey, including finding talented CEOs that they can entrust to run the family companies if they determine that their own children are not well-suited to run corporations of such overwhelming magnitude versus being suited to amplify and manage their philanthropic future. The question begs, as phrased by one Saint John businessman, will the seventh generation have the 'royal jelly' to continue family management of the endless stream of businesses under their influence. K. C.'s great-grandson Jamie might turn out to be a great newspaper publisher and one or more of his cousins might be great at some other form of enterprise, but will they be able to meet the same level of expectations beset over the decades onto the shoulders of all those men who came before them.

There will be lawyers and accountants lined up from Saint John to Kingdom Come to help manage the family's succession when the sixth generation retires from active business. But before they shift into full-time philanthropy, Jim, Kenneth, and Robert, as the key Irving figures over the next fifteen to twenty years, have much to do to put their corporate matters in order. Jim must get through the immediate tough years and decide what to do with J. D. Irving Ltd. and associated companies under his control over the long term, including the eventual possibility of going public. Kenneth must finish his LNG terminal, build the second oil refinery, and work to give Irving Oil the scale required to make Saint John a true energy hub. And Robert, prolific business growth aside, must win the Memorial Cup. When he does, the 'Irving Cup' can also be hoisted in a salute to George, the impoverished

1833 immigrant who took eleven years to scrape together enough money to secure New Brunswick lot number 3734, the soil on which the Irving legacy was built.

On the day in October 2006 when J. K. gave his personal tour of Bouctouche and the hidden thicket and pond once known as Irvingdale, something very subtle and telling occurred. Although he seemed to enjoy the experience of sharing personal stories, there was an unexpected strangeness to that day. Relaxed and reflective, he spoke with immense pride about the Irvings as entrepreneurs and industrialists as if they existed only in some past tense. That's not the case, of course, because they are still such a vital force and are guaranteed to remain so for the duration of the current generation. But weeks later, while sifting through notes and transcripts, I started to glimpse the forthcoming Irving reality. Based on the reflections of J. K., on intuitions, on the evidence that emerges from research and interviews, and on the patterns of entrepreneurial and industrial history, it seems likely that after 150 years in business, the widening Irving clan will grow more and more disparate, which threatens their main strategic business advantage: closeness of family. Fathers, sons, and brothers are one thing; uncles, nephews, nieces, cousins, and second cousins are quite another. The Irvings entered the twenty-first century believing they were still one single family, all attendees at the metaphorical "Irving family picnic." But in the space of a single generation, they have become several families spread all over the place. It's naturally harder to get everybody to the Irving family picnic, assuming everyone even wants to go. This is nothing to fret about. It is natural and happens to most families.

By most people's standards, the Irvings were fortunate to have kept their dynasty alive as far as K. C., let alone three generations more. The record shows that business families rarely make it beyond that three-generation plateau, sometimes even falling victim to a painful rags to riches to rags scenario. The Irvings have so far bucked all trends and seem capable of rewriting the saga of the typical large business family. If the twenty-first-century Irvings can manage to get along with one another and realize all of their possibilities, theirs can be a good-news story. The trick will be knowing when to shift their interests to outside professionals, when to put sound management ahead of pride, thereby creating a climate in which they can continue focusing more of their energies and immense wealth on projects that matter to them in their communities. For their story is not just one about stockpiling wealth. It has become a story about creating and sharing wealth for the greater public good, for a region and a people that need it more than the Irvings will ever really know.

Acknowledgements

The idea that it was time for a new book about the Irvings came from Nimbus Publishing marketing man Dan Soucoup. The writing was guided by Nimbus managing editor Sandra McIntyre, who is at once inspirational, insightful, and—thankfully—one tough cookie. Dan and Sandra have opened doors for me that otherwise would never have been opened. I cannot thank them enough. Thanks also to Nimbus's Penelope Jackson, Diane Faulkner, Terrilee Bulger, and Heather Bryan, and to freelance editor James MacNevin.

Technical and research assistance was provided by Karen Garrett and Billy Fong of Fredericton, New Brunswick, and Darlene Pound of North River, Prince Edward Island. I wish to thank the following people for their cooperation in agreeing to on-the-record interviews: Lisa Hrabluk, Steve Carson, Willa Mavis, Terry Totten, Joel Levesque, Derek Oland, and Andrew Oland, all of Saint John, New Brunswick; Donald Savoie and Louis LaPierre of the University of Moncton; Denis Losier, Jean Brousseau, David Hawkins, and George Bouchard of Moncton, New Brunswick; Jim Scott, Mike MacBride, Art Doyle, Burton Glendenning, and Francis McGuire of Fredericton, New Brunswick; Robert Morrissey of Tignish, Prince Edward Island; David Ganong of St. Stephen, New Brunswick; Steve Parker and David Holt of Halifax, Nova Scotia; Thane Stenner and David Bentall of Vancouver, British Columbia; Brad McCully of Truro, Nova Scotia; Louis Branch of Bathurst, New Brunswick; and Jean-Guy Levesque of St. Anne, New Brunswick. A number of credible sources were also interviewed anonymously. Their insights provide valuable background and information without impinging on the integrity or character of the Irving family members. Many others graciously declined interviews out of concern for their business and/or personal relationships with Irving family members.

I am humbled by the continuous encouragement and support toward my writing efforts by the following individuals: Jim and Linda Gourlay and Heather White at *Saltscapes* magazine; Pamela Scott-Crace of *Progress* magazine; David Holt; Tim Gordon of General Store Publishing House in Renfrew, Ontario; and Ann Louise Kenney, whose love, insight, and moral high ground are evident on every page of this book.

Extracts were referenced from the Canadian Broadcasting Corporation documentary *Unlocking the Mystery* (2001); Douglas How and Ralph Costello, *The Biography of K. C. Irving* (Toronto: Key Porter, 1993); John L. Ward, *Perpetuating the Family Business: 50 Lessons From Long-Lasting, Successful Families in Business* (New York: Palgrave, 2004); and Erin Steuter, "The

Irvings Cover Themselves: Media Representations of the Irving Oil Refinery Strike, 1994–1996," *Canadian Journal of Communication* 24, no. 4 (1999).

The foreword was written by my close friend and associate, Francis McGuire, of Fredericton—pollster and political addict, idealist, chef, wine connoisseur, explosive personality, and, next to the Irvings, the hardest-working individual I've ever met.

Finally, I am extremely grateful to J. K. Irving of Saint John, Bouctouche, and Irvingdale. Mr. Irving provided unencumbered access to his personal experiences, viewpoints, and philosophies, as well as to the genealogical information contained within the Irving family history authored by Burton Glendenning.